Bench Joinery

W/D

The NVQ Construction series titles are:

WOOD OCCUPATIONS by Peter Brett
(covers all wood occupations at Level 1)

A BUILDING CRAFT FOUNDATION (2nd edition) by Peter Brett
(covers the common core units at Levels 1 and 2)

SITE CARPENTRY AND JOINERY (2nd edition) by Peter Brett
(covers the Site Carpentry units at Level 2)

BENCH JOINERY by Peter Brett
(covers the Bench Joinery units at Level 2)

**Nelson Thornes
Construction NVQ Series**

**Level
2**

Bench Joinery

Peter Brett

Text © Peter Brett 2002

Original illustrations © Nelson Thornes Ltd 2002

Published in 2002 by:
Nelson Thornes Ltd
Delta Place
27 Bath Road
CHELTENHAM
GL53 7TH
United Kingdom

04 05 06 / 10 9 8 7 6 5 4 3 2

A catalogue record for this book is available from the British Library

ISBN 0 7487 6533 6

Illustrations in Chapters 2, 4 and 6 by Peters and Zabransky (UK) Ltd
Page make-up by Florence Production Ltd, Stoodleigh, Devon

Printed in Great Britain by Scotprint

Contents

Acknowledgements

The author wishes to thank the following:

Elizabeth Whiting Associates for the photograph of wet rot.

Rentokil Property Care for the photographs of dry rot.

My sincere thanks go to: my wife Christine for her assistance, support and constant encouragement; my daughter Sarah and my son James for their patience particularly at weekends; my colleagues and associates past and present for their continued support and motivation.

Word-square searches were kindly produced by James Brett.

Finally, all the best for the future to those who use this book.

National Vocational Qualifications – NVQs

The work of a skilled person in the construction industry can be divided into various tasks: build a brick wall; fix plasterboard; prepare and paint surfaces; assemble a door; hang a door, etc. These tasks along with many others are grouped into '**units of competence**'. You can consider these units of competence as a menu to select from, according to your own or employer's skill requirements.

Traditional barriers to gaining a qualification such as age, length of training, mode of training, how and where skills are acquired have been removed. Individuals may acquire units of competence in any order as and when and where they want. Units of competence are accredited individually and may be transferred to any appropriate NVQ award.

Credits for units of competence, which can be accumulated over any period of time, may be built into a full NVQ award at three levels.

NVQ Level 1   Introduction to industry, a 'foundation' common core plus occupational base skills, e.g. Wood occupations, Trowel occupations and Decorative occupations, etc.

NVQ Level 2   A set number of units of competence in a recognisable work role, e.g. Carpentry and joinery, Sitework, Benchwork and brickwork, etc.

NVQ Level 3   A more complex set of units of competence again in a recognisable work role including some work of a supervisory nature.

The Qualification and Curriculum Authority QCA is the accrediting body for NVQ qualifications in the construction industry.

The Construction Industry Training Board CITB establish standards for the units of competence and the qualification structure for the industry.

Collecting evidence

You will need to collect evidence of your satisfactory performance in each element of a unit of competence.

This evidence can be either:

● **Work-based**. This will be evidence from your employers and supervisors, etc. that confirms you have demonstrated the full range of practical skills required for a unit. This should be supported by drawings, photographs and other associated documentation used/ produced as part of the activity.

- **Simulation**. Where work-based evidence is not available or appropriate, simulated activities may be undertaken in a training or assessment environment. Again, supporting documentation will be required as with work-based evidence, so that the total provides sufficient evidence to infer that you can repeat the skills competently in a work-based environment.

- **A combination of work-based and simulation evidence**. Again with supporting documentation to infer competence.

Introduction

This book you are about to start is one of the *Construction Competence* series, and is aimed at those working, intending to work or undergoing training as a carpenter and joiner. The workplace will mainly be at the bench in a joinery workshop undertaking purpose-made joinery for new building work and refurbishment. However, some site measurement, installation and maintenance work is also included. The completion of this book can be used as evidence towards job knowledge achievement which, coupled with acceptable evidence or a demonstration of practical skills, can lead to the full NVQ Level 2 award.

The following eight units make up the NVQ Level 2 Carpentry and Joinery Sitework option.

Mandatory core units (common to all construction craft options)

Unit No. 07   Store resources ready for work

Unit No. 08   Erect and dismantle working platforms

Unit No. 09   Contribute to efficient working practices

Sitework option units

Unit No. 146   Produce joinery setting out details

Unit No. 147   Mark out joinery from setting details

Unit No. 148   Manufacture joinery products

Additional units

Unit No. 160   Maintain internal and external timber components

Unit No. 161   Produce timber and timber-based products (circular saw)

The mandatory core units are fully covered in the companion book, *A Building Craft Foundation,* to which reference should be made.

All of the benchwork option units and both of the additional units are fully covered in this book with a chapter being dedicated to each.

How to use this book

This is a self-study package designed to be supported by:

- tutor reinforcement and guidance
- group discussion
- films, slides and videos
- text books
- practical learning tasks.

You should read/work through each section of a chapter, one at a time as required. Discuss its content with your group, tutor, or friends wherever possible. Attempt to answer the *Questions for you* in that section. Progressively read through all the sections, discussing them and answering the questions and other learning tasks as you go. At the same time you should be either working on the matching practical learning task/assessment set by your college/training centre or, alternatively, be carrying out the practical competence and recording its successful completion in the workplace.

This process is intended to aid learning and enable you to evaluate your understanding of the particular section and to check your progress through the chapters and entire package. Where you are unable to answer a question, further reading and discussion of the section is required.

Throughout this learning package, 'Jimmy' the joinery manager will prompt you regarding important details.

The *Questions for you* in this package are either multiple choice or short answer.

Multiple-choice questions consist of a statement or question followed by four possible answers. Only *one* answer is correct, the others are distracters. Your response is recorded by filling in the line under the appropriate letter.

Example

This indicates that you have selected (b) as the answer.

If after consideration you want to change your mind, fill in the box under your first answer and then fill in the line under the new letter.

This changes the answer from (b) to (d).

Short-answer questions consist of a task to which a short written answer is required. The length will vary depending on the 'doing' word in the task, *Name* or *List* normally require one or two words for each item, *State*, *Define*, *Describe* or *Explain* will require a short sentence or two, *Draw* or *Sketch* will require an illustration. In addition sketches can be added to any written answer to aid clarification.

Example

Name the intermediate vertical member of a framed door used to reduce panel width.

Typical answer: Muntin.

Example

Define the term 'weathering' when applied to joinery.

Typical answer: The slope given to horizontal surfaces to allow rain-water to run off.

Example

Produce a **sketch** to show the difference between a stuck and planted mould on a joinery section.

Typical answer:

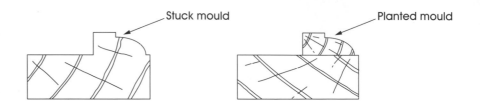

In addition this learning package also contains *Learning tasks*. Follow the instructions given with each exercise. They are intended to reinforce the work undertaken in this package. They give you the opportunity to use your newly acquired awareness and skills before attempting the *Questions for you*.

In common with NVQ knowledge and understanding assessments, the learning exercises in this package may also be attempted orally. You can simply tell someone your answer, point to a diagram, indicate a part in a learning pack or text book, or make sketches, etc.

1 Basic skills

READ THIS CHAPTER, WORKING THROUGH THE 'QUESTIONS FOR YOU'

In order to successfully complete the main practical activities in each Level 2 Unit of Competence, you will require an understanding of a range of enabling skills and supporting job knowledge, e.g. interpretation of drawings and oral/written instructions, adoption of safe working practices, loading and unloading materials, use of tools and general knowledge.

You may have already achieved some or all of these skills and knowledge either in industry or as a result of training at Level 1 or similar. Thus this basic skills chapter has been included in the form of typical questions for you to undertake. Questions are divided into topic areas. Where you cannot answer any particular question, further study should be undertaken using either the information source indicated, other appropriate text books, or talk it through with your tutor or a workmate.

This chapter should be studied on its own, or alongside other chapters according to your need.

Persons with prior achievement may wish to use these questions on basic skills as a refresher to support other chapters as required.

Interpreting instructions and planning own work

These two topics are covered in *A Building Craft Foundation* under 'Communications' and 'Materials'. These should be referred to if you have difficulty in answering the following questions.

Questions for you

1. State the reason why construction drawings are drawn to a scale and not full size.

_____

_____

2. Mark on the scale rule shown below 4.550 m to a scale of 1:50.

Metric   **JAKAR**   **315 PL.**   British Made

3. Produce sketches to show the standard symbols used to represent: brickwork, blockwork, concrete, sawn and planed timber.

THE TERMS 'UNWROT' AND 'WROT' ARE SOMETIMES USED INSTEAD OF SAWN AND PLANED TIMBER

4. State what is meant by orthographic projection.

_____

_____

5. Define the terms: plan, elevation and section when applied to a drawing of an object.

_____

_____

_____

6. State the purpose of specifications and schedules.

_____

_____

7. State why messages must be relayed accurately.

_____

_____

8. State the meaning of the following standard abbreviations:

bwk _____   bldg _____

DPC _____   dwg _____

hwd _____   swd _____

9. State the action to be taken when damaged goods are received from a supplier.

_____

_____

10. State **ONE** reason why you as an employee should plan how to carry out work given to you.

_____

_____

11. Name the person you should contact in the event of a technical problem occurring at work.

_____

_____

12. State the reason why dust sheets should be used when working internally in occupied premises.

_____

_____

13. State why it is important to be polite with the customer.

_____

_____

14. State why it is important to be co-operative and helpful with work colleagues.

_____

_____

REFER BACK TO THE INDICATED SOURCES IF YOU HAVE ANY PROBLEMS

Adopting safe working practices

This topic is covered in *A Building Craft Foundation* under 'Health and Safety' and 'Scaffolding'. These should be referred to if you have difficulty in answering the following questions.

TRY TO
ANSWER THESE

——— Questions for you ———

15. State **TWO** duties expected of you as an employee under the Health and Safety at Work Act.

_____

_____

16. State **TWO** objectives of the Health and Safety at Work Act.

_____

_____

17. State **TWO** main powers of a Health and Safety Executive Inspector.

_____

_____

18. State **TWO** situations where protective equipment must be used. Name the item of equipment in **EACH** case.

_____

_____

19. State the reason for keeping work areas clear and tidy.

_____

_____

20. Name a suitable fire extinguisher for use on a flammable liquid or gas fire.

_____

_____

21. Describe the correct body position for lifting a large box from ground level.

_____

_____

22. Name the type of safety sign that is contained in a yellow triangle with a black border.

_____

23. Describe the role of a site Safety Officer.

_____

_____

24. State the purpose of a toe board on a scaffold platform.

_____

_____

25. Name **TWO** parts of a ladder.

_____

_____

26. List **THREE** checks that should be made before using a scaffold.

_____

_____

27. State the correct working angle of a ladder.

_____

_____

28. State the immediate action to be taken if a scaffold is found to be defective.

_____

_____

29. State where the flattened end of a putlog is inserted.

_____

REFER BACK TO THE INDICATED SOURCES IF YOU HAVE ANY PROBLEMS

Identifying, maintaining and using hand tools

This topic is covered in *Wood Occupations*. This should be referred to if you have difficulty in answering the following questions.

TRY TO
ANSWER THESE

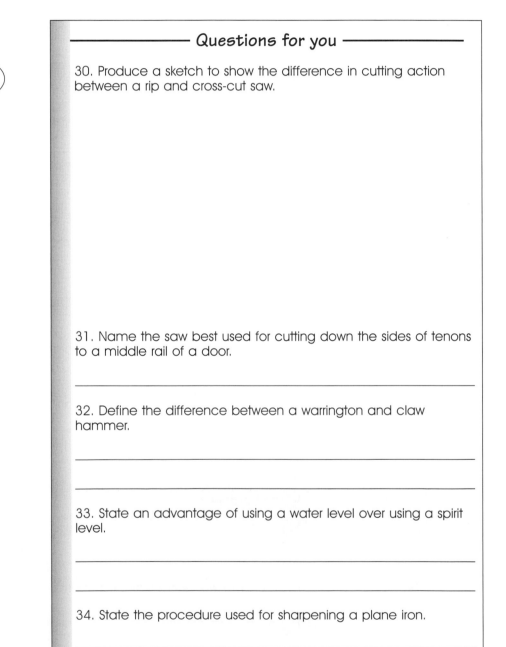

———— Questions for you ————

30. Produce a sketch to show the difference in cutting action between a rip and cross-cut saw.

31. Name the saw best used for cutting down the sides of tenons to a middle rail of a door.

_____

32. Define the difference between a warrington and claw hammer.

_____

_____

33. State an advantage of using a water level over using a spirit level.

_____

_____

34. State the procedure used for sharpening a plane iron.

_____

_____

35. When sharpening saws the following operations are carried out: setting, shaping, sharpening and topping. State the order in which these are carried out.

_____

_____

36. Explain the operations carried out when preparing a piece of sawn timber to PAR by hand.

_____

_____

37. State the purpose of using oil when sharpening plane and chisel blades.

_____

_____

38. Name the type of work for which a panel saw is most suitable.

_____

_____

39. Name the type of work for which a bullnose plane is most suitable.

_____

_____

40. Name **THREE** different types of chisel and state a use for **EACH**.

_____

_____

_____

41. State the purpose of a bradawl.

_____

HOW'S
IT
GOING?

42. Produce a sketch to show a mitre template and state a situation where it may be used.

_____

_____

43. Name a tool that can be used to draw large diameter curves.

_____

44. State the reason for taking off the corners of a smoothing plane iron after sharpening.

_____

_____

REFER BACK TO
THE INDICATED SOURCES
IF YOU HAVE ANY
PROBLEMS

Setting up and using portable power tools

This topic is covered in *Wood Occupations*. This should be referred to if you have difficulty in answering the following questions.

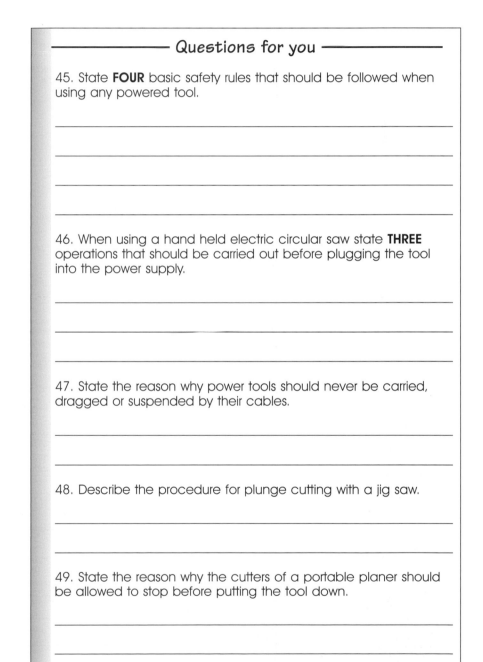

TRY TO ANSWER THESE

Questions for you

45. State **FOUR** basic safety rules that should be followed when using any powered tool.

_____

_____

_____

_____

46. When using a hand held electric circular saw state **THREE** operations that should be carried out before plugging the tool into the power supply.

_____

_____

_____

47. State the reason why power tools should never be carried, dragged or suspended by their cables.

_____

_____

48. Describe the procedure for plunge cutting with a jig saw.

_____

_____

49. State the reason why the cutters of a portable planer should be allowed to stop before putting the tool down.

_____

_____

50. State how cutters are held in a portable powered router.

_____

_____

51. Describe the **THREE** basic work stages when using a plunging portable powered router.

_____

_____

_____

52. Produce a sketch to show the correct direction of feed for a router in relation to the rotation of the cutter.

HOW'S
IT
GOING?

53. State the purpose of using 110 volt power tools.

_____

_____

54. What type of power tools does not require an earth wire?

_____

_____

55. State the correct location of an extension cable used in conjunction with a transformer that steps 240 volts mains supply down to 110 volts.

_____

_____

56. Which of the following sanders is best used for fine finishing work: circular, orbital, belt?

_____

57. A cartridge-operated fixing tool is to be used for fixing timber grounds to a concrete ceiling. List **THREE** items of equipment that are recommended for the operator to wear.

_____

_____

_____

58. The cartridge-operated fixing tool you are using on site has been supplied with **THREE** colours of cartridge: red, black and yellow. List them in order of decreasing strength.

_____

_____

_____

59. State the action that the operator should take if a power tool is not working correctly or its safety is suspect.

_____

_____

_____

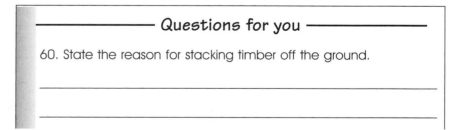

REFER BACK TO THE INDICATED SOURCES IF YOU HAVE ANY PROBLEMS

Handling timber-based materials and components

This topic is covered in *A Building Craft Foundation* under 'Materials'. This should be referred to if you have difficulty in answering the following questions.

─────── **Questions for you** ───────

60. State the reason for stacking timber off the ground.

_____

_____

61. State **TWO** reasons why materials storage on site should be planned.

_____

_____

62. State **THREE** personal hygiene precautions that may be recommended by a manufacturer when handling materials.

_____

_____

_____

63. State the reason for using piling sticks or cross-bearers when stacking carcassing timber.

_____

_____

64. Give the reason for stacking sheet materials flat and level.

_____

_____

65. Explain why joinery should be stored under cover after delivery.

_____

_____

66. State the reason why the leaning of items of joinery against walls is not to be recommended.

_____

_____

67. State the reason why new deliveries are put at the back of existing stock in the store.

_____

_____

68. Explain why liquids should not be kept in any container other than that supplied by the manufacturer.

_____

_____

69. Explain why veneered sheets of plywood are stored good face to good face.

_____

_____

REFER BACK TO THE INDICATED SOURCES IF YOU HAVE ANY PROBLEMS

General knowledge

1) Timber and manufactured boards
2) Preservatives
3) Adhesives
4) Fixings
5) Calculations

This topic is covered in *Wood Occupations*. Calculations are covered in *A Building Craft Foundation* under 'Numerical skills'. These should be referred to if you have difficulty in answering the following questions.

TRY TO
ANSWER THESE

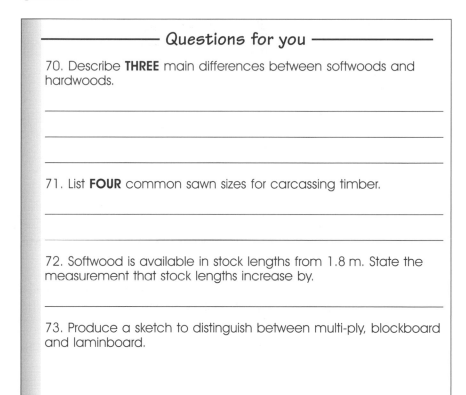

─────── **Questions for you** ───────

70. Describe **THREE** main differences between softwoods and hardwoods.

_____

_____

_____

71. List **FOUR** common sawn sizes for carcassing timber.

_____

_____

72. Softwood is available in stock lengths from 1.8 m. State the measurement that stock lengths increase by.

_____

73. Produce a sketch to distinguish between multi-ply, blockboard and laminboard.

74. Describe what is meant by stress-graded timber and name **TWO** grades.

_____

_____

75. Produce sketches to show the following mouldings: torus, ogee, bullnosed, ovolo, scotia.

HOW'S
IT
GOING?

76. List the **TWO** initial factors that must be present for an attack of dry rot in timber.

_____

_____

77. Describe the **THREE** stages of an attack of dry rot.

_____

_____

_____

78. State the purpose of using preservative-treated timber.

_____

_____

79. Name **TWO** types of timber preservative and state **TWO** methods of application.

_____

_____

80. Produce sketches to show the following timber defects: cup shake, knot, cupping, waney edge and sloping grain.

81. Name **TWO** common wood-boring insects and for **EACH** state the location and timber they will most likely attack.

_____

_____

82. Define what is meant by conversion of timber and produce sketches to show through-and-through and quarter sawn.

_____

_____

83. Define the term seasoning of timber.

_____

_____

84. State a suitable moisture content when installing carcassing timber and explain how a moisture meter measures this.

_____

_____

_____

85. State **TWO** advantages that sheet material have over the use of solid timber.

_____

_____

86. A sheet of plywood has been marked up WBP grade. Explain what this means.

_____

_____

87. Explain the reason why water is brushed into the mesh side of hardboard prior to its use.

_____

_____

88. Define the following terms when applied to adhesives: storage/shelf life, pot life.

_____

_____

89. Explain the essential safety precaution to be taken when using a contact adhesive.

_____

_____

90. Produce a sketch to show the difference between countersunk, round-head and raised-head screws.

HOW'S
IT
GOING?

91. Describe a situation where **EACH** of the following nails may be used: wire nail, oval nail, annular nail and masonry nail.

_____

_____

_____

_____

92. Define with the aid of sketches **EACH** of the following types of nailing: dovetail, skew, and secret.

93. Describe a situation where a non-ferrous metal plug would be specified for screwing into rather than a fibre or plastic one.

_____

_____

94. Add together the following dimensions 750 mm, 1.200 m, 705 mm, 4.645 mm.

95. 756 joinery components are produced by a manufacturer. 327 are to be preservative treated, the remainder require painting. State how many are to be painted.

96. Nine pieces of timber are required to make an item of joinery. How many pieces of timber are required to make 17 such items?

97. A rectangular room measures 4.8 m × 5.2 m. Calculate the floor area and the length of skirting required. Allow for **ONE** 900 mm wide door opening.

98. Five semi-circular pieces of plywood are required. Calculate the cost of plywood at £4.55 per square metre if the radius of **EACH** semi-circular piece is 600 mm.

99. A 105 m run of carcassing timber is required for a project. You have been asked to allow an additional 15% for cutting and wastage. Determine the amount to be ordered.

100. A triangular piece of plywood has a base span of 1.4 m and a rise of 500 mm. Determine in metres square the area of five such pieces.

101. A semi-circular bay window has a diameter of 2.4 m. Determine the length of skirting required for this window.

102. A door 1980 mm in height is to have a handle fixed centrally. A security viewer is to be positioned 350 mm above this height. Determine the height of the viewer.

103. A carpenter earns £65.60 per day. The apprentice is paid 30% of this amount. Determine the wage bill for five days, for both people if the employer has to allow an additional 17.5% for on-costs.

104. Use a calculator or tables to solve the following:
(a) 457 divided by 239
(b) 6945 multiplied by 1350
(c) 336 raised to the third power
(d) The square root of 183.

WELL, HOW DID YOU DO?

REFER BACK TO THE INDICATED SOURCES IF YOU HAVE ANY PROBLEMS

2 Setting out for joinery

READ THIS CHAPTER, WORKING THROUGH THE 'QUESTIONS FOR YOU'

In undertaking this chapter you will be required to demonstrate your skill and knowledge of the following joinery processes:

- Gathering and interpreting information.
- Selecting and preparing appropriate materials.
- Setting out details for internal and external joinery products.

You will be required practically to:

- Set out joinery products for new and or alteration contracts, including:
  – doors, door frames and linings
  – windows
  – staircases
  – wall and floor units.
- Produce cutting lists.
- Undertake calculations for quantity, measurement or costs.
- Discuss work with machinists and joiners.

Design of joinery

READ THIS PAGE

A large proportion of the joinery used in the building industry today is mass-produced by large firms who specialise in the manufacture of a range of items (doors, windows, stairs, and units) to standard designs and specifications. However, there is still a great need for independent joinery works to produce joinery for high quality work, for repair and replacement and one-off items to individual designs.

The design of this joinery is normally the responsibility of either an architect or designer, who should supply the joinery works with a brief consisting of scaled working drawings, full size details and a written specification, of their client's requirements. See Figure 2.1 However, these joinery details are often little more than a brief outline, leaving the construction details to the joinery works.

Often the best joinery is produced when the architect or designer discusses their design at an early stage with the joinery manufacturer, so that each can appreciate the requirements and difficulties of the other, and amend the design accordingly. This communication between the two parties enables the work to be carried out efficiently and therefore have a noticeable effect on the finished joinery item. In addition the joinery manufacturer may also be involved in the joinery design for small works directly with the customer when an architect or designer has not been employed.

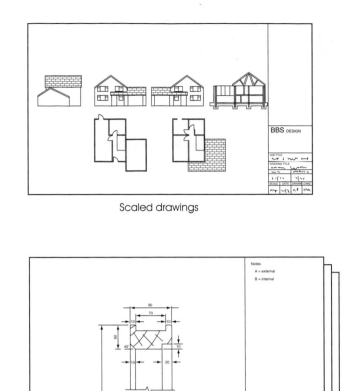

Scaled drawings

Specification

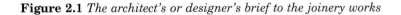

Joinery design details

Figure 2.1 *The architect's or designer's brief to the joinery works*

When designing and detailing joinery three main aspects must be taken into account as illustrated in Figure 2.2. These are:

● function
● production and materials
● aesthetics.

All of these design aspects are important although, depending on the nature of the work in hand, more or less priority may be given to any aspect in order to achieve a satisfactory design.

Function

This aspect is the first to be considered and concerns the general efficiency of an item. The designer will consider this by asking himself/herself a series of questions, such as:

Figure 2.2 *Design considerations*

- What are the main functions of the item, e.g. access, security, ventilation, seating, etc?
- Who will mainly use the item, e.g. adults, teenagers or small children, etc. Each will have a different size requirement.
- In what environment will it be used, e.g. temperature, humidity, weather, likelihood of vandalism, harsh treatment, etc?
- What statutory regulations might affect the design, e.g. stairs, fire doors, etc.?

Table 2.1 *Functional design considerations*

Joinery requirement	*Kitchen/rear access door and frame to new house*
Main functions	• Access from kitchen to garden for a disabled person (wheelchair access required) • Through vision • Daylight admission • Weather exclusion • Security
Special functions	• Wider than standard door width (to accommodate wheelchair) • Inward opening off ramp • Standard door height • Low-level glazing with clear glass (toughened) at line-of-sight when seated • Threshold flush with internal floor and outside ramp • Solid rebated frame • 5-lever security mortise lock fixed lower than standard height
Environment	• Domestic usage (may take additional abrasion at low level) • Adequate space both internally and externally • Aspect of door exposed to weather
Special features	• Hardwood door and frame for increased resistance to abrasion • Kick plates fitted to both sides • Water bar at threshold with the minimum projection • Additional weather strips fitted to frame • Canopy roof desirable over ramp
Statutory regulations	• See Building Regulations
Design	• This is mainly fixed by the above specification • Materials requirements • Production requirements • Aesthetic requirements

An analysis of the answers to these questions will point to suitable **materials** and **construction details**, such as sizes and finishes, resulting in a satisfactory functional design. However this functional design may require further amendment after considering the **production** and **aesthetic** aspects. This analysis can be applied to even the most simple or common joinery requirements. Although this can be a mental process, Table 2.1 shows a typical checklist for use as the design is committed to paper.

Production

This consideration is vital to the economic production of joinery. Construction details should be designed not only to avoid unnecessary handwork, enabling the maximum possible use of machinery and power tools, but also to utilise the minimum amount of material to the best possible effect.

Standard sections – The size and profile of a section will be determined by the functional considerations and the desired finished appearance. Figure 2.3 illustrates a range of standard joinery profiles, which can be economically produced by machine.

Figure 2.4 illustrates the typical application of various standard profiles to produce one section. This may be described in a specification as a 'three-times grooved, once chamfered, rebated, throated, weathered and pencil-rounded sill section'.

The design and proportions of the profile should also take into account the type of joint to be used at intersections, as additional handwork can be involved at joints. Figure 2.5 illustrates a number of profiles and their suitability for machine scribed joints. Pencil-rounded and steeply chamfered profiles are best hand mitred, as the razor edge produced by scribing them is difficult to machine cleanly and is easily damaged during assembly. These problems are avoided by the use of a sunk chamfer or ovolo profile. It is impossible to scribe bead or other undercut profiles, so hand mitring is the only option.

Routing – An alternative to both scribing or hand mitring is the technique of routed profiles – see Figure 2.6 where rectangular sections are framed up and assembled, prior to being worked with a router.

Stopped rebates (see Figure 2.7) should be avoided whenever possible, as they are expensive to produce. This is because they require a separate machine operation, and also the curve left by the cutter on exit has to be squared by hand.

Materials

Nature of timber – When considering both the functional design and production of joinery items an understanding of the nature of the material is essential. Timber is a **hygroscopic** material; this means it will readily absorb or give up moisture, depending on the surrounding environment. Before use timber should be dried out to a moisture content that is approximately equal to the surrounding atmosphere in which it will be used. This is known as the **equilibrium moisture content** and, providing the moisture content and temperature remain the same, the timber will be stable. Table 2.2 shows typical moisture content ranges for a number of joinery situations.

HAND MITRING OF JOINTS IS MORE EXPENSIVE THAN MACHINE SCRIBING

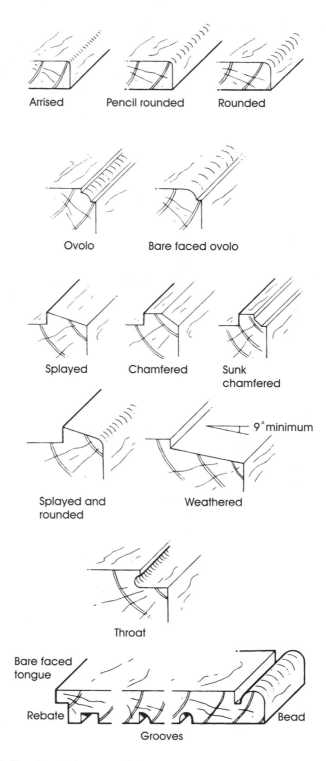

Figure 2.3 *Standard joinery profiles*

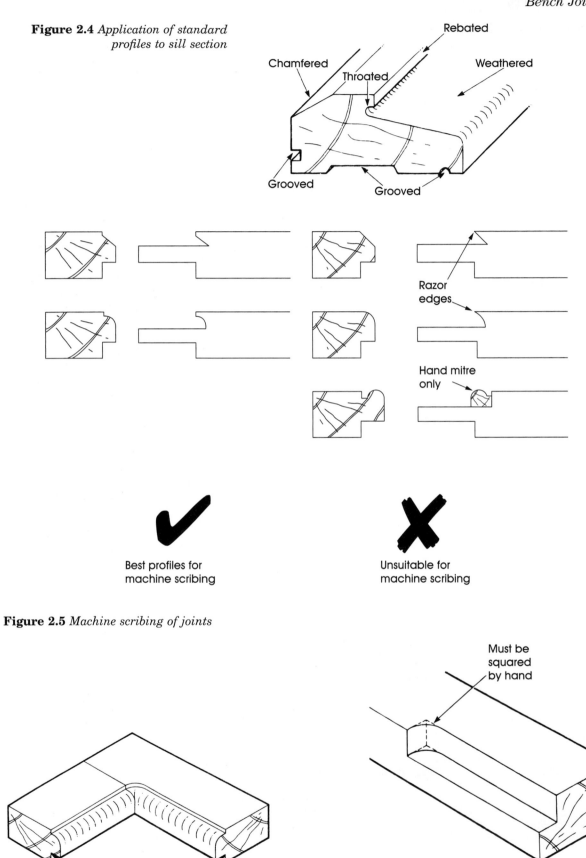

Figure 2.4 *Application of standard profiles to sill section*

Chamfered
Rebated
Throated
Weathered
Grooved
Grooved

Razor edges

Hand mitre only

Best profiles for machine scribing

Unsuitable for machine scribing

Figure 2.5 *Machine scribing of joints*

Must be squared by hand

Figure 2.6 *Routed profile applied after framing*

Figure 2.7 *Stopped rebate*

Table 2.2 *Moisture content for joinery*

Situation	Moisture content range
Internal joinery over or near sources of heat	6–10%
Internal joinery in centrally heated building	10–15%
Internal joinery in building with intermittent heating	13–17%
External joinery	15–20%

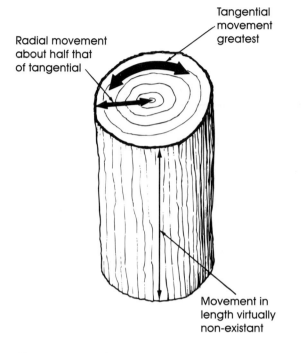

Figure 2.8 *Timber movement caused by moisture*

Changes in moisture content will result in dimensional changes in timber. Loss of moisture results in shrinkage and an increase will cause swelling. This movement is not the same in all directions, it differs (**differential movement**) relative to the growth structure of the tree from which it was cut. The directions of movement are tangential, radial and longitudinal, see Figure 2.8. The majority of movement takes place tangentially, in the direction of the annual rings. Radial movement at right angles to the annual rings is about half that of tangential. Longitudinal movement is virtually non-existent and can be disregarded. This differential movement causes distortion to take place in the timber. If it is remembered that in effect movement occurs along the annual rings, then the likely results of movement can be predicted.

Illustrated in Figure 2.9 are the typical results after drying out, of different sections cut from a tree:

- The tangential section shrinks much in width and is prone to cup
- The radial section shrinks less in width and remains stable in shape
- The square section with annual rings diagonal looses its squareness whereas with annual rings at right angles, the section shrinks but remains stable.

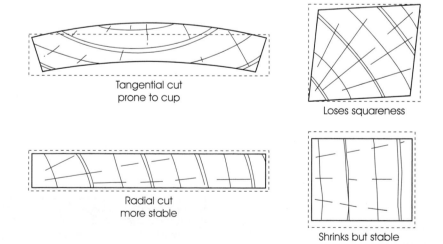

Figure 2.9 *Different shrinkage in sections on drying*

Timber species – The amount of movement also varies with the species of timber. Table 2.3 lists four common joinery timbers and compares the amount of movement expected as the moisture fluctuates between 12 and 20%. It can be seen that a piece of European Redwood 100 mm wide would be expected to vary in width by 2.3 mm when cut tangentially, but only 1 mm when cut radially, as the moisture content moves between 12 and 20%.

Table 2.3 *Movement in timber over 12 and 20% moisture content ranges (mm per 100 mm width)*

Species	Tangential	Radial
European Redwood	2.3	1.0
Douglas Fir	1.5	1.0
Sapele	1.8	1.2
Utile	1.7	1.4

Design allowances for moisture movement – It is inevitable that a certain amount of moisture movement will take place in the finished item of joinery, which must be allowed for in design. The following are typical points of consideration:

- Figure 2.10 shows that wide boards show a bigger open joint as a result of shrinkage than do narrow ones. It is preferable to incorporate some form of feature that conceals the movement.
- Tongued joints and cover moulds can be used to mask the effects of movement. Figure 2.11 illustrates typical situations.
- Wide tangentially sawn boards always cup away from the heart. Greater stability can be achieved by using narrower boards, or ripping wider boards and joining up with alternate heart side up heart side down as shown in Figure 2.12.
- Made-up wide boards, such as solid tabletops and countertops, act as one board with any movement taking place, over the total width. The use of slot-screwed battens on the underside is desirable to prevent distortion whilst still allowing movement. Round or slotted steel washers may be used for added strength in conjunction with the battens (see Figure 2.13).

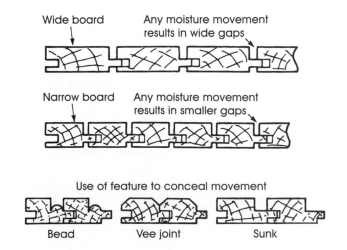

Figure 2.10 *Moisture movement in T&G boarding*

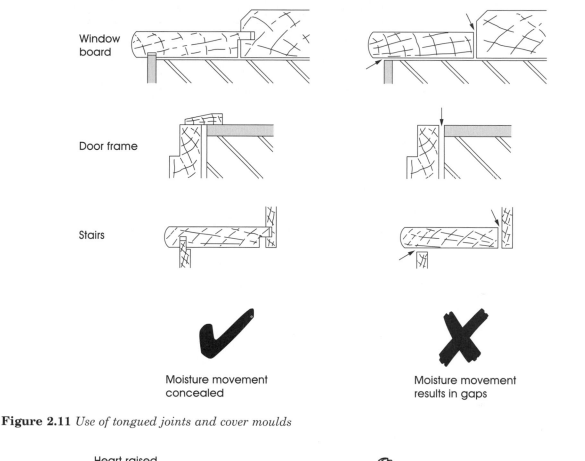

Window board

Door frame

Stairs

Moisture movement concealed

Moisture movement results in gaps

Figure 2.11 *Use of tongued joints and cover moulds*

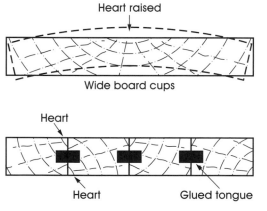

Heart raised

Wide board cups

Heart

Heart   Glued tongue

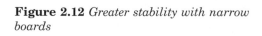

Figure 2.12 *Greater stability with narrow boards*

Round or slotted steel washers

Slot-screwed batten

Figure 2.13 *Slot-screwed batten on underside of solid tops*

- When fixing solid timber tops, differential movement between the top and frame or carcass should be allowed for by using buttons or metal shrinkage plates as shown in Figure 2.14.
- Figure 2.15 illustrates typical design points to be considered to allow for movement, when constructing cabinets in solid timber.
- Tenon widths in framed joinery should be restricted to a maximum of five times their thickness. Wide tenons should be avoided as they

29

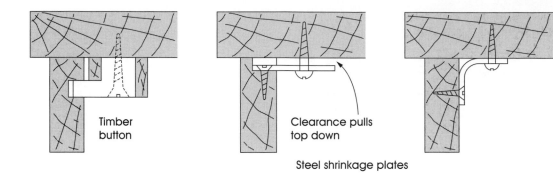

Timber button

Clearance pulls top down

Steel shrinkage plates

Figure 2.14 *Fixings to solid tops which allow for movement*

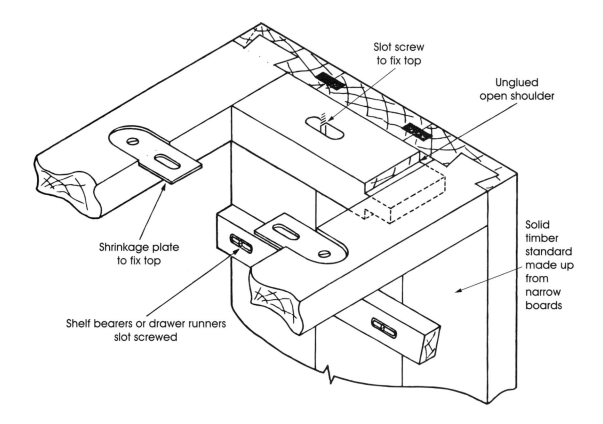

Slot screw to fix top

Unglued open shoulder

Shrinkage plate to fix top

Shelf bearers or drawer runners slot screwed

Solid timber standard made up from narrow boards

Figure 2.15 *Solid timber cabinet construction*

are prone to a large amount of movement. The use of a haunch reduces their effective width, thus minimising movement. Movement at shoulders is avoided by using full length wedges or draw pinning near the shoulder. (See Figure 2.16)

- Bolection moulds should be slot-screwed through a panel in order to prevent the panel splitting. A planted mould used to cover the screw holes should be fixed to the framing and not to the panel. (See Figure 2.17)
- Planted mouldings such as glazing beads and panel beads should never finish flush with the framing, as an unsightly gap will result. Figure 2.18 illustrates how they may be set back, set proud or have a decorative feature incorporated to break the joint.

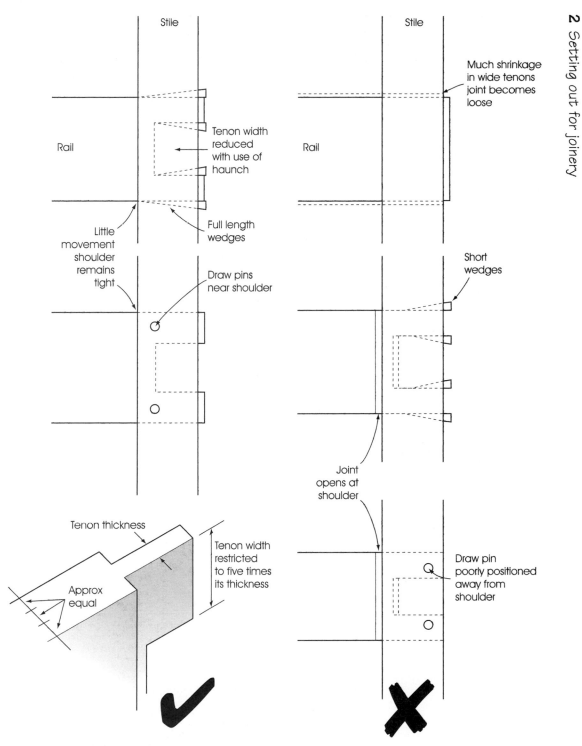

Figure 2.16 *Joint detailing.*
Note: the thickness of a tenon is set to the nearest size chisel.

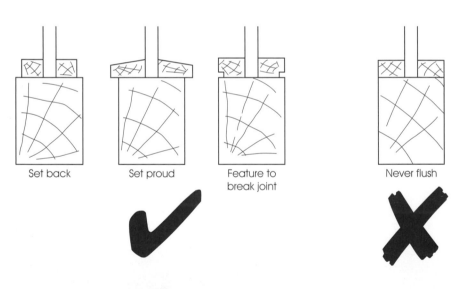

No glue in
panel groove

Bolection mould
slot screwed
through panel

Planted moulding pinned
into framing not panel

Figure 2.17 *Fixing bolection mould*

Set back

Set proud

Feature to
break joint

Never flush

Figure 2.18 *Detailing planted mouldings*

Weathering – External joinery must be designed to shed water and prevent capillarity, which would otherwise collect on horizontal surfaces and be attracted through fine spaces. See Figure 2.19. Refer to Chapter 6 for further information on capillarity

● Top surfaces such as rails and sills should be 'weathered' or splayed at an angle of 9° minimum.
● Under-surfaces such as sills and cappings should incorporate drip grooves, or undercut splay.
● Where components join such as bottom rail of casement and sill, wide gaps are more effective than narrow ones in excluding water.

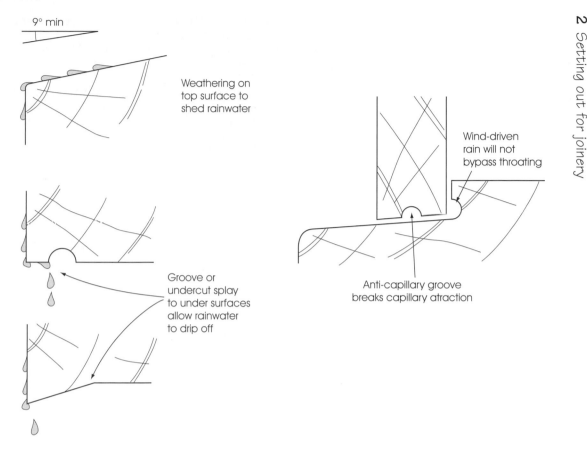

Figure 2.19 *Weathering treatment of external joinery*

- The use of anti-capillary grooves and throatings in these locations is effective against wind-driven rain.

Key points – From these notes on the nature of timber it can be seen that careful consideration at the design and setting-out stages is required. Otherwise an item of joinery may quickly deteriorate, become unsightly or even become unfit for its purpose. The key factors which must always be borne in mind are:

- select an appropriate species of timber;
- specify an appropriate method of conversion;
- specify an appropriate moisture content (this must be maintained during production and delivery);
- use construction details that both minimise effects of movement, yet allow movement to take place without damage.

Aesthetics

This is concerned with the appearance or 'beauty' of an item and can thus be down to individual opinion. What is in good taste or acceptable to one person may be the complete opposite to another.

The aesthetics of joinery is the province of the architect or designer who has a sensitive trained eye and can consider the complexities of proportion, shape, harmony, finish and compatibility to produce a design that will have the desired effect.

33

In addition the aesthetic effect can be considerably enhanced or marred in the joinery works by the degree of enthusiasm and craftsmanship exercised by the machinist and joiner during each stage of manufacture and installation.

Many joinery works operate an internal **quality control** procedure, whereby the joiners are responsible for checking their own work on completion and attaching a quality label to it. Illustrated in Figure 2.20 is a typical quality label which identifies the job and the person undertaking the checks. In addition to the quality checks undertaken by the joiner random sample quality checks are normally carried out by a foreman or manager on a daily or regular basis. This provides a further quality control measure.

A typical company's quality check sheet for joinery assembly work is shown in Figure 2.21. It contains guidance for making the quality check and includes a grading system which can be used as statistical quality evidence.

> YOU ARE RESPONSIBLE FOR QUALITY – GET IT RIGHT FIRST TIME

BBS Quality Assured Joinery

Another Quality Joinery Product
Supplied by BBS. Tel. 01159434343

Part No. _____ Date. _____
Description. _____
Order No. _____
Checked by. _____

Figure 2.20 *Quality check label*

Site measurement

Before working drawings and rods can be produced, it is often necessary to make a site survey to check the actual measurements. It is preferable for this to be carried out by the joinery manufacturer's setter-out, since it is he or she who will later use the information when setting out the rod, deciding the allowances to be made for fitting and fixing, in addition to maximum made-up sizes for access.

Joinery items for existing buildings and rehabilitation work will always require a site survey, whereas the need for a site survey for joinery in new buildings will depend on the specification.

Specification methods – The two main methods of specifying joinery items are:

● *Built-in joinery* – Where the joinery item is specified as 'built-in' or positioned during the main construction process, the work can normally be carried out directly from the architect's drawings and specifications without any need to take site dimensions. In many cases these may not even exist at the time.

BBS Quality Assured Joinery

JOINERY STANDARDS

- ❑ All joinery, units and sub-assemblies to be clean and free of shavings etc.
- ❑ All items to be free of surplus glue
- ❑ All seen surfaces and edges to be free from scratches and blemishes
- ❑ All seen surfaces and edges to be free from machine marks and excessive sanding marks. No cross grain sanding marks on clear finished work
- ❑ All joints and mitres to be tight fitting
- ❑ All sharp arrises to be removed
- ❑ All glass, mirrors and other brightwork to be cleaned and smear-free
- ❑ All doors, drawers and other moving parts should operate smoothly
- ❑ All ironmongery should operate correctly
- ❑ All dimensions to be within + or – 1 mm
- ❑ All items to be square where applicable
- ❑ All finished items should conform to all details supplied
- ❑ All finished items should carry a completed quality label

Quality control check % rating

ELEMENT	CONFORMS		Non-conforming
	YES	NO	Reduction %
Overall dimensions and squareness			–10%
Joints and mitres			–10%
Door and drawer operation			–10%
Ironmongery operation			–5%
Surface and edge finish			–10%
Cleanliness			–3%
Correct to detail			–10%
Quality label			–3%
	Total Rating		%

Comments:

Inspected by:_____ Date:_____

Figure 2.21 *Typical quality check sheet*

- ● *Fixed-in joinery* – In cases where the joinery item is specified as 'fixed-in' or inserted in position after the main construction process, it is the joinery manufacturer's responsibility to take all measurements required for the item from the building and not the architect's drawings.

The extent of the measurements and details taken during the site survey will depend on the nature of the work in hand. It can clearly be seen that the requirements of a survey for a small reception desk in a new building will be completely different to those of a survey for the complete refurbishment of an existing office block. The details taken may range from a single dimensioned sketch to a full external and internal survey of the whole building.

Survey procedure – Each survey is considered separately, and sufficient measurements and details are taken in order to fulfil the survey's specific requirements. However a methodical approach is always required to avoid later confusion. The following survey procedures can be used to advantage in most circumstances.

Drawings – The floor plans and details supplied by the architect for joinery items will form the basis of the survey. The relevant measurements, etc. are taken and recorded on these. Before the actual survey, the building should be looked over, both internally and externally to determine its general layout and any likely difficulties.

External survey – Sketch an outline plan and elevations of the building and then add the measurements. Wherever possible **running dimensions** are preferred to separate dimensions for plans, since an error made in recording one separate dimension will throw all succeeding dimensions out of place and also make the total length incorrect (see Figure 2.22). Running dimensions are recorded at right angles to the line, an arrow head indicating each cumulative point. To avoid confusing the position of the decimal point an oblique stroke is used to separate metres and millimetres. **Separate dimensions** are recorded on the line, its extent being indicated by arrow heads at either end.

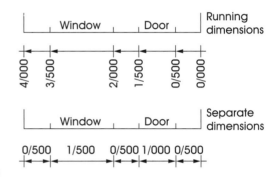

Figure 2.22 *Outline dimensions*

It is important that this distinction between the two methods is observed, because in certain situations it may be necessary to use both on the same sketch. Typical external survey sketches are shown in Figure 2.23.

Running dimensions are taken in a clockwise direction around the building. Vertical dimensions on the elevations are taken from a level datum, often the damp proof course. Where measurements cannot be taken because they are inaccessible, they can be estimated by counting the brick courses and relating this to brickwork lower down that can be accurately measured.

All external details of materials and finishes, etc. should be recorded on the elevation sketches.

Where the survey is for a shop front or similar, accurate dimensions of the opening will be required. Vertical measurements should be taken at either end and at a number of intermediate positions. Horizontal measurements at the top and bottom are required. The diagonals should be taken to check the squareness and accuracy of the opening. Also the reveals should be checked for plumb and straightness (see Figure 2.24). In addition the head of the opening should also be checked for level and the slope of the pavement or exterior surface measured. The slope can be determined by means of a long straight edge, spirit level and rule as shown in Figure 2.25. Where the opening is too wide the slope can be measured in several stages using the same method.

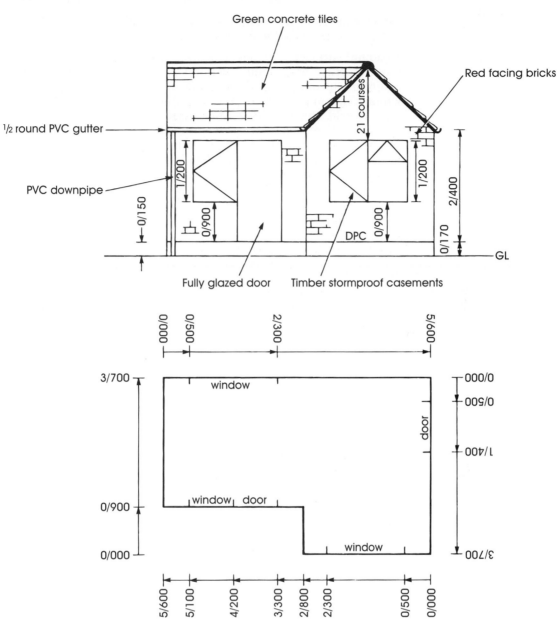

Figure 2.23 *Typical external survey sketches*

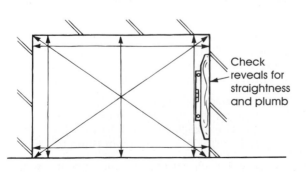

Figure 2.24 *Measuring an internal opening*

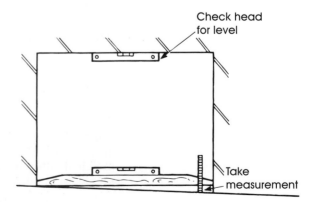

Figure 2.25 *Checking slope of ground across an opening*

CIRCLED DIMENSIONS SHOW FLOOR TO CEILING HEIGHTS

Photographs of the elevations are often taken as a back-up to the sketches, especially for fine or intricate details.

Internal survey – Dimensioned sketches are made of each floor or room starting at ground level. These sketches are traced from the external outline plan of the building, measuring through door or window openings to determine the thickness of the walls. Each floor plan should show a horizontal section through the building, about 1 m above floor level. Measurements should be taken and recorded on the sketches in a clockwise direction around each room. Diagonal measurements from corner to corner check the shape of the room and enable one to redraw it later. Floor to ceiling heights are circled in the centre of each room. Floor construction and partition wall details are also shown on the floor plans. The floorboards run at right angles to the span of floor joists. The lines of nails indicate joist spacing (see Figure 2.26).

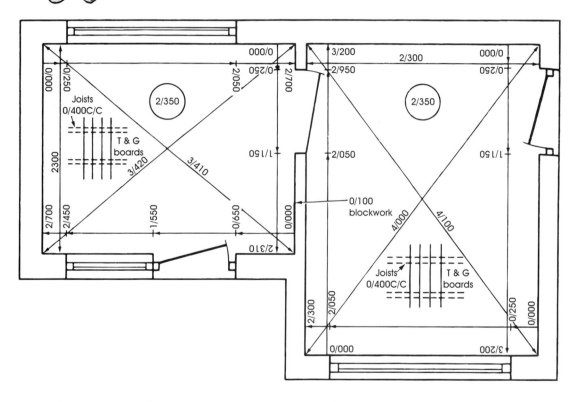

Figure 2.26 *Internal survey floor span*

Pattern staining on walls and ceilings can sometimes indicate positions of grounds or battening and ceiling joists (see Figure 2.27).

Walls can be identified by sounding them. When tapped with the fist, brick walls sound solid, thin blockwork walls tend to vibrate, stud walls sound solid over the studs and hollow between them. Walls should also be checked for straightness and plumb and any irregularities noted.

Where joinery items are to be repaired or replaced, full-sized details of the sections and mouldings must be made to allow them to be matched later at the workshop. The exact location from which the moulding is taken should be noted as this may vary from room to room.

Using sketches – Sketches of internal elevations or photographs may be required especially where intricate details are concerned.

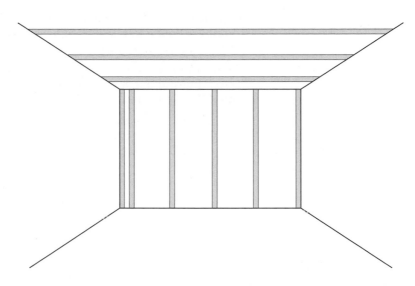

Figure 2.27 *Pattern staining can indicate position of timber behind*

Sketches of the vertical sections taken at right angles to the building's external walls complete the main sketches. A typical section is shown in Figure 2.28. Sections should include door and window heights, as well as the internal height of the roof. The thickness of upper floors and ceilings can be measured at the stairwell or loft trap door opening.

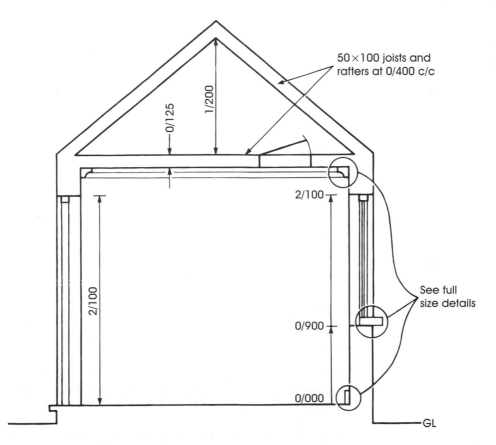

Figure 2.28 *Vertical section sketch*

Only details that can be seen and measured are sketched. No attempt should be made to guess details, so foundations, floor construction and lintels etc. are not shown.

Using datum lines – It is often advantageous, particularly in large areas, to establish a datum line around the interior at this stage. They should be indicated thus: ⊼

The datum line is established at a convenient height (about 1 m above the finished floor level). From this position all height measurements may then be taken, up or down as required. This reveals any differences in the floor to ceiling heights, any slope in the floor or ceiling, as well as the heights of the openings and beams, etc. as shown in Figure 2.29.

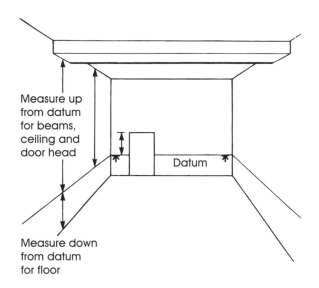

Figure 2.29 *Use of a datum line*

To establish the datum line transfer a level position to each corner of the room using a water level as shown in Figure 2.30. Having established the corner positions, stretch a chalk line between each of the two marks in turn and spring it in the middle, leaving a horizontal chalk dust line on the wall. The water level must be prepared well in advance of using it. This is done by filling it from one end with water, taking care not to trap any air bubbles. Check by holding up the two glass tubes side by side. The levels of the water should settle at the same height. Alternatively an optical or laser level may be used to establish the datum.

Specifying stairs – Where a new flight of stairs is required the total rise and total going should be measured.

The total rise is the vertical distance from the finished floor level at the bottom of the flight to the finished floor level at the top. The total going is the overall horizontal distance of travel from the nosing of the bottom step to the nosing of the upper floor or landing. Other items to check are the length and width of the opening in the floor, the position of the doorways either end of the stairs and finally the floor level (see Figure 2.31)

Other details – Internal openings, and areas or recesses for screens, partitions or fitments are measured in the same way as external openings.

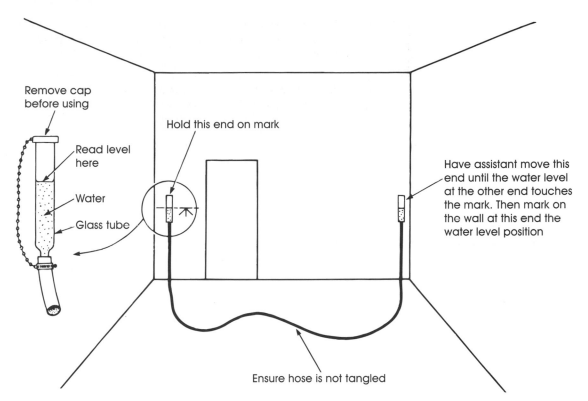

Figure 2.30 *Using a water level to establish datum line*

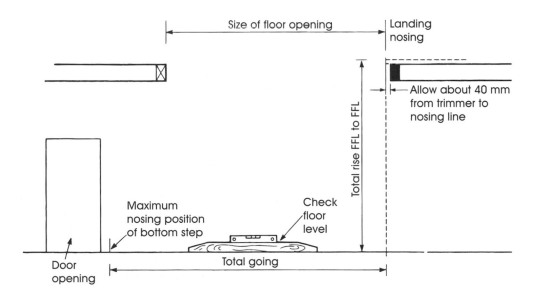

Figure 2.31 *Site measurement for stairs*

Depending on the nature of the survey, service details such as outlets, sockets and switches for gas, water, electricity, television, telephone, etc., may be shown, although these are often recorded on separate, service plans, to avoid overloading and confusing the main floor plans.

Using notes – In addition, when undertaking surveys for refurbishment purposes, brief notes should be taken, recording details of structural defects and signs of decay and deterioration. This may entail lifting several floorboards and the partial removal of panelling or casings. See Chapter 6 Maintenance of Buildings for further details regarding surveys undertaken for this type of work.

Scale drawings – On returning to the workshop or office the sketches can be drawn up to produce a set of scale drawings and any brief notes used to form the basis of the survey report. It is at this stage that the necessity of taking all the dimensions and details is realised. One vital missing dimension can be costly, as it will result in a further visit to the building at a later stage to take the dimension.

Workshop rods

SETTING OUT MAY BE UNDERTAKEN ON A COMPUTER USING CAD SOFTWARE

Before making anything but the most simple, one-off item of joinery, it is normal practice to set out a workshop rod. This is done by the **setter-out** who translates the architect's scale details, specification and their own survey details into full-size vertical and horizontal sections of the item. In addition, particularly where shaped work is concerned, elevations may also be required. Rods are usually drawn on either thin board, thin plywood, white painted hardboard or rolls of decorator's lining paper.

When the job with which they are concerned is complete and they are no longer required for reference, boards may be planed or sanded off and used again. Plywood and hardboard rods may be painted over with white emulsion.

Sizing – Although paper rods are often considered more convenient, because of their ease in handling and storage, they are less accurate in their use. This is because paper is more susceptible to dimension changes as a result of humidity and also changes due to the inevitable creasing and folding of the paper. In order to avoid mistakes, the critical dimensions shown in Figure 2.32 should be included where paper rods are used. Sight size is the dimension between the innermost edges of the components, also known as daylight size as this is the height and width of a glazed opening which admits light. Shoulder size is the length of the member (rail or muntin) between shoulders of tenons. Overall size (O/A) is the extreme length or width of an item.

Where figured dimensions are different from the rod, always work to the stated size.

Rodding windows and doors – A typical rod for a casement window is shown in Figure 2.33. The drawings on the rod show the sections

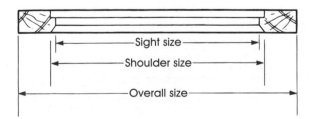

Figure 2.32 *Critical dimensions*

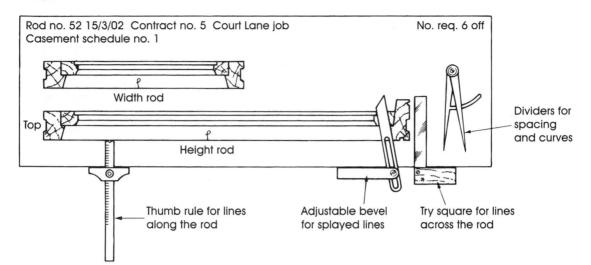

Rod no. 52 15/3/02 Contract no. 5 Court Lane job
Casement schedule no. 1

No. req. 6 off

Width rod

Top

Height rod

Dividers for spacing and curves

Thumb rule for lines along the rod

Adjustable bevel for splayed lines

Try square for lines across the rod

Figure 2.33 *Rod for a casement window*

and positions of the various window components on a height and width rod. All of the component parts of the window can then be marked accurately from the rod. The rod should also contain the following information:

- rod number;
- date drawn;
- contract number and location;
- the scale drawing from which the rod was produced;
- the number of jobs required.

The drawing equipment the setter-out will use to produce the rod is also shown in Figure 2.33.

- A thumb rule for lines along the rod.
- An adjustable bevel for splayed lines.
- A try square for lines across the rod.
- Dividers for spacing and curves.

It is standard practice to set out the height rod first, keeping the head or top of the item on the left of the rod and the face of the item nearest the setter-out.

Illustrated in Figure 2.34 is a workshop rod for a framed, ledged and braced door. In this rod the position of the mortises have been indicated by crosses, as is the practice in many workshops. The rear elevation has also been included for the joiner's information when fitting the braces.

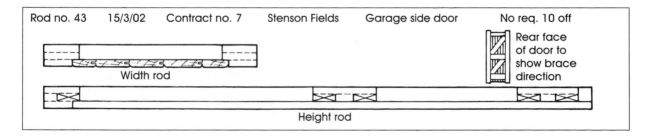

Rod no. 43 15/3/02 Contract no. 7 Stenson Fields Garage side door No req. 10 off

Rear face of door to show brace direction

Width rod

Height rod

Figure 2.34 *Rod for framed, ledged and braced door*

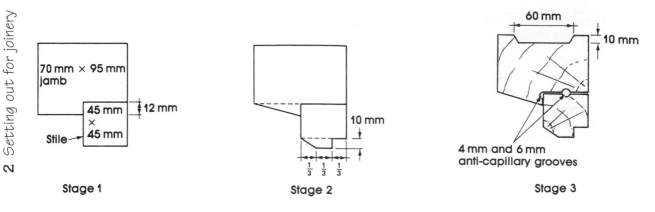

Figure 2.35 *Building up a drawing*

Preparation stages – Figure 2.35 shows the three easy stages, which can be used to build up a detailed section. This method can be used when producing both workshop rods and scale drawings:

- Stage 1. The components are drawn in there rectangular sections.
- Stage 2. The square and rectangular sections are added.
- Stage 3. All other details are then added including hatching.

It is good practice to keep the square and moulded sections the same depth. This eases the fitting of the joint, as the shoulders will be in the same position.

Sometimes it is not practical to set out the full height or width of very large items. In such cases the section may be reduced by broken lines and inserting an add-on dimension between them for use when marking out as shown in Figure 2.36.

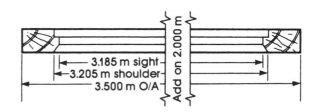

Figure 2.36 *Add-on dimensioning*

Preparation for openings – When determining details for doors and windows the setter-out must take into account their opening radius. A number of applicable door and window sections are illustrated in Figure 2.37.

- *Detail A* shows that the closing edge must have a leading edge (bevelled off) to prevent jamming on the frame when opened.
- *Detail B* applies to the use of parliament and easy-clean hinges which both have extended pivot points. Here both the opening edge and frame jamb have been bevelled off at 90° to a line drawn between the pivot point and the opposite inner closing edge.
- *Detail C* shows how splayed rebates are determined for narrow double doors, bar doors and wicket gates, etc.

Illustrated in Figure 2.38 is a workshop rod for a glazed door with diminished stiles and a shaped top rail. As the stiles section is different

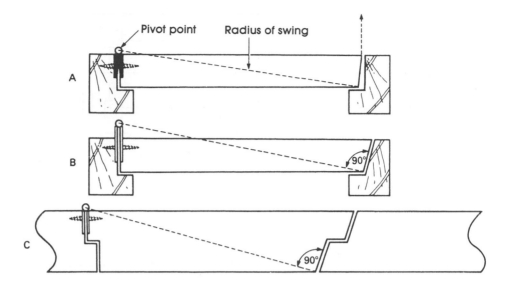

Figure 2.37 *Opening details (doors and windows)*

above and below the middle rail, two width rods are required. Also included on the rod is a half elevation of the curved top rail as its shape is not apparent from the sections.

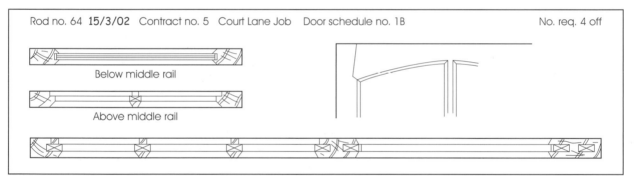

Figure 2.38 *Rod for half-glazed doors*

Rodding tables and cabinets – Rods for three-dimensional joinery items such as tables and cabinets are drawn using broken details and add-on dimensions for one or more of the sections. This is in order to represent their three, often considerable, framed dimensions on a narrow rod.

Figure 2.39 illustrates a rod for a dining table. The length and height sections are shown in full along the rod, with the full width section being positioned under the length.

Figure 2.40 illustrates a rod for a cabinet (floor unit), to be constructed from melamine-faced chipboard (MFC) with hardwood trims. A circled detail (not part of the rod) shows that the carcass is rebated out and screwed together. The hardwood trims are glued and pinned in position after assembly to conceal the screw fixings. Also included on this rod are notes on assembly for use by the marker-out and joiners.

Rodding stairs – Rods for stairs are often drawn showing the top and bottom details, with the width section positioned between them. See Figure 2.41.

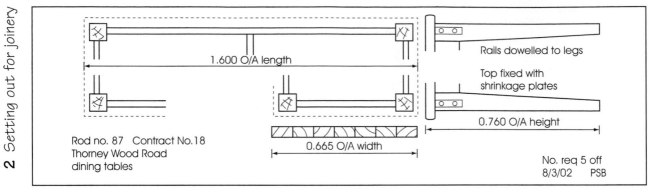

Figure 2.39 *Rod for three-dimensional item (dining table)*

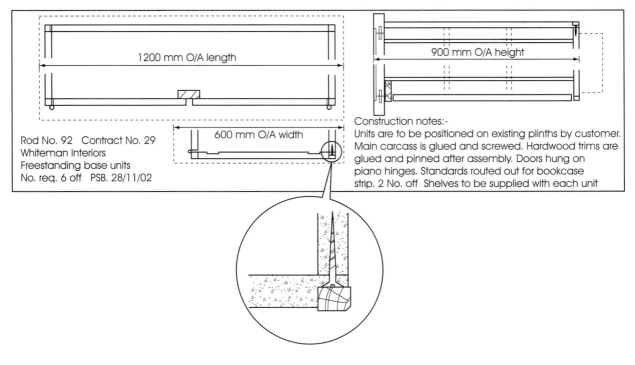

Figure 2.40 *Rod for cabinet (floor unit)*

Where newels form part of the construction these should be drawn to show the housings for the treads and risers, and mortises for the string. To accompany these details the setter-out should supply storey and going rods on timber battens, as shown in Figure 2.42. These are set out using the total rise and going of the stair taken during the site survey. Further information is not required, as the marker-out will make a set of templates from these details in order to complete the task.

Before setting out storey and going rods for a flight of stairs, it is necessary to determine the individual rise and going for each step.

The rise of each step is determined by dividing the total rise (vertical measurement from finished floor to finished floor) by the number of risers required.

The going of each step is determined by dividing the total going (horizontal measurement from bottom step nosing to landing nosing) by the number of treads required (one less than the number or risers).

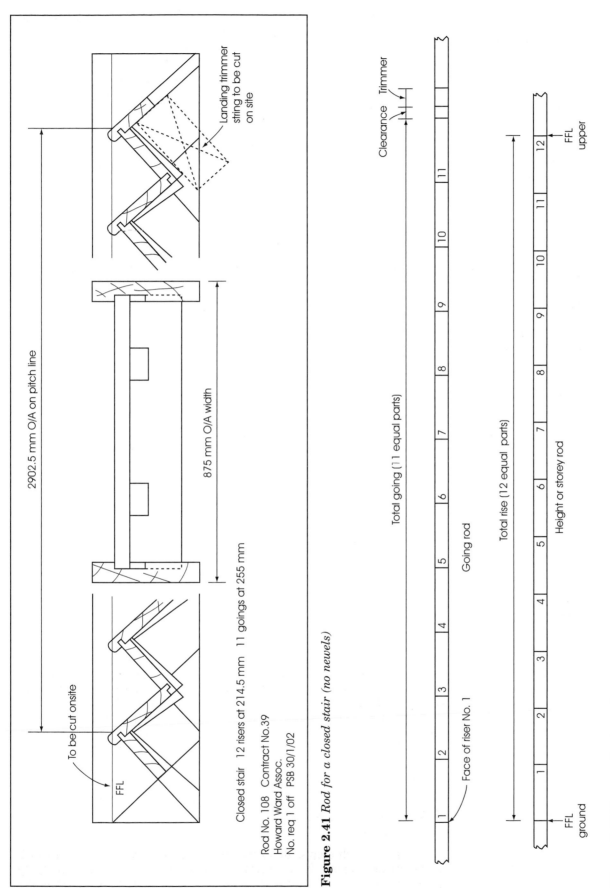

Landing trimmer string to be cut on site

2902.5 mm O/A on pitch line

875 mm O/A width

To be cut onsite

FFL

Closed stair 12 risers at 214.5 mm 11 goings at 255 mm

Rod No. 108   Contract No.39
Howard Ward Assoc.
No. req 1 off   PSB 30/1/02

Figure 2.41 *Rod for a closed stair (no newels)*

Total going (11 equal parts)

| 1 | 2 | 3 | 4 | 5 | 6 | 7 | 8 | 9 | 10 | 11 |

Face of riser No. 1

Going rod

Clearance   Trimmer

Total rise (12 equal parts)

Height or storey rod

| 1 | 2 | 3 | 4 | 5 | 6 | 7 | 8 | 9 | 10 | 11 | 12 |

FFL ground

FFL upper

Figure 2.42 *Storey and going rods*

These dimensions are controlled by the Building Regulations. Chapter 4, Manufacture Joinery Products, contains details for typical situations.

Example

Internal flight for a dwelling house with a total rise of 2574 mm and a restricted going of 2805 mm, assuming that the minimum number of steps are required:

- Minimum number of risers = total rise ÷ maximum permitted rise for location of stair (220 mm in this case) = 2574 mm ÷ 220 mm = 11.7, say 12 (each measuring less than the maximum permitted).

- Individual rise = total rise ÷ number of risers = 2574 mm ÷ 12 = 214.5 mm.

- Individual going = total going ÷ number of treads (always one less than the number of risers) = 2805 mm ÷ 11 = 255 mm.

- Maximum pitch (in this case) = 42°. Draw rise and going full size and check the angle with a protractor, see Figure 2.43. In this case it measures 40°, which is permissible.

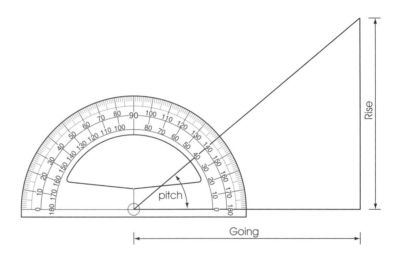

Figure 2.43 *Use of protractor to check pitch of stairs*

Where the pitch measures greater than 42° it can be reduced by introducing an extra rise and going, thereby slackening the pitch. However, this will increase the total going, so that stairs with restricted goings (such as those with a doorway at the bottom of the stairs) will require a total re-design in order to comply, possibly by the introduction of a landing to change the direction on plan.

Computer-aided setting out

READ THIS PAGE

Many medium to large joinery firms now utilise computers as an aid to producing workshop rods. Setters-out input the job details into a CAD (computer-aided design) software programme, to produce both scale and full size drawings/rods. These can be printed out on a plotter for workshop use. The use of CAD in this way has the added advantage for specifying future jobs. Standard details can be stored in the computer for a range of commonly produced joinery items, requiring only dimensions to be added/adjusted in order to customise the rod before printing out for each new job.

Illustrated in Figure 2.44 is a typical joinery shop standard data sheet for an external glazed door. The computer software has been developed so that on inputting the required sizes, the rod will automatically be adjusted to suit and can then be printed off on the plotter. In addition the computer can also be programmed to produce cutting lists at the same time.

Cutting lists

When the rod has been completed the setter-out will prepare a cutting list of all material required for the job. The list will accompany the rod throughout the manufacturing operations. It is used by the machinists to select and prepare the required materials with the minimum amount of waste. The cutting list or a duplicate copy will finally be passed on to the office for job costing purposes.

There is no standard layout for cutting lists, their format varies between firms. However it is important that they contain the following information as a minimum:

- details of the job, job title or description, date, rod and contract number;
- description of each item;
- quantity of each item required (No. off);
- finished size of each item.

A typical cutting list for six casement windows is shown in Figure 2.45. The length of each item shown on the cutting list should be the precise length to be cut. It must include an allowance over the lengths shown on the rod for manufacturing purposes.

- Between 50 mm and 75 mm is the normal allowance for each horn on heads and sills, to take the thrust of wedging up and to allow for 'building in'.
- A horn of at least 25 mm is required at each end of stiles for both wedging and protection purposes.
- An allowance of at least 10 mm in length for rails that are to be wedged.

An alternative more detailed cutting list for the same six casement windows is illustrated in Figure 2.46. In addition to the previous cutting list, it also includes the following:

- An item number that can be crayoned on each piece to allow its easy identification during all stages of manufacture
- The sawn sectional sizes of the items to simplify the timber selection, machining and final costing of the job
- The type of material to be used for each item e.g. softwood, hardwood or sheet material, etc.

49

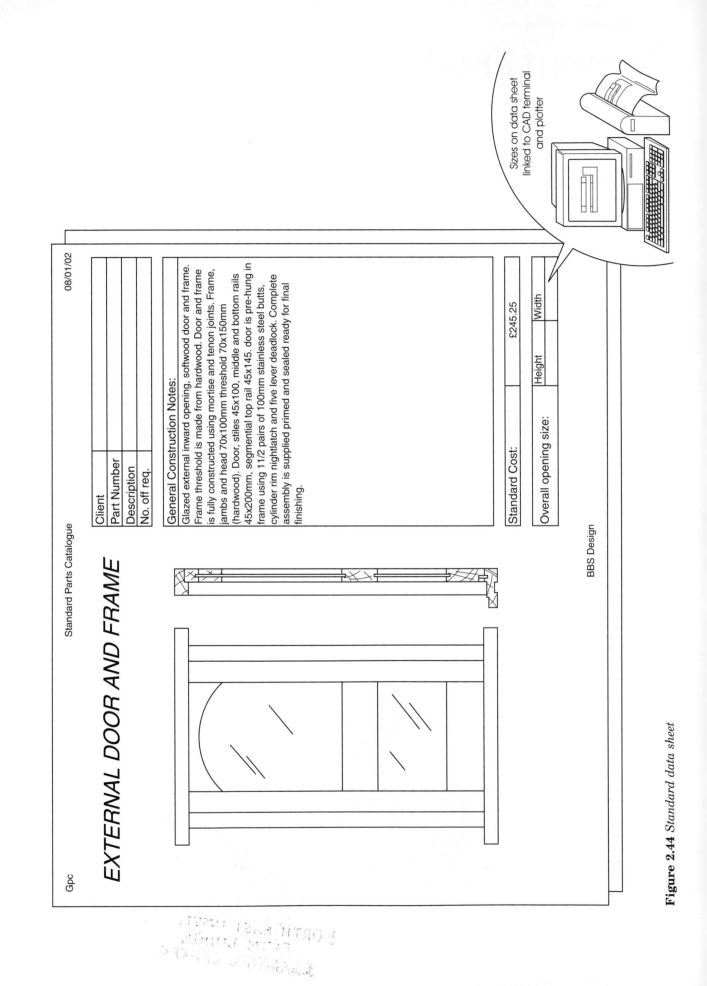

Figure 2.44 *Standard data sheet*

Cutting list		
Rod no. 52 Date		Contact no. 5
Job title Casement window		
Item	No. off	Finished size (mm)
Frame:		
Jambs	12	70×95×1000
Head	6	70×95×700
Sill	6	70×120×700
Casement:		
Stiles	12	45×45×900
Top rail	6	45×45×500
Bottom rail	6	45×70×500

Figure 2.45 *Cutting list*

Cutting list					
Rod no. 52		Date		Contract no. 5	
Job title		Casement window			
Item no.	Item	No. off	Finished size (mm)	Sawn size	Material
	Frame:				
1	Jambs	12	70×95×1000	75×100×1000	Redwood
2	Head	6	70×95×700	75×100×700	Redwood
3	Sill	6	70×120×700	75×125×700	Oak
	Casement:				
4	Stiles	12	45×45×500	50×50×500	Redwood
5	Top rail	6	45×45×900	50×50×900	Redwood
6	Bottom rail	6	45×70×500	50×75×500	Redwood

Figure 2.46 *Detailed cutting list*

READ THE INSTRUCTIONS
AND COMPLETE
THE TASK

—— Learning task ——

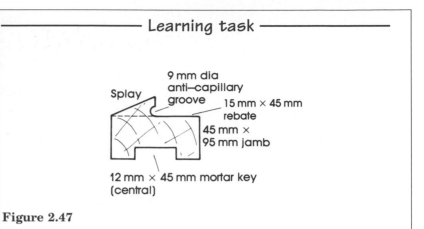

Figure 2.47

Draw full size the jamb of a doorframe shown in Figure 2.47.
(Draw the rectangular sections first, then add the details.) Add
lines to the above section to show the door frame head. Indicate
the mortise position.

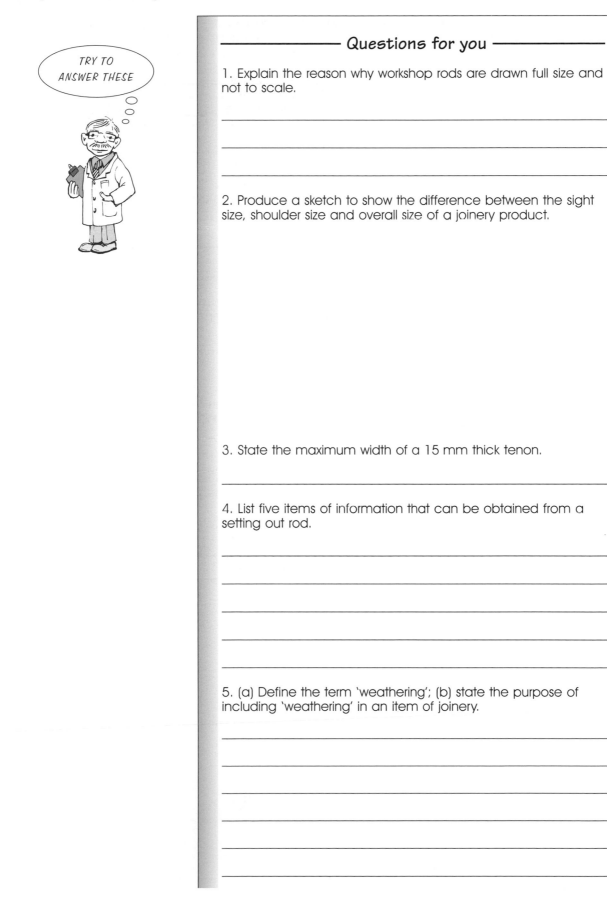

TRY TO ANSWER THESE

Questions for you

1. Explain the reason why workshop rods are drawn full size and not to scale.

_____

_____

_____

2. Produce a sketch to show the difference between the sight size, shoulder size and overall size of a joinery product.

3. State the maximum width of a 15 mm thick tenon.

_____

4. List five items of information that can be obtained from a setting out rod.

_____

_____

_____

_____

_____

5. (a) Define the term 'weathering'; (b) state the purpose of including 'weathering' in an item of joinery.

_____

_____

_____

_____

_____

WELL, HOW DID YOU DO?

WORK THROUGH THE SECTION AGAIN IF YOU HAD ANY PROBLEMS

6. A cross is used on a timber section shown on a workshop rod to denote a: (a) tenon, (b) mortise, (c) rebate (d) groove.

7. Describe a circumstance where add-on dimensions may be used on a rod.

_____

_____

8. Calculate the individual rise of a step for a staircase that has 14 risers and a total rise of 2740 mm.

_____

_____

9. Setting out details may be produced using a CAD system. Define what this abbreviation means.

_____

10. Explain why it is good practice to keep square and moulded sections the same depth when designing joinery items.

_____

_____

COMPLETE THE WORD SQUARE

WORD-SQUARE SEARCH

Hidden in the word square are 20 words associated with *'setting out'*. You may find the words written forwards, backwards, up, down and diagonally. Solve the clues and then see if you can find the words.

SETTING OUT	VERTICAL	AESTHETICS
FUNCTION	HORIZONTAL	MITRING
DESIGNER	BUILT-IN	ASSEMBLED
ARCHITECT	DATUM	CUTTING LIST
WORKSHOP ROD	MEASUREMENT	COMPONENT
SHOULDER	PRODUCTION	SURVEY
DIMENSION	PROFILE	

Draw a ring round the words, or line-in using a highlight pen, thus:

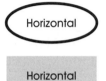

Horizontal

Horizontal

```
S A R C I S S W G T C E T I H C R A
H E Q U L M E A S U R E M E N T S J
O G T T H J D I M G J T E G J S Z P
U A L T D G E H F S D O P R F H R D
L E H I I F S L F S J A D I P O E A
D S I N M N I F A U U F T K D L U T
E T Y G E D G X T C D R H U B O Y E
R H R L N C N O G Y I D C M M O T Z
D E Q I S J E H U D G T E K L D F I
G T A S I G R R J T I S R H F Y G S
J I D T O T E K I O S S D E S J H R
N C G T N E L K N A D S U R V E Y E
I S N H D A I W O R K S H O P R O D
T H I M B F F C V N L L Y B E K S L
L W D U J N O I T C N U F G Q J Z O
I S X I H O R I Z O N T A L F D U H
U C F G J O P G S F H E D A E G K S
B V M I T R I N G C O M P O N E N T
```

WELL, HOW MANY DID YOU GET?

3 Marking out for joinery

READ THIS CHAPTER, WORKING THROUGH THE 'QUESTIONS FOR YOU'

In undertaking this chapter you will be required to demonstrate your skill and knowledge of the following joinery processes:

- Gathering and interpreting information.
- Selecting and preparing appropriate materials.
- Marking out details for internal and external joinery products.

You will be required practically to:

- Mark out joinery products for new and or alteration contracts, including:
  - doors, door frames and linings
  - windows
  - staircases
  - wall and floor units.
- Produce cutting lists.
- Undertake calculations for quantity, measurement or costs.
- Discuss work with machinists and joiners.

Definitions

Marking out – Referring to design drawings, workshop rods and cutting lists produced during the setting-out process, the selection and marking out of timbers, to show the exact position of joints, mouldings, sections and shapes. In addition may also include the making of jigs for later manufacturing or assembly operations.

Manufacturing operations – The basic operations that are undertaken during the small to medium scale production of joinery items, follow the traditional sequence of working by hand. However machinists undertake most of the work, with the joiner only being involved at assembly. These operations are briefly described in Table 3.1. They are listed in workshop sequence and apply to traditional solid timber, framed joinery manufacture. Typical machines for the smaller joinery works are listed. Larger works will have additional or alternative machines, such as: a multi-head planer and moulder; a double-ended tenoning machine; or even CNC (computer numerical control) machines.

Table 3.1 *Typical sequence of operations for a small joinery works*

Operation	Description	Typical machine used
1. Setting out	The translation of design drawings and specification into production drawings, rods and cutting lists.	
2. Cross-cutting	The selection and cutting to length of timber shown on the cutting list.	Pull over cross-cut saw
3. Ripping	The cutting of listed timber to its sawn or 'nominal' width and thickness.	Circular rip saw bench
4. Surface planning	The accurate preparation of the face side and edge.	Surface planer or combination planer
5. Thicknessing	The preparation and reduction in size of the material to the required width and thickness.	Panel planer or combination planer
6. Marking out	The selection and marking out of timbers, to show the exact position of joints, mouldings, sections and shapes.	
7. Mortising	The cutting of mortises and haunches.	Chisel or chain mortiser
8. Tenoning	The cutting of tenons to suit mortises and the production of scribed shoulders.	Single-ended tenoner
9. Moulding	The running of mouldings and other sections.	Spindle moulder
10. Assembly	The fitting of joints, gluing, cramping, squaring and final cleaning up of an item of joinery.	

Timber selection

Radial sawn sections are normally preferred for joinery as these remain fairly stable, with little tendency to shrink or distort see Figure 3.1. However, for clear finished work this factor may take second place, as the important consideration will then be which face of a particular timber is the most decorative. For example as illustrated in Figure 3.2:

- radial face oak gives figured or silver grain;
- tangential face Douglas fir gives flame figuring.

Grain – The timber's grain and defects must also be considered when marking out and machining. Careful positioning of a **face mark** (the leg of the mark points towards the face edge) may allow defects such as knots, pith and wane etc. to be machined out later by a rebate or a moulding as shown in Figure 3.3. Knots and short graining should be avoided, especially near joints or on mouldings.

Grain direction must be considered also when marking up faces, in anticipation of later machining operations. For the best finish diagonal grain should slope into the cutter rotation as shown in Figure 3.4. The grain will tend to break out if marked the other way.

The visual effect of grain direction and colour shading for painted work is of little importance, but careful consideration is required for hardwood and other clean finished joinery.

FACE MARKS LOOK LIKE A FIGURE '9' WITH THE LEG POINTING TOWARDS THE FACE EDGE

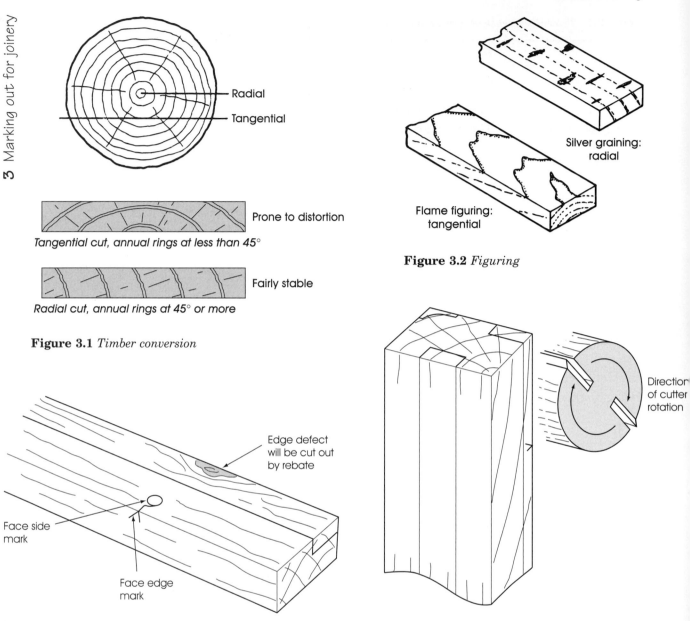

Radial

Tangential

Prone to distortion

Tangential cut, annual rings at less than 45°

Fairly stable

Radial cut, annual rings at 45° or more

Figure 3.1 *Timber conversion*

Silver graining: radial

Flame figuring: tangential

Figure 3.2 *Figuring*

Edge defect will be cut out by rebate

Face side mark

Face edge mark

Figure 3.3 *Positioning of face mark*

Direction of cutter rotation

Figure 3.4 *Grain direction and cutter rotation*

Decorative matching – The aim is to produce a decorative and well-balanced effect. Figure 3.5 illustrates a pair of well-matched panel doors. The meeting stiles have been cut from one board so that their grain matches. Likewise, adjacent rails have been cut from one continuous board to provide a continuity of grain. Any heavily grained, or darker shaded timber is best kept to the bottom of an item for an impression of balance and stability. If these were placed at the top, the item would appear to be 'top-heavy'. Panels should be matched and have their arched top grain features pointing upwards. See Figure 3.6.

Edge jointed members are best matched by deeping a thicker section and opening out, just as the pages of this book are opened, as shown in Figure 3.7. This method of timber matching is termed 'book matching'. Where this is not possible, different boards should be positioned edge-to-edge to obtain the best match, and marked up for machining. See Figure 3.8.

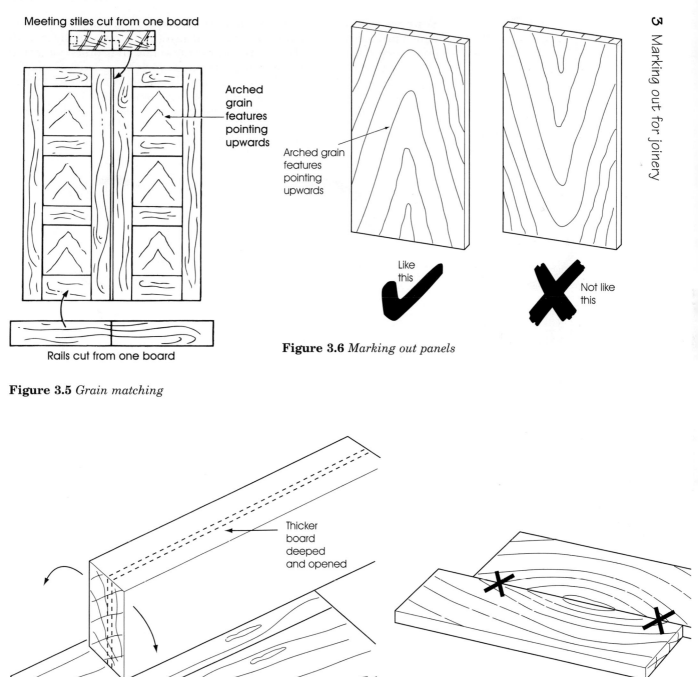

Meeting stiles cut from one board

Arched grain features pointing upwards

Rails cut from one board

Figure 3.5 *Grain matching*

Arched grain features pointing upwards

Like this ✔

Not like this ✘

Figure 3.6 *Marking out panels*

Thicker board deeped and opened

Figure 3.8 *Grain matched and marked for jointing*

Figure 3.7 *Book matching for solid panels*

Veneers – Plywoods are mostly manufactured using rotary cut veneers which produce a widely varying grain pattern that is not usually considered very decorative. Therefore, when plywoods and other veneered sheet materials are used for clear finished work their surface should be veneered with a radially or tangentially sliced veneer. See Figure 3.9. When hand veneering for table tops and panels, etc., there are a number of different ways in which veneers may be matched in order to create different decorative effects. A number of typical matching arrangements are illustrated in Figure 3.10.

 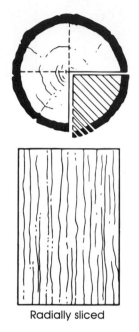 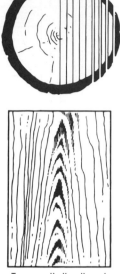

| Rotary peeled | Radially sliced | Tangentially sliced |

Figure 3.9 *Veneer cutting*

Book matching   Quarter matching   Slip matching

Figure 3.10 *Veneer matching*

READ THIS PAGE

Marking out

After the timber has been prepared and faces marked, the actual marking out of the item can be undertaken. Depending on the size of joinery works and the volume of work it handles, setting out and marking out may either be undertaken by one person or treated as separate roles to be undertaken by different people.

Framed joinery – A workshop rod for a glazed door is illustrated in Figure 3.11. It shows how a stile and rail are laid on the rod, the sight,

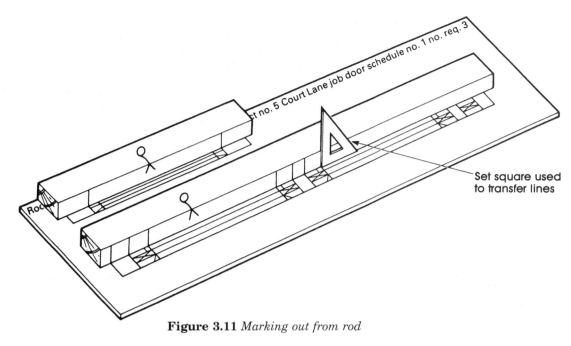

Set square used
to transfer lines

Figure 3.11 *Marking out from rod*

Figure 3.12 *Marked-out stile*

shoulder and mortise position lines are squared up with the aid of a set square. The mortises, tenons and sections, etc., are marked out as shown in the completed stile, Figure 3.12. Most details are simply pencilled on, however mortises should be marked with gauge lines and the shoulders of tenons marked with a marking knife.

In many joiners' shops it is standard practice to sketch the section on a member to enable all who handle it to instantly see how it should look when finished. The marked-out member is also marked up with the rod or job number, so that it may be identified with the rod/job, throughout manufacturing operations.

Where a paired or handed member is required (stiles and jambs) the two pieces can be placed together on a bench with their face sides apart, as all squaring should be done from the face side or edge for accuracy. The lines can then be squared over onto the second piece as shown in Figure 3.13. When pre-sectioned timber has to be marked out, a box square, as shown in Figure 3.14, can be used to transfer the lines around the section.

Using a pattern – Whenever more than one joinery item of a particular design is required, the first to be marked out becomes a pattern for the rest of the job. After checking the patterns against the rod for accuracy, they can be used to mark out all other pieces, and set up the machines. The positions of the mortises are normally marked out on every member, as it is not economical to spend time setting up chisel or chain mortising machines to work to stops, except where very long runs are concerned. Shoulder lines for tenons are required on the pattern only, as tenoning machines are easily set up to stops enabling

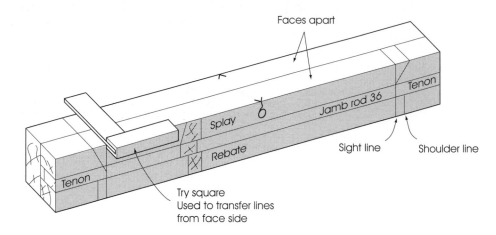

Faces apart

Splay

Jamb rod 36

Tenon

Rebate

Sight line

Shoulder line

Tenon

Try square
Used to transfer lines
from face side

Figure 3.13 *Transferring marks to the second of a pair*

FOR ACCURACY, MARKING OUT SHOULD BE DONE FROM THE FACE SIDE OR FACE EDGE ONLY

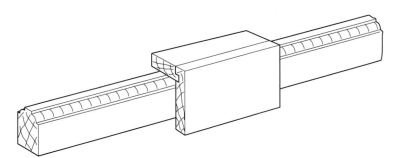

Figure 3.14 *Use of a box square*

all similar members with tenons in a batch to be accurately machined to one setting.

Information for the machinist should be included on the pattern, as to how many or how many pairs are required. Illustrated in Figure 3.15 are the pattern head and jamb for a batch of 10 doorframes.

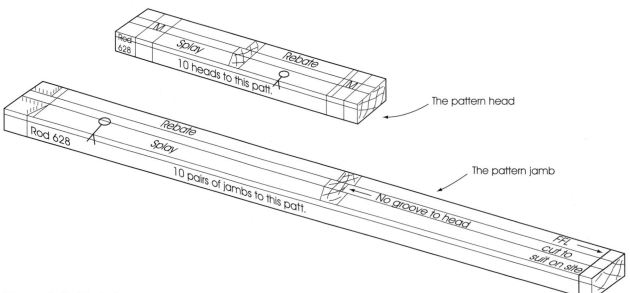

Rod 628

M

Splay

Rebate

10 heads to this patt.

M

The pattern head

Rebate

Rod 628

Splay

10 pairs of jambs to this patt.

No groove to head

The pattern jamb

FFL

cut to suit on site

Figure 3.15 *Marked-out patterns*

Figure 3.16 shows a pattern being used to mark out a batch of paired stiles. As any distortion of the timber could result in inaccuracies they must be firmly cramped together.

The use of this method ensures greater accuracy than if each piece were to be individually marked from the rod. Alternatively, a batch of stiles can be cramped between two patterns and the positions marked across with the aid of a short straight edge. At the end of a run the patterns can be machined, fitted and assembled to produce the final item.

Figure 3.16 *Marking out batch of paired stiles from pattern*

Three-dimensional joinery

JIGS AND TEMPLATES SAVE TIME WHEN MARKING OUT AND WORKING LARGE BATCHES

Marking out for three-dimensional items follows the methods used for framed joinery. Each component part having its own individual pattern containing information for the machinist. Where sheet material is concerned this may be marked out on the actual component part or a thin plywood or MDF **template/jig** may be produced. Illustrated in Figure 3.17 is the design drawing for a base unit, a data sheet for one of its standards and a plywood template marked up and drilled out, to be used as a machining jig.

Joinery works with computer-controlled boring or routing facilities, will programme the machines directly from the data sheet, without any need to mark out panels or make templates.

Stairs

The marker-out will make a number of templates out of thin plywood or MDF to assist in the marking out of stairs. See Figure 3.18.

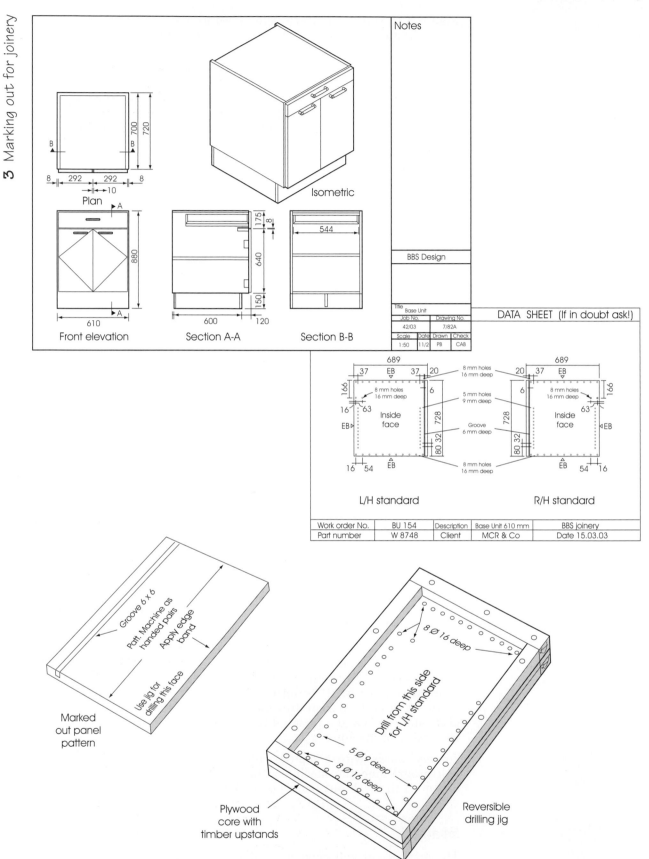

Figure 3.17 *Base unit details*

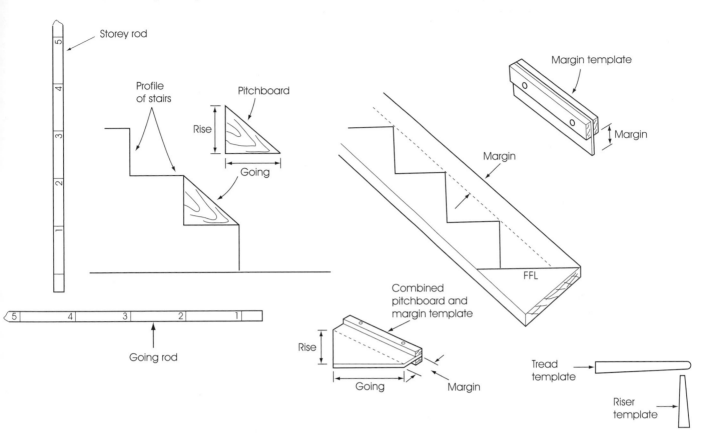

Figure 3.18 *Marking out templates*

Pitchboard – is an accurately prepared right-angled triangle with its two shorter sides conforming precisely to the individual rise and going dimensions of those on the rods.

Margin template – is made as a tee piece, with its projection equal to the distance above the tread and riser intersection to the upper edge of the string.

Combined pitch and margin template – may be made as an alternative and is often preferred for ease of use.

Tread and riser templates – are equal to the shape of the tread and riser plus the allowance for wedging. It is good practice to make the slope for the wedge the same on both templates, so that only one type of wedge needs to be used when the stairs are assembled.

Marking out strings

These are marked out as a left and right handed pair for closed stairs, or as a handed wall and open string for stairs open on one side. See Figure 3.19.

- Mark face side and edge on machined timber. Place paired strings on the bench, face sides up and face edges apart.
- Pencil on pitch or margin line on strings, using either margin template or adjustable square.
- Set pair of dividers to hypotenuse (longest side) of pitchboard and step out along the margin line. This establishes the tread and riser

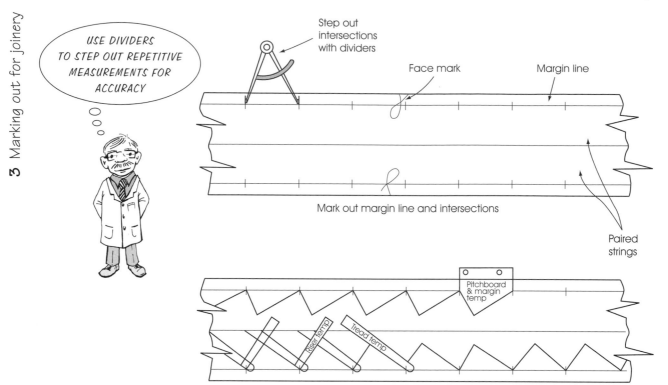

Figure 3.19 *Marking out strings for housing*

intersection points. It is good practice to step out the intersections rather than just rely on the pitchboard, as each step could progressively grow by the thickness of the pencil line.

- Line up pitchboard and margin template on each stepped out position in turn and pencil on the rise and going of each step.
- Using the tread and riser templates, pencil their housing positions on to the strings. It is normal practice to leave the ends of strings long and square for cutting to suit on site. The outer string for an open side stair will require marking out at both ends for tenons. See Figure 3.20.
- Mark out tenon at bottom of stair. A bull-nosed step is being used in this case. The face of the second riser in this case is taken to be the centre line of the newel. Measure at a right angle to the riser, half the newel thickness. Mark a plumb line using the riser edge of the pitchboard. This will give the shoulder line of the tenon. On occasions the shoulder is recessed into the newel face by about 5 mm to conceal shrinkage, if this is the case the shoulder will require extending forwards to allow for it. Alternatively a barefaced tenon may be specified to conceal shrinkage on one face.
- Repeat the previous stage at the top end of the string, except this time the centre line of the newel will be the face of the top riser.
- From the shoulder line measure at a right angle again, three-quarters of the newel thickness, to give the tenon length. Divide the tenon as shown to give a twin tenon with a central haunch. The bottom end of the string will have an additional haunch at its lower edge, whilst the upper part of the tenon at the top end of the string will be cut off level. This arrangement of tenons is to avoid undercutting the mortises or weakness caused by short grain, if other arrangements are used.

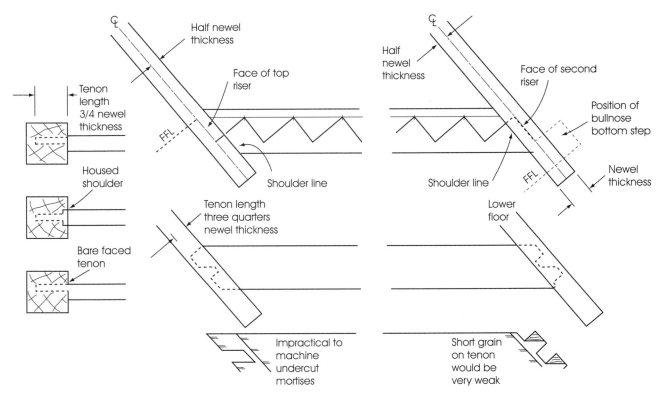

Figure 3.20 *Marking out string for tenons*

Marking out newels

The marking out is illustrated in Figure 3.21. The four faces of the newel are drawn out to show the housing and mortise positions. The upper edges of both newels will also require mortising to receive the handrail.

Marking out handrail and balustrade

The overall height of the handrail on the stairs is 900 mm above the pitch line. On upper landings this is either 900 mm or 1000 mm above the floor level, depending on the use of the building. See Figure 3.22

- Handrails are normally tenoned into the mortised newels. The shoulder angle and line of the handrail tenons (and capping if used) will be the same as the string. Balusters may be either stub tenoned into the edge of the string, or fitted in a groove run into a string capping, which itself is grooved over the string. At their upper end they are normally pinned into the groove run on the underside of the handrail, or again they may be stub tenoned. Distance pieces may be cut between balusters and pinned into the grooves to maintain the baluster spacings.
- Determine the number of balusters required. Allow two per tread and one where there is a newel. Say an 11-going flight with a bottom bullnose step. There will be eight full treads and two part treads between newels, thus 18 balusters will be required.
- Determine the horizontal distance between balusters. Divide the horizontal distance between the newels (less space taken up by total width of all balusters) by the number of balusters plus one. There will always be one more space than the number of balusters.

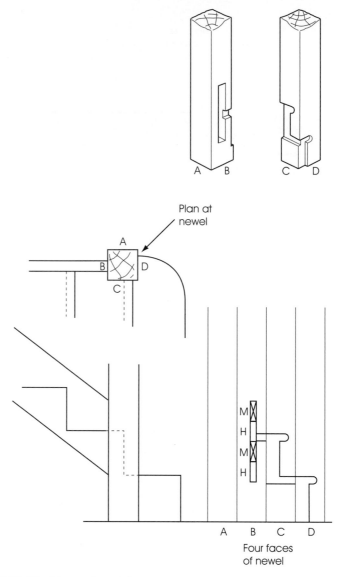

Figure 3.21 *Marking out newel*

Example

Distance between newels   = 10 treads x going – newel width
                                             = (10 × 255) – 100
                                             = 2450 mm

Space taken by balusters   = number of balusters × width
                                             = 18 × 40
                                             = 720 mm

Distance between balusters   =

           $$\frac{\text{Distance between newels – space taken by balusters}}{\text{Number of balusters + 1}}$$

                                             = 2450 – 720 ÷ 19
                                             = 91 mm

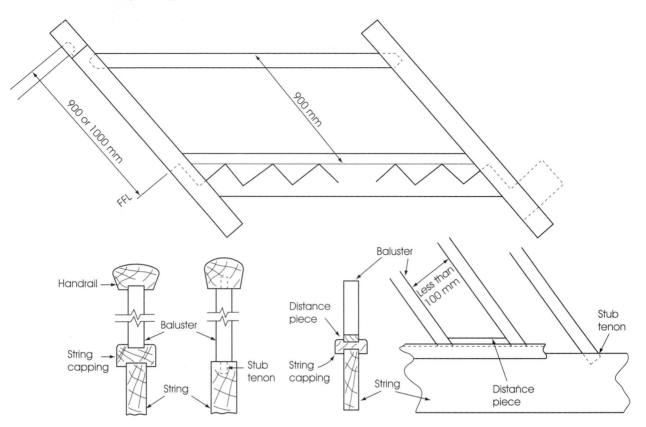

Figure 3.22 *Marking out for handrail and balustrade*

The maximum distance between balusters should be such that a 100 mm sphere (less than a small child's head) is not able to pass between them. At 91 mm this example is acceptable for straight balusters. However, if turned balusters were to be used the space between the turned sections may exceed 100 mm. If this were the case an additional baluster should be added and the distance between re-calculated.

Methods, briefings and costings

Method statement

At some stage in the setting and marking out process, a method statement is often produced. This sets out the main operations that have to be undertaken in order to complete a specific task. Illustrated in Figure 3.23 is a typical joinery method statement for a batch of floor units. This would be passed onto the joiners for guidance prior to them starting the task.

JOINERY METHOD STATEMENT

Works Order Number	15350		Del. Date	30-1-03		Part Number	BU14 MEW

Description	BASE UNIT 610 mm					Client	MEAL-E-WAY

Unit Time hrs	1·95		Quantity	10 off		Total Time hrs	19·5

No.	Operations
1	Assemble unit carcass to assembly details, using cascamite glue and dowels. Fix back of unit to base and sub top using 25 mm ring shank nails.
2	Assemble plinth using cascamite glue and plated screws. Fix to unit using 8 off white plastic modesty blocks.
3	Assemble drawer and install in unit, using bottom mounted steel runners. Fix slab front and ironmongery as detailed.
4	Hang doors and fit ironmongery as detailed.
5	Insert shelf studs and shelf.
6	Remove all arrises and wipe down all surfaces.
7	Undertake final quality check, label and transfer to pallet.
8	
9	
10	

Figure 3.23 *Joinery methods statement (not definitive – provided as a guide only)*

Workshop briefing

It is standard practice in many joinery companies for a workshop briefing to take place prior to starting a task. This is particularly the case where prototypes for new designs, intricate assembly or specific technical issues are concerned.

The briefing meeting normally held by the setter/marker-out will often bring together the machinist and joiner to familiarise themselves with the task and its specific requirements. A further briefing may take place once the materials have been machined prior to assembly, to consider methods and give assembly-specific instructions.

Determining costs

The setter-out/marker-out is in many organisations responsible for determining shop floor costs. This may involve both the calculation of material costs and the cost of labour.

Material costs – are determined by taking off the m³ of solid timber and m² of sheet materials required for a job from the cutting list. Plus the cost of any ironmongery (an allowance is not normally made for consumables such as glue, nails and screws, etc.).

A percentage is added to these quantities for cutting and waste, before the purchasing price of the materials is applied.

Example

Figure 3.24 shows a cutting list for a batch of ten external doors and frames. Also included on the bottom of the list are the ironmongery requirements.

- It is company standard practice to add 50 mm to the finished component length, to allow for squaring off ends. The normal 5 mm has been allowed on the sectional size for planning.
- 15% is added to the m³ quantities for cutting and waste.
- Use the sawn (also known as breakout) sizes to determine volume of each component.
- Total volume of like materials and add percentage for cutting and waste.
- Multiply by cost using figures below.

   US Redwood = £246.50 m³
   FAS Oak = £695.75 m³
   100 mm stainless steel hinges = £5.90 per pair
   Night latch (stainless steel case) = £28.42 each
   5 lever mortise deadlock (stainless steel foreplate) = £32.40 each
   6 × 25 mm stainless steel water bar = £15.90 per 3 m length

Volume of softwood:

Head	10 × 1.2 × 0.1 × 0.075	= 0.09 m³
Jambs	20 × 2.25 × 0.1 × 0.075	= 0.3375 m³
Top rail	10 × 0.96 × 0.15 × 0.05	= 0.072 m³
Mid rail	10 × 0.96 × 0.225 × 0.05	= 0.108 m³
Bottom rail	10 × 0.96 × 0.225 × 0.05	= 0.108 m³
Stiles	20 × 2.19 × 0.1 × 0.05	= 0.219 m³

CUTTING LIST

Client:	A. J. SIMS PLC		Part Number:			AJS 1/4	Description:			EXTERNAL DOOR & FRAME			

Component Number:	Quantity required:	Component Description:	Breakout Sizes (sawn)			Material Description:	Finished sizes:			Remarks:
			Length	Width	Thickness		Length	Width	Thickness	
EDF 1.1	10	Head	1200	100	75	US Redwood	1150	95	70	MTD
EDF 1.2	10	Threshold	1200	150	75	FAS Oak	1150	145	70	MTD
EDF 1.3	20	Jambs	2250	100	75	US Redwood	2200	95	70	MTD
EDF 1.4	10	Top rail	960	150	50	US Redwood	910	145	45	MTD
EDF 1.5	10	Middle rail	960	225	50	US Redwood	910	220	45	MTD
EDF 1.6	10	Bottom rail	960	225	50	US Redwood	910	220	45	MTD
EDF 1.7	20	Stiles	2190	100	50	US Redwood	2140	95	45	MTD
IRONMONGERY										
HSS100	30	100 mm hinge				Stainless steel				
CRNL2	10	Night latch				Stainless steel casing				
MDL4	10	Mortise deadlock				5 lever SS fore plate				
WB1	10	Water bar				Stainless steel	1000	25	6	Joiners cut to length

* MTD = Machine to detail   NFM = No further machining

Figure 3.24 *Cutting list for costing example*

Total volume softwood	$= 0.9345 \text{ m}^3$
Cutting and waste allowance	$= 0.9345 \times 1.15$ $= 1.075 \text{ m}^3$ (to 3 decimal places)
Total cost of softwood	$= 1.075 \times £246.50$ $= £264.99$

Volume of hardwood:

Threshold	$10 \times 1.2 \times 0.15 \times 0.075 = 0.135\text{m}$
Cutting and waste allowance 15%	$= 0.135 \times 1.15$ $= 0.155 \text{ m}^3$
Total cost of hardwood	$= 0.155 \times £695.75$ $= £107.84$

Other costings:

Total cost of timber	$= £264.99 + £107.84$ $= £372.83$
Cost of 30 hinges at £5.90 per pair	$= 15 \times £5.90$ $= £88.50$
Cost of 10 night latches at £28.42 each	$= 10 \times £28.42$ $= £284.20$
Cost of 10 deadlocks at £32.40 each	$= 10 \times £32.40$ $= £324.00$
Cost of 10 × 1 m lengths of water-bar at £15.90 per 3 m for say 4 lengths	$= 4 \times £15.90$ $= £63.60$
Total cost of ironmongery	$= £88.50 + £284.20$ $+ £324.00 + £63.60$ $= £760.30$
Total cost of materials (timber and ironmongery)	$= £372.83 + £760.30$ $= £1133.13$

Labour costs – are determined from the estimated length of time required to complete a task. These may be derived from:

- Company standard times.
- Records of past performance.
- Built-up using a task procedure, costing sheet.

Illustrated in Figure 3.25 is a task procedure sheet developed by a joinery company for assembly work. It is used as a computer spread sheet. The task is analysed and broken down into its individual elements and entered on the sheet for a one-off. The times for each task are calculated by the software and multiplied by the batch size (number off required), giving the total assembly time required.

The actual labour cost per hour charged by a company will be far in excess of the hourly rate paid to its employees. It will be the full cost of employing a person and is made up of the following:

ENTER TIMES FOR A 1 OFF ASSEMBLED, SHEET WILL ADJUST FOR BATCH QUANTITY

DESCRIPTION
PART NUMBER
QUANTITY

JOINERY ASSEMBLY

ACTIVITY	QTY	DESCRIPTION	MEASURE	Mins	TOTAL Mins
GENERAL ASSEMBLY Pick up and position component part		LARGE - ABOVE 1 m	PER PIECE	1.00	
		MEDIUM - ABOVE 0.5 m	PER PIECE	0.70	
		SMALL - BELOW 0.5 m	PER PIECE	0.35	
Framed joints		FIT SINGLE MORTISE AND TENON JOINT	PER JOINT	2.25	
		HAND SCRIBE OR MITRE MOULDING AT JOINT	PER JOINT	3.00	
FIXINGS					
Nails/Pins/Dowels		GLUE AND POSITION WOODEN DOWEL	PER OCCASION	0.50	
		INSERT PIN OR NAIL	PER OCCASION	0.25	
		FILL PIN OR NAIL HOLE USING FILLER, INC SAND OFF	PER OCCASION	0.30	
Screws		POSITION AND SECURE SCREW	PER SCREW	0.50	
		FILL SCREW HOLE USING PELLET, INC SAND OFF	PER SCREW HOLE	1.25	
HAND & POWER TOOLS		USE CHOP SAW	PER CUT	0.75	
		USING POWER ROUTER	PER LIN M	1.25	
		USE HAND PLANE	PER LIN M	1.00	
		CUT GROOVE, APPLY GLUE, FIT BISCUIT	PER BISCUIT	1.25	
GLUE & CRAMPS		APPLY GLUE - PER BEAD	PER LIN M	0.75	
		SECURE AND REMOVE CRAMP	PER OCCASION	1.25	
Drawer		ASSEMBLE AND FIT DRAWER	PER ASSEMBLY	22.00	
Unit doors		ASSEMBLE AND FIT SWING DOOR TO UNIT	PER DOOR	12.50	
		ASSEMBLE AND FIT SLIDING DOORS TO UNIT	PER PAIR	14.75	
Building door		HANG C/W 2 No HINGES, LEVER FURN, AND LOCK/LATCH	PER DOOR	85.00	
IRONMONGERY Unit handles		FIT "D" TYPE HANDLE	EACH	2.10	
Unit catch		FIT BALESOR MAG. CATCH	EACH	2.50	
Surface bolt		FIT TOWER BOLT	EACH	2.75	
Additional hinges		FLUSH HINGE	PER HINGE	1.25	
		BUTT HINGE	PER HINGE	2.50	
		PIANO HINGE	PER LIN M	17.25	
Glass & metalwork		UNWRAP AND POSITION	PER ITEM	1.50	
SANDING & FINISHING		SAND - FACE	PER SQ. MTR	9.25	
		SAND - EDGE OR DE-ARRIS EDGE	PER LIN. MTR.	0.50	
LAMINATE & EDGING		APPLY FACE LAMINATE	PER SQ. MTR	30.00	
		APPLY LAMINATE EDGING	PER LIN. MTR.	12.50	
		APPLY TAPE EDGING (brush glue or iron-on)	PER LIN. MTR.	7.50	
		APPLY TIMBER EDGING	PER LIN. MTR.	17.50	

ESTIMATED ITEMS		DESCRIPTION	UNIT	TIME	
Estimated time for work required, but not included in sheet					
EXAMINE & LABEL		EXAMINE, AFFIX QUALITY LABEL TRANSFER TO PALLET	PER OCCASION	2.50	

OCCASIONAL ELEMENTS

Recieve parts, ironmongery, check measurements, cutting list, plan method and sequence of work, consult on details, rectify faults, sort tools on bench or at workplace, turn work over or around on bench or workplace, examine assembly, machine items - grind off hardware to fit, find tools, pallets etc and clock on and off.

Percentage already included in rates shown above

TOTAL MINS. PER ITEM

TOTAL MINS. FOR COMPLETE BATCH QUANTITY

TOTAL HOURS FOR COMPLETE BATCH QUANTITY

Figure 3.25 *Typical computer-based joinery task procedure – costing spreadsheet*

BSS Joinery

JOB RECORD

Description	Panel door	Client	P. BRAND	Job No. PBI
Operation	Employee	Date	Time (from–to)	Total mins
SAW	I. HUNT	11-11-02	10·15/11·45	90
PLANER	G. BOLT	"	12·00/1·50	110
MORTISE	P. HARE	12-11-02	8·00/10·45	165
TENON	P. HARE	12-11-02	2·10/4·15	125
MOULD	G. BOLT	13-11-02	8·00/11·05	185
ASSEMBLE	J. JONES	14-11-02	8·00/4·30	480
ASSEMBLE	J. JONES	15-11-02	8·00/10·15	135

← Manually completed forms

BSS Joinery

EMPLOYEE TIMESHEET

Employee No. BBS47	Name	JIM JONES		Week No. 48
Operation	Job No.	Date	Time (from–to)	Total time (mins)
CLEAN UP & FIT	PBI	14-11-02	8·00/12·00	240
ASSEMBLY	PBI	14-11-02	12·30/4·30	240
ASSEMBLY/FINISH	PBI	15-11-02	8·00/10·15	135

BSS Joinery

BSS47 J JONES

Electronic 'Smartcard' linked to computer base management information system

BOOKINGS BY JOB NUMBER   **PB1**

Operation	Centre	Date	Employee	Time Booked	Standard Time	Variance
010	Mill	11-11-02	Hunt	90	95	−5
020	Mill	11-11-02	Bolt	110	105	5
030	Mill	12-11-02	Hare	165	180	−15
040	Mill	12-11-02	Hare	125	135	−10
050	Mill	13-11-02	Bolt	185	200	−15
		Total for Mill		675	715	−40
060	Join	14-11-02	Jones	240		
060	Join	14-11-02	Jones	240		
060	Join	14-11-02	Jones	135	600	15
		Total for Joinery		615	600	15
		Total for Job		1290	1315	−25

Figure 3.26 *Time collection*

- *Direct costs* – of employing the hourly paid operatives, mainly wood machinists and joiners, including the cost of insurance and holidays, overtime rates and bonus payments, etc.
- *Indirect costs* – of employing both hourly paid operatives, such as general operatives and packing/despatch operatives, etc. Salaried staff including workshop foreman, managers, the setter/marker-out and other technical staff, again including the cost of insurance and holidays, etc.

The typical cost of employing a person is two to three times the hourly rate paid and this does not include other overheads and profit.

Each firm will have their own system for recording the amount of time spent by hourly paid operatives on a particular task. Typical methods of time collection include (see Figure 3.26):

- *Job records* – showing who has worked on a particular job. These are completed by the foreman.
- *Timesheets* – kept by individual operatives, showing on a daily basis the type and duration of tasks undertaken.
- *Electronic smartcards* – which are being increasingly used even by smaller concerns. The card is 'swiped' into the system by an operative who enters a job code each time they undertake a different task.

In addition to determining the labour cost of a job, the information collected may also be used to:

- compare the actual cost with the estimated cost;
- compile standard times for tasks;
- compare individual performance against a standard time;
- calculate financial incentive scheme payments;
- compile statistical information on productivity and downtime.

Overall costs – Overheads and profits are added to the actual material and labour costs to determine the total price charged to the customer for a particular job. Typical costs recovered in overheads are:

- salaries of administrative staff, senior support staff and directors;
- building maintenance and running costs;
- plant and machinery costs;
- consumable material costs.

READ THE INSTRUCTIONS AND COMPLETE THE TASK

Learning task

The cutting list for a casement window showing finished sizes is illustrated in Figure 3.27.

Complete the columns to show the material requirements for a batch of twelve. Allow 5 mm for planing on each section size, when entering the sawn sizes.

Using the sawn sizes calculate the total cost of material required for the batch of twelve, if the cost of US softwood is £235 52 per m³. Add cutting and wastage allowance of 20%.

You have determined a target time of 2.25 hours for manufacturing each window. Calculate the total time required to manufacture the batch of twelve, including an addition of 15% for planning and contingencies.

Determine the total cost of materials and labour for the batch of twelve to be charged to the customer, if the company's labour charge-out rate is £15.65 per hour and 35% is added to both material costs and labour rates for overheads and profit.

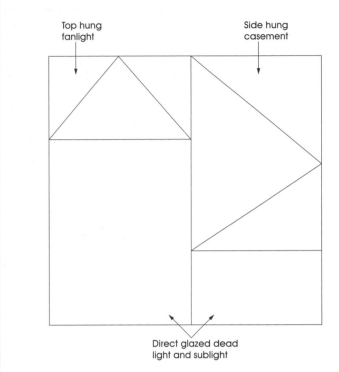

Figure 3.27

Cutting list					
Rod no.		Date		Contact no.	
Job title		Casement window			
Item no.	Item	No. off	Finished size (mm)	Sawn size	Material
	Frame:				
1	Jambs		70×95×1220		Redwood
2	Head		70×95×1350		Redwood
3	Sill		70×95×1350		Redwood
4	Transoms		70×95×600		Redwood
	Casement:				
5	Stiles		45×45×900		Redwood
6	Top rail		45×45×550		Redwood
7	Bottom rail		45×70×550		Redwood
	Fanlight:				
8	Stiles		45×45×300		Redwood
9	Top rail		45×45×550		Redwood
10	Bottom rail		45×70×550		Redwood

Total cost of material =

Total time to manufacture =

Selling price =

TRY TO ANSWER THESE

——— Questions for you ———

1. Define the term 'marking out' and state how it differs from setting out.

_____

_____

_____

_____

2. Explain the reason for using patterns when marking out joinery components.

_____

_____

_____

3. Briefly describe **TWO** main considerations made before placing a face mark on a piece of timber.

_____

_____

_____

_____

4. The tool/piece of equipment best used when squaring over lines on a pre-moulded piece of timber is: (a) steel square; (b) combination square; (c) box square; (d) set square.

a	b	c	d

5. Produce a sketch to show the veneer arrangement for a table top that is specified as quarter matched.

6. State the reason why a batch of paired stiles may be cramped to the pattern for marking out.

_____

_____

_____

7. Explain why radial sawn timber sections are more stable than tangential sawn sections.

_____

_____

_____

8. Define the following terms related to stair construction: margin; rise; going.

_____

_____

_____

_____

_____

9. Sketch a typical pattern head for an external door frame, marked up ready for machining.

WELL, HOW DID YOU DO?

WORK THROUGH THE SECTION AGAIN IF YOU HAD ANY PROBLEMS

10. State how the best possible grain match could be achieved for the meeting stiles of a pair of doors that are to receive a clear finish.

_____

_____

_____

COMPLETE THE WORD SQUARE

WORD-SQUARE SEARCH

Hidden in the word square are 20 words associated with *'marking out'*. You may find the words written forwards, backwards, up, down and diagonally. Solve the clues and then see if you can find the words.

MARKING OUT	INACCURACIES	MORTISE
BATCH	REBATE	CAD/CAM
PATTERN	PREPARED	BOX SQUARE
SECTIONAL	RECTANGULAR	SHOULDER LINES
GOING	CHAMFER	PAIRED
ACCURACY	HANDED	STRAIGHT EDGE
SQUARED	FACE SIDE	

Draw a ring round the words, or line-in using a highlight pen, thus:

Handed

Handed

WELL, HOW MANY DID YOU GET?

```
S E C W H A N D E D A E E T A B E R
B T A I A S F G H L S S F R J L W Q
A C R N T B O X S Q U A R E G F C S
T P B A G O I S D G I U C C A C A C
S R O C I Z X G N I O G R T N V D V
E E X C D G D S A I J G E A R O C G
N P S U F U H K J C N H D N E F A J
I A T R H H U T I R A C X G T F M E
L R R A R C U P E R Q M X U T S E A
R E A C A H T P Z D A Y E L A E C G
E D S I H J V A X R G R E A P C W E
L P E E G A S J B E F E X R U T F D
D A R S N J M D B S F R Z R R I Y I
U A F K G T Y F C I C Q A E F O U S
O K M A R K G C E T S C B W E N C E
H L P A I R E D L R Y R H D Q A B C
S P Q A D G F H J O F Y X C Z L S A
T U O G N I K R A M D E R A U Q S F
```

4 Manufacture of joinery products

READ THIS CHAPTER, WORKING THROUGH THE 'QUESTIONS FOR YOU'

In undertaking this chapter you will be required to demonstrate your skill and knowledge of the following joinery processes:

- Interpreting information.
- Selecting and preparing appropriate materials.
- Fitting, assembling and finishing components for internal and external joinery products.

You will be required practically to:

- Fit, assemble and finish components to form internal and external joinery products, including:
  – doors, door frames and linings
  – windows
  – staircases
  – wall and floor units.
- Undertake calculations for quantity, measurement or costs.
- Discuss work with setter-out/marker-out.

Task planning

Pre-task work

Before starting a job you will be involved in planning and organising the work. You may ask yourself the following questions:

- What is to be done?
- How is it to be done?
- When is it to be done?
- Where is it to be done?

In answering these questions, which is part of the planning process, you will refer to: drawings, specifications, setting-out rods, method statements and the actual machined components, etc. Any discrepancies must be resolved before proceeding with the work, as any mistakes are more costly to rectify the further on they go unnoticed.

Depending on your employer's line of communication, this may be directed via your workshop foreman/manager or direct with the setter-out/marker-out.

The means of communication will again vary depending on your organisation's line of communication and may involve direct face-to-face contact, a telephone call, e-mail or memo, or use of a standard form. The spoken word is often used as a quick and informal first point of

Figure 4.1 *Pre-task planning*

contact. However, a written confirmation should be sought as evidence and as a means of updating information for the future.

Resolving irregularities – On checking the machined components with the drawings and details, you notice that the data sheet for a veneered standard shows a vertical grain direction. Whereas, the actual standard has been machined with a horizontal grain direction. See Figure 4.2.

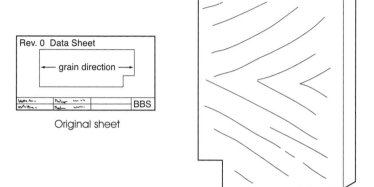

Figure 4.2 *Irregularities between data sheet and cut panel*

Your first action should be to speak directly or via the telephone with either you foreman/manager or setter-out/marker-out, to find whether there has been a last minute change or the standard has been incorrectly machined.

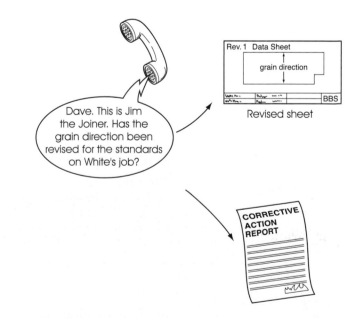

Figure 4.3 *Resolving irregularities*

If the data sheet has been revised and the grain direction as machined is correct, a new data sheet should be issued as confirmation.

If the data sheet is correct you may be required to complete a corrective action report form. This will have the effect of re-ordering the 'incorrectly' machined part (Figure 4.4).

BSS Joinery

CORRECTIVE ACTION REPORT

Raised by:	JIM. JONES		Job number:	WC12		Date raised:	8-11-02
Description:	BASE UNIT					Client:	WHITES & CO.

Defect or Improvement					
Manufacturing		Design		Details	
Saw:		Drawings:		General:	
Plane:		Specification:		*DATA SHEET FOR STANDARD,*	
Joint:		Data sheet:		*SHOWS VERTICAL GRAIN, BUT HAS*	
Mould:		Method statement:		*BEEN CUT HORIZONTALLY. CHECKED*	
Bore:		Setting out:		*WITH DESIGN, DATA SHEET IS*	
Assembly:		Marking out:		*CORRECT.*	
Handling damage:		Improvement:			
Other:	✔	Other:			

Suggested Corrective Action: (originator to complete)	Issued to:
RE-MACHINE 10 NEW STANDARDS TO DATA SHEET. **J.J.**	*MACHINE SHOP*
	Data received:
Corrective Action Taken: (recipient to complete)	Action taken by:
	Data completed:

☑ Tick appropriate box

Figure 4.4 *Corrective action report form*

Checking components – All materials and ironmongery should be inspected before use:

- Check you have the correct number of components shown on the cutting list.
- Inspect all components for damage. Any scratches on sheet material or bowing, shakes and other defect in timber, should be brought to the attention of your foreman/manager, who will decide whether thy are acceptable for use or require replacement.
- Ensure all ironmongery and other fittings are as specified and working correctly. Return defective items to the store for replacement.

Work tasks

Look at the method statement if provided, or write down a list of main tasks to be done, in the order that they will be undertaken. An example is shown over:

- Apply hardwood edge to batch of worktops and overlay with laminate.
- Mitre edging at returns.
- Glue and loose tongue, edge to top.
- Clean edge flush with face.
- Overlay with laminate.
- Trim off laminate and profile edge
- Sand up edging ready for finishing.

Tools and equipment

Look at the method statement or your work tasks list. Ensure you have all the correct specialist tools and equipment ready to undertake the task. Make a list. Items, which you do not have may require requisition from your stores, or even hiring from an outside supplier for the duration of the job. An example tools and equipment list is shown below:

- chop saw;
- 900 mm sash cramps (10 off);
- 'Jay' roller;
- hand-powered router and profile cutter;
- orbital sander.

Work timing

The time required to complete a task will depend on your skill level and how familiar you are with it. You may be given either a target time to do the work or a required completion date.

You will have to consider whether you can complete the task on your own within the deadlines, if not request assistance (Figure 4.5).

Review of task

On completion of the task, you should undertake a review. Think of any problems that occurred and steps you took to make things easier. Remember these and incorporate in future tasks. Figure 4.6 illustrates the planning, task and review procedure.

Figure 4.5 *Work timing*

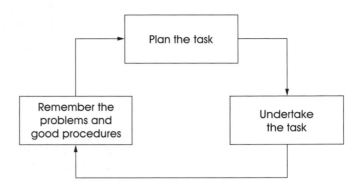

Figure 4.6 *Planning, task and review procedure*

Windows

A window is a glazed opening in a wall used to admit daylight and air and also to give the building's occupants an outside view. They are classified into different types by their method of opening, which is illustrated in Figure 4.7.

- *Casements* – which are either top or side hung on hinges.
- *Pivot hung* – which can be either horizontally or vertically hung.
- *Sliding sashes* – which can slide either horizontally or vertically.

The recommended method of indicating on a drawing the type of window and its method of opening is shown in Figure 4.8.

Figure 4.9 illustrates the principle of determining the size of rectangular window openings, with well balanced proportions. The method used is to draw a square with sides equal to the smallest dimension and then to swing the diagonal down to give the longest side. This method is equally suitable to determine the proportions of other items of joinery where a pleasing balanced effect is required.

Casement windows

A casement window comprises of two main parts: the frame and opening casement or casement sash.

The frame – consists of head, sill and two jambs. Where the frame is subdivided, the intermediate vertical members are called mullions and the intermediate horizontal member is called a transom.

The opening casement – consists of top rail, bottom rail and two stiles. Where the casement is subdivided, both the intermediate vertical and horizontal members are called glazing bars. Opening casements which are above the transom are known as fanlights. Fixed glazing is called a dead light and glazing at the bottom of a window, normally below a casement, is a sub-light. Where glass is bedded in the main frame itself, it is called direct glazing.

The elevation of a four-light casement window is shown in Figure 4.10 with all the component parts named. The 'four' refers to the number of glazed openings or lights in the window.

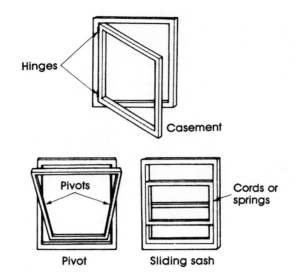

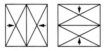

Figure 4.7 *Types of window*

Sliding: arrows indicate direction of opening

Casements: point of arrow indicates the hanging stile or rail

Pivot windows: lines indicate pivot points

Figure 4.8 *Direction of opening of doors and windows*

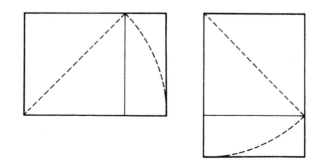

Figure 4.9 *Setting out rectangular openings*

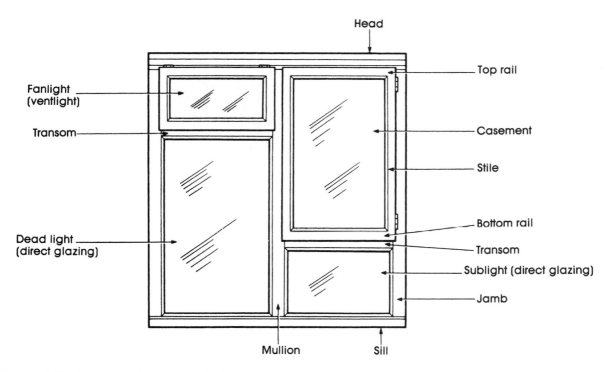

Figure 4.10 *Four-lighted casement window*

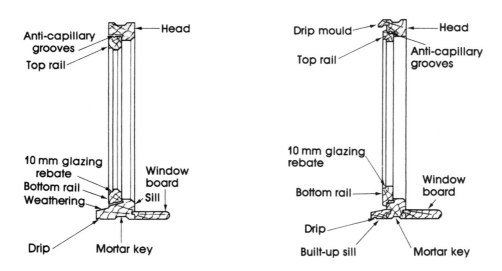

Figure 4.11 *Traditional casement and (right) stormproof casement*

Casement windows can further be divided into two types, traditional and stormproof depending on their method of construction. See Figure 4.11.

Traditional casement – A vertical section through a traditional casement window is illustrated in Figure 4.12. Anti-capillary grooves are incorporated into the frame and the opening casements, in order to prevent the passage of water into the building. Drip grooves are made towards the front edges of the transom and sill to stop the water running back beneath them.

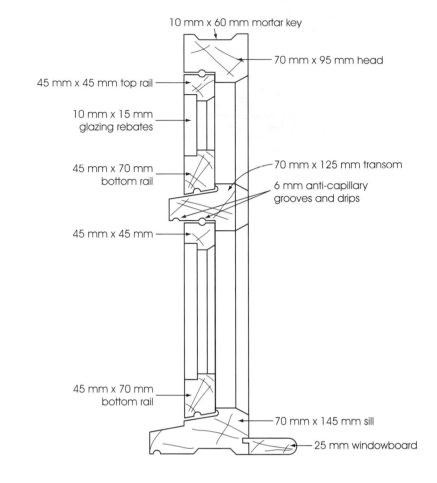

10 mm x 60 mm mortar key

70 mm x 95 mm head

45 mm x 45 mm top rail

10 mm x 15 mm glazing rebates

45 mm x 70 mm bottom rail

70 mm x 125 mm transom

6 mm anti-capillary grooves and drips

45 mm x 45 mm

45 mm x 70 mm bottom rail

70 mm x 145 mm sill

25 mm windowboard

Figure 4.12 *Traditional casement window (vertical section)*

A mortar key groove is run on the outside face of the head, sill and jambs. The sill also has a plough groove for the window sill to tongue into. Both transom and sill incorporate a throat to check the penetration of wind-assisted rain. In addition this feature may be continued up the jambs. Finally the front of the transom and sill is weathered: it has a nine degree slope for the rainwater to run off.

Figure 4.13 is a part horizontal section through a traditional casement window. It also shows the sizes and positions of the rebates, grooves and moulding in the jambs, mullion and casement stiles.

All joints used in traditional casement window construction are mortise and tenons. Standard haunched mortise and tenons (Figure 4.14) are generally used for the actual casements, although a sash haunch (Figure 4.15) is preferable where smaller sections are used. As a matter of good practice, the depth of the rebates should be kept the same as the depth of the mouldings. This simplifies the jointing as the shoulders of the tenons will be level.

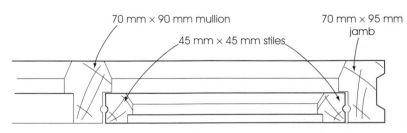

70 mm × 90 mm mullion

70 mm × 95 mm jamb

45 mm × 45 mm stiles

Figure 4.13 *Traditional casement window (part horizontal section)*

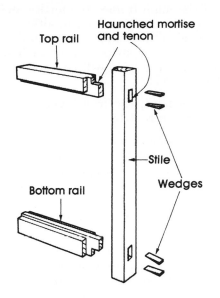

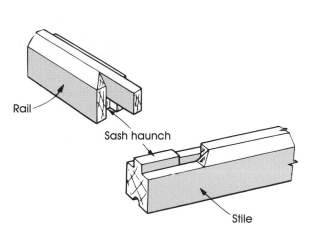

Figure 4.14 *Haunched mortise and tenon joint secured with wedges*

Figure 4.15 *Joint detail (sash haunch)*

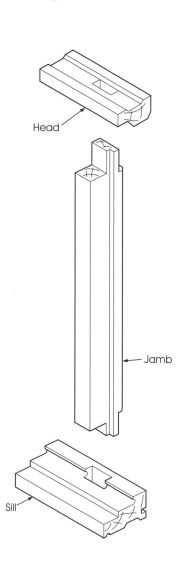

Figure 4.16 *Main frame joints*

The jointing of head, jamb and sill of the main frame are mortise and tenons (see Figure 4.16). These joints are normally wedged, although the use of draw pins or star dowels is acceptable and even preferable where the horn is to be later cut off. In addition, by offsetting the hole in the tenon slightly towards the shoulder, the joint will be drawn up tight as the pin is driven in (see Figure 4.17).

In order to make a better weatherproof joint, the front edge of the transom is housed across the jamb (see Figure 4.18).

Stormproof casement – Stormproof casement windows incorporate two rebates, one round the main frame, and the other round the casement. These rebates, in conjunction with the drip, anti-capillary grooves and throat make this type far more weatherproof than traditional casements (see Figure 4.19).

The jointing of the main frame of the stormproof casement window is often the same as that of the traditional casement, except for the transom which is not housed across the face of the jambs since it is usually of the same width. Comb joints can also be used, although they leave no horn for building in. Comb joints fixed with metal star dowels (see Figure 4.20) are normally used for jointing the actual casements, although mortise and tenon joints can be used.

Assembly procedure – The main frame and casement should be assembled dry to check the fit of joints, sizes, square and winding.

Squaring up – of a frame is checked with a squaring rod which consists of a length of rectangular section timber with a panel pin in its end as shown in Figure 4.21. The end with a panel pin is placed in one corner of the frame (see Figure 4.22). The length of the diagonal should then be marked in pencil on the rod. The other diagonal should then be checked. If the pencil marks occur in the same place, the frame must be square. If the frame is not square, then sash cramps should be angled to pull the frame into square as shown in Figure 4.23.

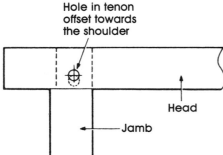

Figure 4.17 *Draw pinning*

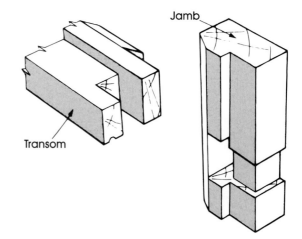

Figure 4.18 *Transom joint detail*

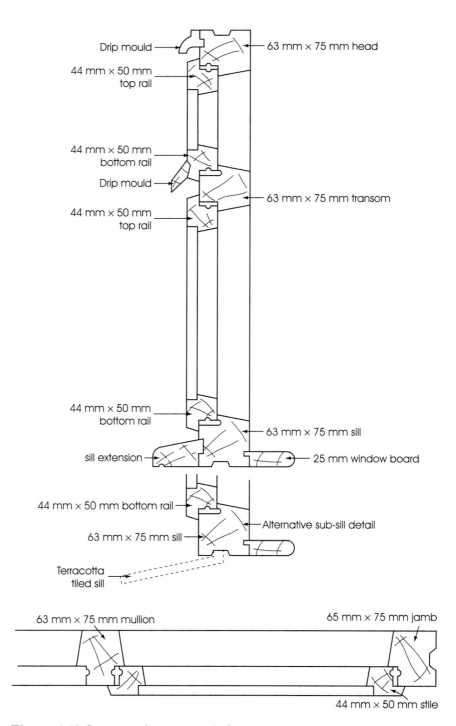

Figure 4.19 *Stormproof casement window*

Winding – of a frame is checked with winding strips (see Figure 4.24). These are two parallel pieces of timber. With the frame laying flat on a level bench, place a winding strip at either end of the job. Close one eye and sight the tops of the two strips as shown in Figure 4.25. If they appear parallel the frame is flat or 'out of wind'. The frame is said to be winding, in wind or distorted if the two strips do not line up. Repositioning of the cramps or adjustment to the joints may be required.

4 Manufacture of joinery products

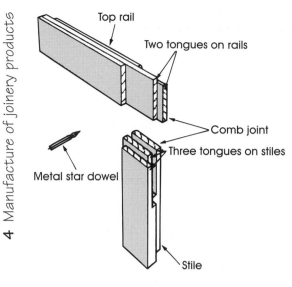

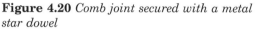

Figure 4.20 *Comb joint secured with a metal star dowel*

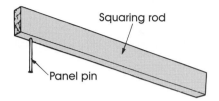

Figure 4.21 *Squaring rod*

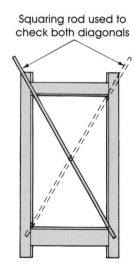

Figure 4.22 *Checking the frame for square*

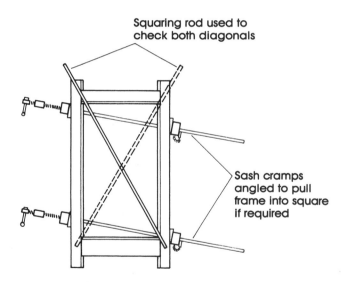

Figure 4.23 *Pulling the frame into square using cramps*

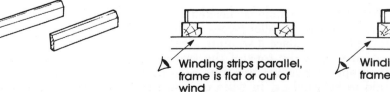

Figure 4.24 *Winding strips used to check frame for winding*

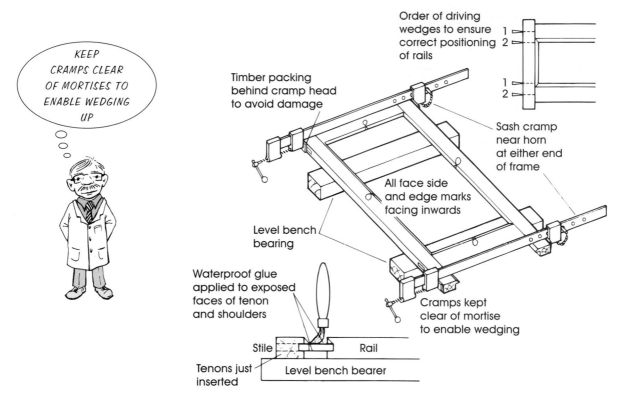

Figure 4.25 *Assembling casement sash*

Glue up – assemble and lightly drive wedges. A waterproof adhesive should be used for external joinery or where it is likely to be used in a damp location. Ensure the overall sizes are within the stated tolerances. Re-check for square and wind. Assuming all is correct, finally drive wedges and insert star dowels as appropriate.

Pivot windows

The vertical and horizontal sections of a traditional pivot window is shown in Figure 4.26. Both the surrounding frame and the pivoting sash are constructed using mortises and tenons. The sash is hung on pivot pins about 25 mm above its center line height to give it a self-closing tendency. The pivot pin usually is fixed to the frame and the socket to the sash. The planted stops which form the rebates serves to weatherproof the window. Those above the pivots are nailed or screwed to the frame on the outside and the sash on the inside, whereas those below are fixed to the frame on the inside and the sash on the outside. The actual positions of intersections of the beads needs to be precisely determined, especially where the sash is required to be removable without taking off any beads. This is shown in the vertical section. The sash stile and its planted top bead must be grooved as shown to allow removal of the sash. The head and top rail is splayed to give sufficient opening clearance. This is provided at the sill by its weathering.

Stormproof pivot window – Details of a stormproof centre-hung pivot window is shown in Figure 4.27. This is an improvement on the type described above. The joints used in the frame are mortise and tenons. Comb joints are used for the sash. Face fixing friction pivots or back flap hinges are used for hanging the sash.

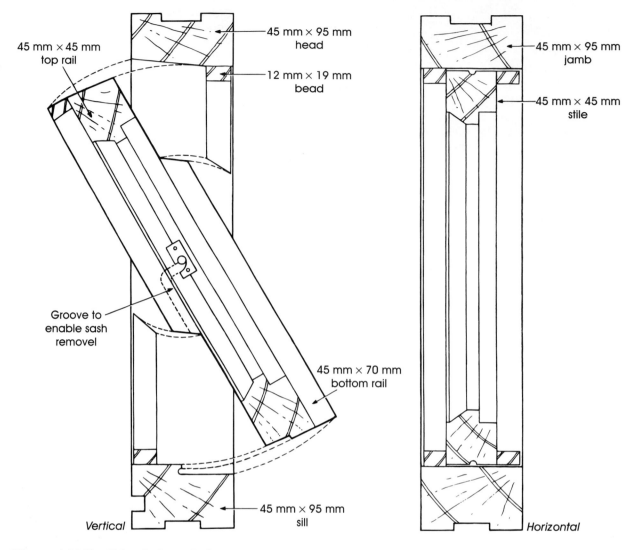

4 Manufacture of joinery products

45 mm × 45 mm top rail

45 mm × 95 mm head

12 mm × 19 mm bead

45 mm × 95 mm jamb

45 mm × 45 mm stile

Groove to enable sash removel

45 mm × 70 mm bottom rail

45 mm × 95 mm sill

Vertical

Horizontal

Figure 4.26 *Traditional pivot window sections*

The moulded stop, which is mitred around the frame and cut on the pivot line, is glued and pinned to the top half of the frame and the bottom half of the sash.

Sash windows

Vertical sliding sashes – consist of two sashes which slide up and down in a main frame. They are also known as double hung sliding sash windows. There are two different forms of construction for these types of window: those with boxed frames and those with solid frames.

Boxed frames – this type of window is the traditional pattern of sliding sashes and for many years has been superseded by casements and solid frame sash windows. This was mainly due to the high manufacturing and assembly costs of the large number of component parts. An understanding of their construction and operation is essential and they will frequently be met in renovation and maintenance work. See Chapter 6 Maintenance of Buildings for further details.

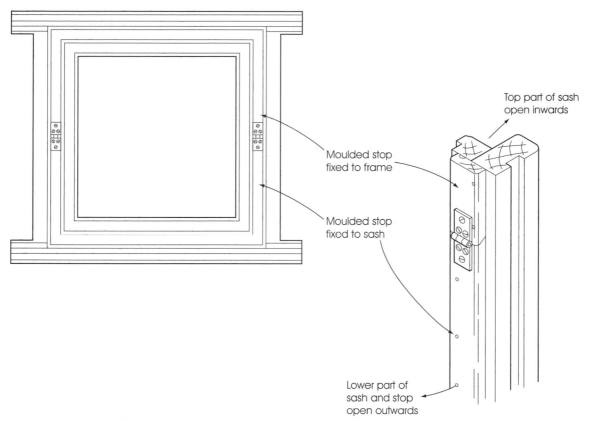

Figure 4.27 *Stormproof pivot window*

Solid frame sash windows – The elevation, horizontal and vertical section of a solid frame sliding sash window are illustrated in Figure 4.28. Both the frame and sashes can be jointed using mortise and tenon joints, or alternatively comb joints held with metal star dowels. For lightweight domestic sashes, the spring balances are accompanied in grooves run in the back of the sash stiles. The spring balances for heavyweight industrial sashes are accommodated in grooves which are run in the actual jamb of the frame.

Hanging casement sashes – Stormproof casements fit on the face of the frame and normally require no fitting at all. The only operation necessary to hang the casement is the screwing on of the hinges. See Figure 4.29

Traditional casements fit inside the frame and require both fitting and hanging. This is often thought of as a difficult task but by following the procedure given and illustrated in Figure 4.30, the task is greatly simplified.

Fitting and hanging procedure –

1. Mark the hanging side on both the sash and the frame.
2. Cut off the horns.
3. 'Shoot in' (plane to fit) the hanging stile.
4. Shoot the sash to width.
5. Shoot in the top and bottom of the sash.
6. Mark out and cut in the hinges.
7. Screw one leaf of the hinges to the sash.
8. Offer up the sash to the opening and screw the other leaf to the frame.
9. Adjust fit if required and fix any other ironmongery.

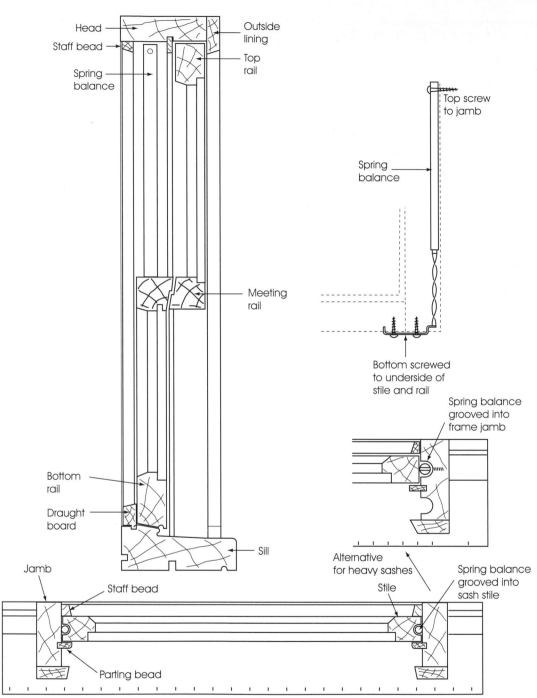

Figure 4.28 *Sash window sections*

The two stiles when planed should have a 'leading edge' (slightly out of square). This allows the sash to close freely without binding. The joint on casements should be 2 mm. This is to allow a certain amount of moisture movement and not cause the casement to jam in the frame.

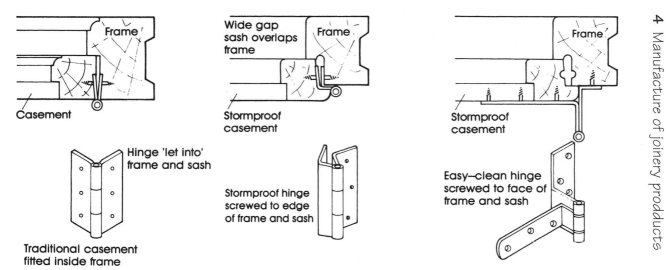

Figure 4.29 *Hanging of casement sashes*

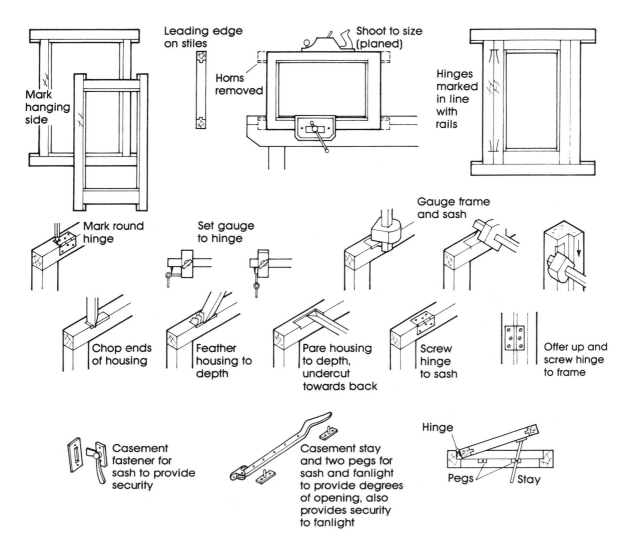

Figure 4.30 *Fitting and hanging a casement sash*

4 Manufacture of joinery products

TRY TO ANSWER THESE

─────── Questions for you ───────

1. Name a suitable piece of ironmongery for the fastening of:
(a) a top-hung casement;
(b) a side-hung casement sash.

_____

_____

2. Outline a typical procedure to follow, for resolving irregularities in work documentation.

_____

_____

_____

_____

3. Name the intermediate vertical member used to divide a casement window frame.

_____

4. State the reason for draw-pinning mortise and tenon joints.

_____

_____

5. Name the type of tenon shown.

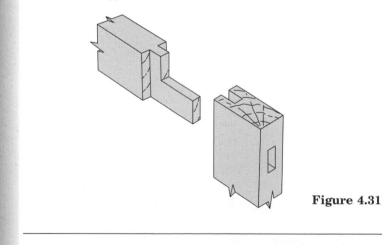

Figure 4.31

_____

6. State the reason why the stiles of a traditional casement window sash are planed with a 'leading edge'.

_____

_____

7. Complete a work task list as part of your pre-task planning to show the sequence of main operations required to assemble and complete a casement window frame and sash.

_____

_____

_____

_____

_____

_____

_____

8. Complete an equipment list for the task in Question 7.

_____

_____

_____

_____

_____

_____

_____

_____

9. On the outline of a casement window, mark the hinge positions.

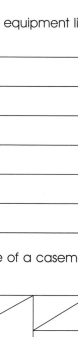

Figure 4.32

10. Sketch or describe the following terms: a) weathering; b) throating; c) rebate; d) groove.

WELL, HOW DID YOU DO?

WORK THROUGH THE SECTION AGAIN IF YOU HAD ANY PROBLEMS

Doors

READ THIS PAGE

A door is a moveable barrier used to cover an opening in a structure. Its main function is to allow access into a building and passage between the interior spaces. Other functional requirements may include weather protection, fire resistance, sound and thermal insulation, security, privacy, ease of operation and durability. Doors may be classified by their method of construction: matchboarded, panelled, glazed, flush, fire resistant, etc., and also by their method of operation: swinging, sliding and folding.

Methods of construction

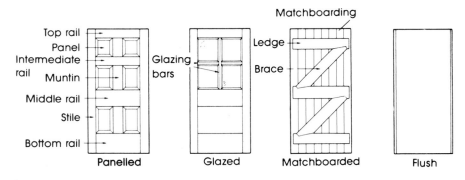

Figure 4.33 *Doors*

Panelled doors – have a frame made from solid timber rails and stiles, which are jointed using either dowels or mortise and tenon joints. The frame is either grooved or rebated to receive two or more thin plywood or timber panels. Interior doors are thinner than exterior doors.

Glazed doors – are used where more light is required. They are made similar to panelled doors except glass replaces one or more of the plywood or timber panels. Glazing bead is used to secure the glass into its glazing rebates. Glazing bars may be used to divide large glazed areas.

Matchboarded doors – are used mainly externally for gates, sheds and industrial buildings. They are simply constructed from matchboarding, ledges and braces clench nailed together. The bottom end of the braces must always point towards the hanging edge of the door to provide the required support. Framed matchboarded doors constructed with the addition of stiles and rails are used where extra strength is required.

Flush doors – are made with outer faces of plywood or hardboard. Internal doors are normally lightweight having a hollow core, solid timber edges and blocks which are used to reinforce hinge and lock positions. New flush doors will have one edge marked 'LOCK' and the other 'HINGE'; these must be followed. External and fire resistant flush doors are much heavier, as normally they have a solid core of either timber strips or chipboard. A variation on flush doors, is to use the same lightweight hollow core but have the faces covered in moulded or embossed facings to give the appearance of a traditional panel door. Internal doors use hardboard facings while plastic facings are mainly for external use.

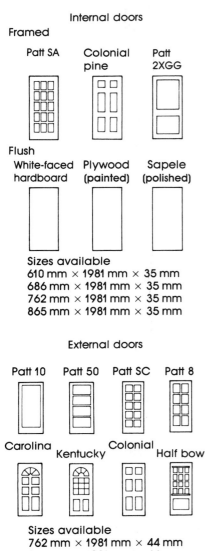

Internal doors

Framed

Patt SA Colonial pine Patt 2XGG

Flush

White-faced hardboard Plywood (painted) Sapele (polished)

Sizes available
610 mm × 1981 mm × 35 mm
686 mm × 1981 mm × 35 mm
762 mm × 1981 mm × 35 mm
865 mm × 1981 mm × 35 mm

External doors

Patt 10 Patt 50 Patt SC Patt 8

Carolina Kentucky Colonial Half bow

Sizes available
762 mm × 1981 mm × 44 mm
835 mm × 1981 mm × 44 mm
813 mm × 2032 mm × 44 mm

Figure 4.34 *Extract from a manufacturer's door list showing range of stock size doors*

Fire resisting doors – The main function of this type of door is to act as a barrier to a possible fire by providing the same degree of protection as the element in which it is located. They should prevent the passage of smoke, hot gases and flames for a specified period of time. This period of time will vary depending on the relevant statutory regulations and the location of the door. Fire doors are not normally purpose-made, as they must have approved fire resistance certification. It is advantageous to use proven proprietary products. Oversize fire door 'blanks' are available for cutting down to size, if required to suit specific situations.

Door sizes

All mass-produced doors may be purchased from a supplier in a range of standard sizes as shown in Figure 4.34. Special sizes or purpose made designs are normally available to order from suppliers with joinery shop contacts.

Manufacture of doors

Matchboarded doors – This group of doors involves the simplest form of construction. They are suitable for both internal and external use, although they are mainly used externally for gates, sheds and industrial buildings.

Ledged and braced door – The basic door shown in Figure 4.35 consists of matchboarding which is held together by ledges. This type is little used because it has a tendency to sag and distort on the side opposite the hinges. In order to overcome this braces are usually incorporated in the construction (see Figure 4.36). The use of braces greatly increases the rigidity of the door. The bottom ends of the braces should always point towards the hinged edge of the door in order to provide the required support. Where these doors are used externally, the top edge of the ledges should be weathered to stop the accumulation of rainwater and moisture.

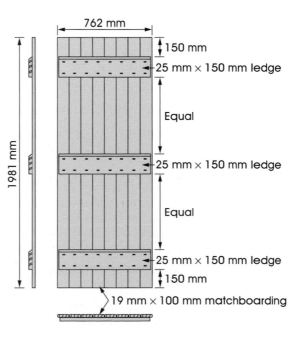

Figure 4.35 *Ledged and matchboarded door*

762 mm
1981 mm
150 mm
25 mm × 150 mm ledge
Equal
25 mm × 150 mm ledge
Equal
25 mm × 150 mm ledge
150 mm
19 mm × 100 mm matchboarding

101

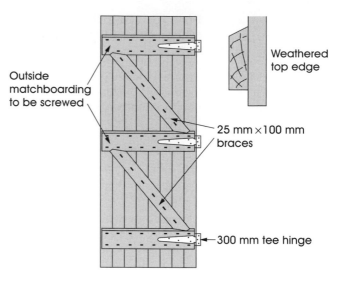

Figure 4.36 *Ledged, braced and matchboarded door showing weathering if door is for external use*

Three ledges are used to hold the matchboarding together. The outside pieces should be fixed with screws, while the remaining lengths of matchboarding are nailed to the ledges. Lost-head nails 6 mm longer than the thickness of the door are used for this purpose. The nails should be punched in and clenched over. Clenching over simply means bending the protruding part of the nails over and punching the ends below the surface as shown in Figure 4.37. The two braces, when used, are also fixed with lost-head nails which are clenched over. The joint detail between the ledges and braces is shown in Figure 4.38.

Figure 4.37 *Clenching over*

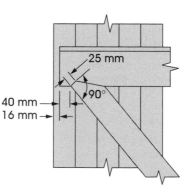

Figure 4.38 *Joint details between ledges and braces*

Framed, ledged, braced and matchboarded door – this type of door is an improvement on the ledged, braced and matchboarded door, as it includes stiles which are jointed to the top, bottom and middle rails with mortise and tenons.

The use of the framework increases the door's strength, and resists any tendency which the door might have to distort. Braces are optional when the door is framed, but their use further increases the door's strength.

Figure 4.39 shows that the stiles and top rail are the same thickness, while the middle and bottom rails are thinner. This is so that the matchboarding can be tongued into the top rail, over the face of the middle and bottom rails, and run to the bottom of the door. As the middle and bottom rails are thinner than the stiles, bare-faced tenons (tenons with only one shoulder) must be used (see Figure 4.40). These joints are normally wedged, although for extra strength draw pins can be used.

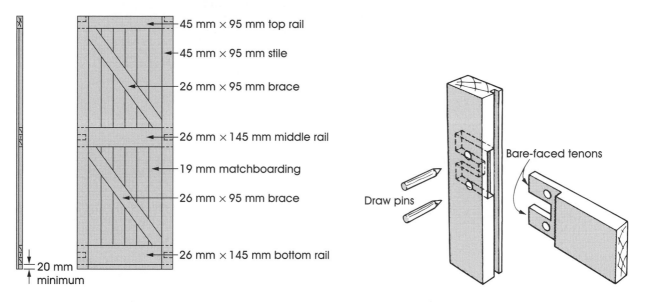

Figure 4.39 *Framed, ledged, braced and matchboarded door*   **Figure 4.40** *Bare-faced tenons joint detail*

Assembly procedure for framed matchboarded doors – This is carried out using a similar procedure to that followed when assembling the casement window. Figure 4.41 shows how the stiles and rails are assembled, glued and wedged before the matchboarding is fixed.

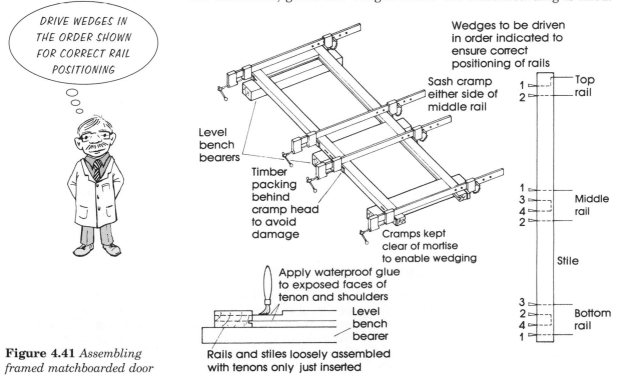

Figure 4.41 *Assembling framed matchboarded door*

The boards should be arranged so that the two outside ones are of equal width. They may either be tongued into the top rail and stiles or simply fit into a housing (see Figure 4.42).

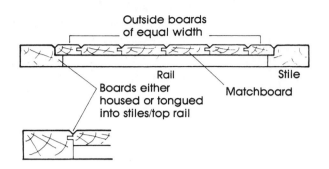

Figure 4.42 *Matchboarding details*

Before assembly the tongues and grooves, the backs of rails and braces and all other concealed surfaces must be treated with a suitable priming paint or preservative.

Arrange the boards on the assembled frame. Locate tongues and grooves so that the boards form an arc between the jambs. Place a short piece of timber across the door at either end. With assistance apply pressure at both ends of the door to fold the boards flat (see Figure 4.43).

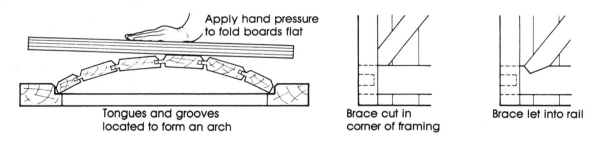

Figure 4.43 *Folding matchboards and fitting braces*

Tap up the boards from the bottom to locate them correctly into the top rail and then clench nail or staple them (using a pneumatic nail gun) to all framing members.

Mark, cut and fix the braces. These may be either cut into the corners of the framework, or let into the rails. The cut in the corner method is simpler; however, it has a tendency to push open the joints between the stiles and the rails.

Panelled and glazed doors

The design and construction of panelled doors are very similar to glazed doors. They consist of a frame which has either a plough groove or rebate run around it to receive the panels or glazing. The framing members for these doors vary with the number and arrangements of the panels. They will consist of horizontal members and vertical members.

Rails, stiles and muntings – All horizontal members are called rails. They are also named according to their position in the door, such as top rail, middle rail, bottom rail, intermediate rail. The middle rail is also known as the lock rail and the upper intermediate rail is sometimes called a frieze rail.

The two outside vertical members are called stiles, while all intermediate vertical members are known as muntins.

Figure 4.44 shows a typical panelled door, with all its component parts named. The middle and bottom rails are of a deeper section as they serve to hold the door square and thus prevent sagging. Muntins are introduced in order to reduce the panel width, therefore reducing the unsightly effect of moisture movement and the likelihood of panel damage.

It is normal to leave at least a 50 mm horn on each end of the stiles. This serves two purposes:

● It enables the joints to be securely wedged without fear of splitting out.
● The horns protect the top and bottom edges of the door before it is hung.

Panels – Figure 4.45 shows a ply panel which is held in a plough groove that is run around the inside edge of the framing. Two ovolo mouldings are also worked around the inside edges of the framing for decorative purposes. They are known as stuck mouldings. The plough groove should be at least 2 mm deeper than the panel. This is to allow for any moisture movement (shrinkage and expansion).

Figure 4.46 again shows a solid or plywood panel which is held in a plough groove that is run around the inside edge of the framing. Here a planted or bed mould has been applied around the panel for decoration. This method avoids the need to scribe or mitre the shoulders of the rails which applies with stuck mouldings.

Planted moulds must not be allowed to restrict panel movement. Therefore they should be pinned to the framing and not the panel.

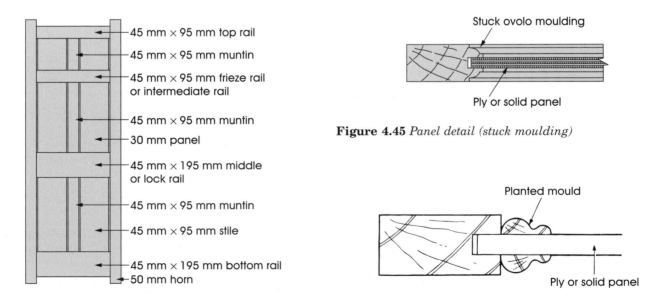

45 mm × 95 mm top rail
45 mm × 95 mm muntin
45 mm × 95 mm frieze rail or intermediate rail
45 mm × 95 mm muntin
30 mm panel
45 mm × 195 mm middle or lock rail
45 mm × 95 mm muntin
45 mm × 95 mm stile
45 mm × 195 mm bottom rail
50 mm horn

Figure 4.44 *A typical panelled door*

Stuck ovolo moulding

Ply or solid panel

Figure 4.45 *Panel detail (stuck moulding)*

Planted mould

Ply or solid panel

Figure 4.46 *Panel detail (planted mould)*

Figure 4.47 shows a timber panel which is tongued into a plough groove in the framing. This type of panel is known as a bead butt panel because on its vertical edges a bead moulding is worked, while the horizontal edges remain square and butt up to the rails.

A thin plywood or glazed panel which is located in the rebate is shown in Figure 4.48. It is held in position by planted beads, which are pinned into the framing. Where this type of door is used externally water tends to get behind them. This makes both the beads and framing susceptible to decay.

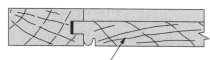

Bead and butt panel

Figure 4.47 *Panel detail (bead butt)*

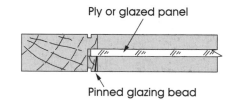

Ply or glazed panel

Pinned glazing bead

Figure 4.48 *Panel detail (planted bead)*

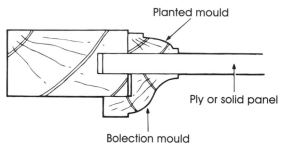

Planted mould

Ply or solid panel

Bolection mould

Figure 4.49 *Panel detail (bolection mould)*

For a neat finish planted beads or moulds should not finish flush with the framing.

Figure 4.49 shows a planted mould that is rebated over the framing in order to create an enhanced feature. This type is known as a bolection mould. In general bolection moulds are fitted on the face and planted bed moulds on the reverse, although in the case of top quality work bolection moulds could be used on both faces.

The bolection mould is fixed through the panel with screws. The holes for the screws should be slotted across the grain to permit panel movement without risk of splitting. The planted bed mould used on the other side to cover the screws should be skew nailed to the framing.

In good quality joinery, refurbishment or restoration work, the panels themselves may be decorated by working various mouldings on one or both of their faces. The portion around the edge of a panel is called the margin and the centre portion is known as the field. The small flat section around the edge of the panel is to enable its correct location in the framing.

Figure 4.50 illustrates the section and part elevation of the main types of decorated panels.

(a) Shows a raised or bevel raised panel.
(b) Shows a raised and fielded panel, also known as bevel raised and fielded, where the margin has been bevelled to raise the field.
(c) Shows a raised, sunk and fielded panel, also known as bevelled, raised sunk and fielded. In this case the margin has been sunk below the field to emphasize it.
(d) Shows a raised, sunk and raised fielded panel, also known as bevelled raised, sunk and bevelled raised fielded panel, where the field itself has been bevelled as a further enhanced detail.

Where bolection moulds or planted moulds are used to finish decorated panels, the small flat section around the panel edge must be extended to provide a flat surface that will accommodate the mouldings.

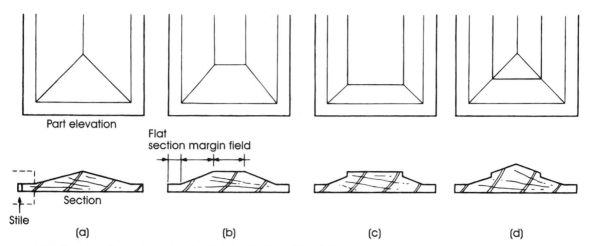

Figure 4.50 *Decorated panels: (a) raised; (b) raised and fielded; (c) raised, sunk and fielded; (d) raised, sunk and raised fielded*

Joints – traditionally the mortise and tenon joint was used exclusively in the jointing of panelled and glazed doors, but today the majority of doors are mass produced and in order to reduce costs the dowelled joint is used extensively.

The use of the dowelled joint reduces the cost of the door in three ways:

- The length of each rail is reduced by at least 200 mm
- The jointing time is reduced as holes only have to be drilled to accommodate the dowel.
- The assembly time is reduced as no wedging, etc., has to be carried out.

Figure 4.51 shows a six-panel door which has been jointed using dowels. These dowels should be 16 mm × 150 mm and spaced approximately 50 mm centre to centre. The following is the minimum recommended number of dowels to be used for each joint:

- Top rail to stile: two dowels.
- Middle rail to stile: three dowels.
- Bottom rail to stile: three dowels.
- Intermediate rail to stile: one dowel.
- Muntin to rail: two dowels.

Figure 4.52 shows an exploded view of a dowelled joint between a top rail and stile. In addition to the dowel, a haunch is incorporated into the joint. This ensures that the two members finish flush. Its use also overcomes any tendency for the rail to twist.

Dowels should be cut to length, chamfered off at either end to aid location and finally a small groove is formed along their length, to allow any excess glue and trapped air escape when the joint is cramped up. Alternatively 'ready-made' dowels may be used. These are available in a range of sizes; they have chamfered ends and multi-grooved sides. See Figure 4.53.

Although the dowel joint is extensively used for mass-produced doors, the mortise and tenon joint is still used widely for purpose-made and high quality door construction.

Figure 4.54 shows an exploded view of the framework for a typical six-panel door. Haunched mortise and tenons are used for the joints between the rails and stiles.

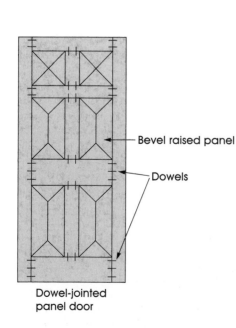

Figure 4.51 *Dowel – jointed panel door*

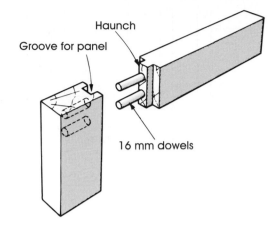

Figure 4.52 *Exploded view of a dowelled joint*

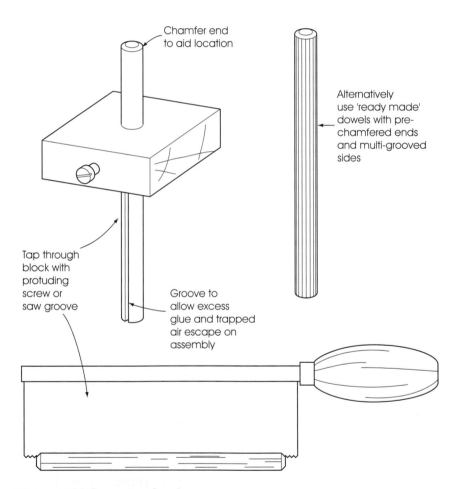

Figure 4.53 *Preparing dowels*

For joints between the muntins and rails, stub mortise and tenons are used. As these joints do not go right through the rails, they cannot be wedged in the normal way. Instead fox wedges are used (see Figure 4.55). These are small wedges which are inserted into the saw cuts in the tenon. When the joint is cramped up the wedge expands the tenon and causes it to grip securely in the mortise.

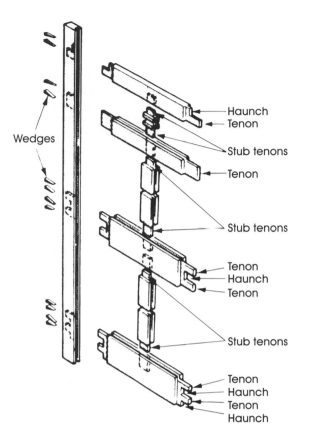

Figure 4.54 *Exploded view of joint details*

A traditional half-glazed door is shown in Figure 4.56. It is constructed with diminishing stiles, in order to provide the maximum area of glass and therefore admit into the building the maximum amount of daylight. This type of door is also known as gun stock stile door because its stiles are said to resemble the stock of a gun. The middle rail has

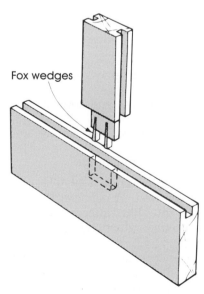

Figure 4.55 *Fox wedged joint*

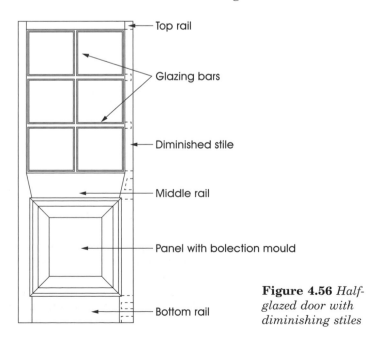

Figure 4.56 *Half-glazed door with diminishing stiles*

splayed shoulders to overcome the change in width of the stiles, above and below the middle rail. An exploded view of this joint is shown in Figure 4.57.

The top half of the door can either be fully glazed or subdivided with glazing bars as shown in Figure 4.58. When glazing bars are used they are normally stub tenoned into the stiles and rails. The joints between the glazing bars themselves could either be stub tenoned or halved and scribed. The bottom half of the door normally consists of a bevel raised sunk and fielded panel with planted bolection mouldings.

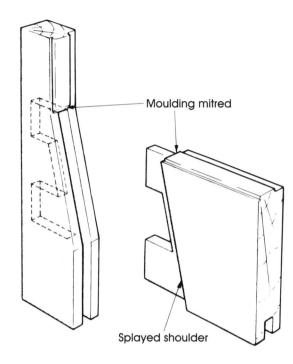

Figure 4.57 *Diminished stile joint detail*

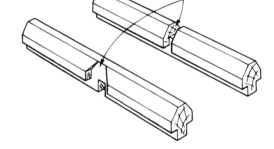

Figure 4.58 *Glazing rail or bar joint detail*

Assembly procedure for panelled and glazed doors – This can be carried out for all types of framed door, using the following assembly procedure:

● Dry assemble to check fit of joints, overall sizes, square and winding.
● Clean up inside edges of all framing components and both faces of panels.
● Glue, assemble, cramp up and wedge. Re-check for square and winding.
● Clean up remainder of item and prepare for finishing.

The assembly of a six-panel door is illustrated in Figure 4.59. The rails and muntins should be glued and assembled first. Panels can then be inserted dry, taking care to ensure that no glue has squeezed into the panel grooves. Next the stiles are positioned, glued, cramped and wedged followed by final cleaning up.

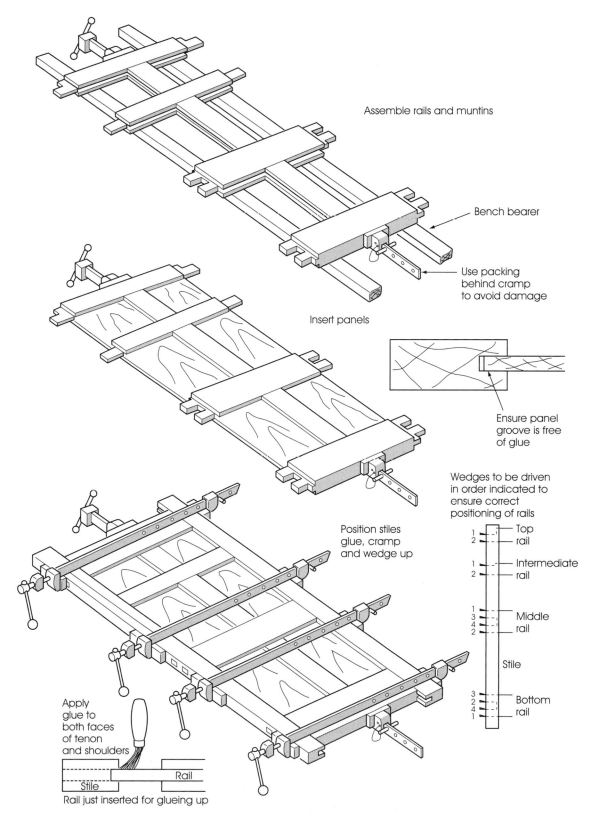

Assemble rails and muntins

Bench bearer

Use packing behind cramp to avoid damage

Insert panels

Ensure panel groove is free of glue

Wedges to be driven in order indicated to ensure correct positioning of rails

1
2 — Top rail

1
2 — Intermediate rail

1
3
4 — Middle rail
2

Stile

3
2 — Bottom rail
4
1

Position stiles glue, cramp and wedge up

Apply glue to both faces of tenon and shoulders

Rail

Stile

Rail just inserted for glueing up

Figure 4.59 *Assembling six-panel door*

111

Flush doors

Joinery works are rarely involved with the manufacture of flush doors, except where special features, not available in standard mass-produced doors, are required.

Figure 4.60 shows a skeleton core door which is suitable in one-off or limited production. It consists of 28 mm × 70 mm stiles, top, bottom and middle rails; 20 mm × 28 mm intermediate rails are used to complete the framework.

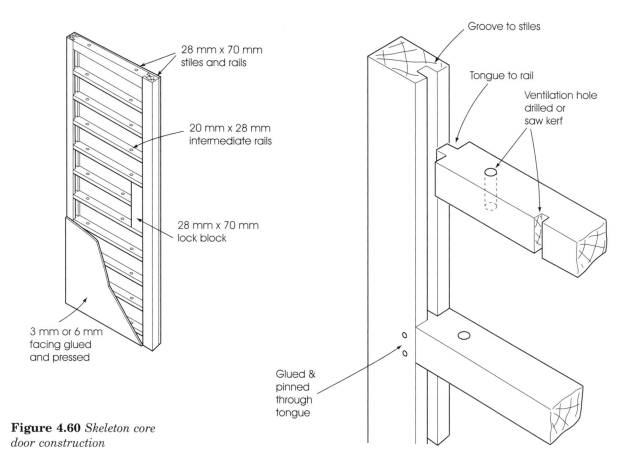

28 mm x 70 mm stiles and rails

20 mm x 28 mm intermediate rails

28 mm x 70 mm lock block

3 mm or 6 mm facing glued and pressed

Groove to stiles

Tongue to rail

Ventilation hole drilled or saw kerf

Glued & pinned through tongue

Figure 4.60 *Skeleton core door construction*

Very simple joints can be used in this type of construction, as its main strength is obtained by firmly gluing the facings both to the framework and to the core. The rails are usually either tongued into a groove in the stiles or butt jointed and fixed with staples or corrugated fasteners. Ventilation holes or grooves must be incorporated between each compartment. This is to prevent air becoming trapped in the compartment when the door is assembled. If this were not done the facings would have a tendency to bulge.

Lippings – are narrow strips of timber which are fixed along the edges of better quality flush doors. Their purpose is to mask the edges of the facings and provide a neat finish to the door. External doors should have lippings fixed to all four edges for increased weather protection.

Plain lipping is acceptable for internal doors, but for better quality internal doors and external doors tongued lipping is preferred, see

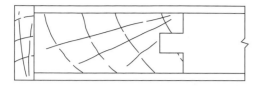

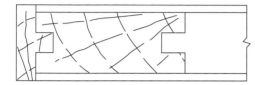

Figure 4.61 *Flush lipping and tongued lipping*

Figure 4.61. Lipping should be glued in position and not fixed with panel pins.

Vision panels – are often required in purpose-made flush doors. Additional framing is required around the opening should be as shown in Figure 4.62. Additional blocking out pieces can be used where other shaped vision panels are required (see Figure 4.63). This framing and blocking is normally done during the construction of the door, although it is possible to form the opening at a later stage.

Glazings beads – are used to hold the glass in place. Figure 4.64 shows glazing beads, suitable for an internal door. Figure 4.65 shows rebated glazing beads, which are more suitable for external doors as they provide a more weather-resistant finish. Figure 4.66 shows a better method for fixing external glazing, as it provides far greater security than the previous method.

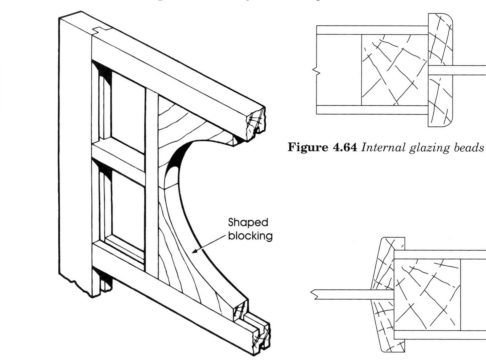

Shaped blocking

Figure 4.64 *Internal glazing beads*

Figure 4.62 *Flush door with vision panel*

Figure 4.63 *Blocking for circular vision panel*

Figure 4.65 *Internal or external glazing beads*

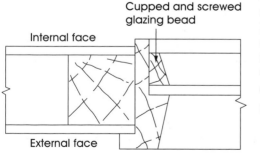

Cupped and screwed glazing bead

Internal face

External face

Figure 4.66 *Alternative external flush door glazing detail*

Glazing beads are normally simply pinned in place. However for better quality work, they can be fixed using countersunk brass screws and recessed cups. This enables the glazing beads to be easily removed and replaced in the event of the glass needing replacement.

Types of door operation – Figure 4.67 shows various methods of door operation: swinging, sliding and folding.

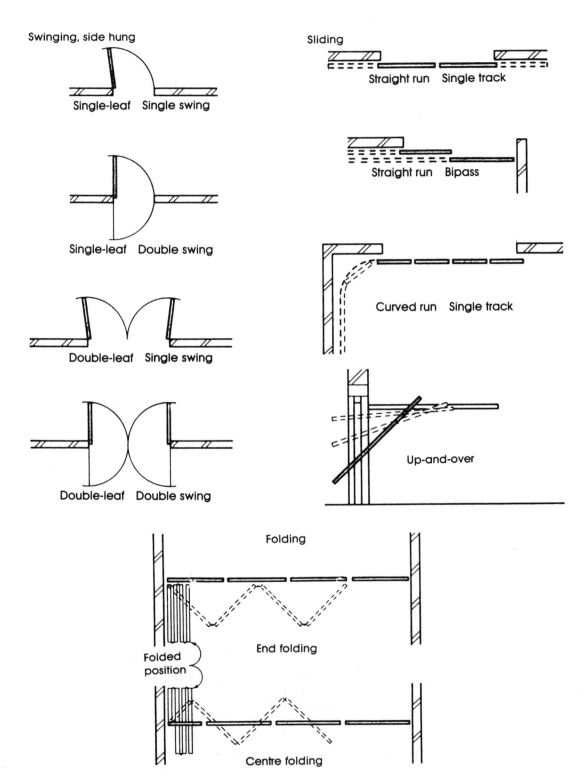

Figure 4.67 *Methods of door operation*

Swinging doors – Side hung on hinges is the most common means of door operation. It is also the most suitable for pedestrian use and the most effective for weather protection, fire resistance, sound and thermal insulation.

Sliding doors – are mainly used either to economise on space where it is not possible to swing a door, or for large openings which would be difficult to close off with swinging doors.

Folding doors – are a combination of swinging and sliding doors. They can be used as either movable internal partitions to divide up large rooms, or alternatively as doors for large warehouses and showroom entrances.

Door ironmongery

WHEN ORDERING IRONMONGERY, YOU ONLY NEED TO STATE:
5.0 = CLOCKWISE CLOSING/OPENING FACE
5.1 = CLOCKWISE CLOSING/CLOSING FACE
6.0 = ANTICLOCKWISE CLOSING/OPENING FACE
6.1 = ANTICLOCKWISE CLOSING/CLOSING FACE

Door ironmongery is also termed **door furniture** and includes hinges, locks, latches, bolts, other security devices, handles and letter or postal plates. The hand of a door is required in order to select the correct items of ironmongery. Some locks and latches have reversible bolts, enabling either hand to be adapted to suit the situation.

View the door from the hinge knuckle side; if the knuckles are on the left the door is left handed, whereas if the knuckles are on the right, the door is right handed. Figure 4.68 shows how doors may also be defined as either clockwise or anticlockwise closing.

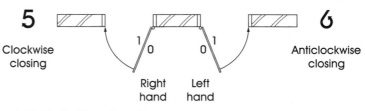

5 Clockwise closing

Right hand   Left hand

6 Anticlockwise closing

Figure 4.68 *Typical handing diagram*

Hinges

Hinges are available in a variety of materials: pressed steel are commonly used for internal doors and brass for hardwood and external doors. Do not use steel hinges on hardwood or external doors because of rusting and subsequent staining problems. Do not use nylon, plastic or aluminium hinges on fire-resistant doors because they melt at fairly low temperatures.

Double washers

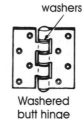

Butt hinge

Washered butt hinge

Parliament hinge

Rising butt

Figure 4.69 *Range of hinges*

115

Butt hinge – is a general purpose hinge suitable for most applications. As a general rule the leaf with the greatest number of knuckles is fixed to the door frame.

Washered butt hinges – are used for heavier doors to reduce knuckle wear and prevent squeaking.

Parliament hinges – have wide leaves to extend knuckles and enable doors to fold back against the wall clearing deep architraves, etc.

Rising butts – are designed to lift the door as it opens to clear obstructions such as mats and rugs. They also give a door some degree of self-closing action. In order to prevent the top edge of the door fouling in the frame as it opens and closes, the top edge must be eased as shown in Figure 4.70. The hand of the door must be stated when ordering this item, as they cannot be reversed (i.e. they cannot be altered to suit either hand of door).

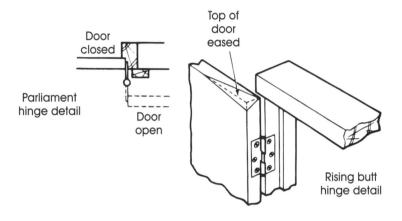

Figure 4.70 *Installation of hinges*

Locks, latches and other furniture (Figure 4.71)

Cylinder rim latches – are mainly used for entrance doors to domestic property but, as they are only a latch, provide little security on their own. When fitted, the door can be opened from the outside with the use of a key and from the inside by turning the handle. Some types have a double locking facility which improves their security.

Mortise deadlock – provides a straightforward key-operated locking action and is often used to provide additional security on entrance doors where cylinder rim latches are fitted. They are also used on doors where simple security is required, e.g. storerooms.

Mortise latch – is used mainly for internal doors that do not require locking. The latch which holds the door in the closed position can be operated from either side of the door by turning the handle.

Mortise lock/latch – is available in the two types, the horizontal one is little used nowadays because of its length, which means that it can only be fitted to substantial doors. The vertical type is more modern and can be fitted to most types of doors. It is often known as a narrow-stile lock/latch. Both types can be used for a wide range of general purpose doors in various locations. They are, in essence, a combination of the mortise deadlock and the mortise latch.

Rebated mortise lock/latch – should be used when fixing a lock/latch in double doors that have rebated stiles. The front end of this lock is cranked to fit the rebate on the stiles.

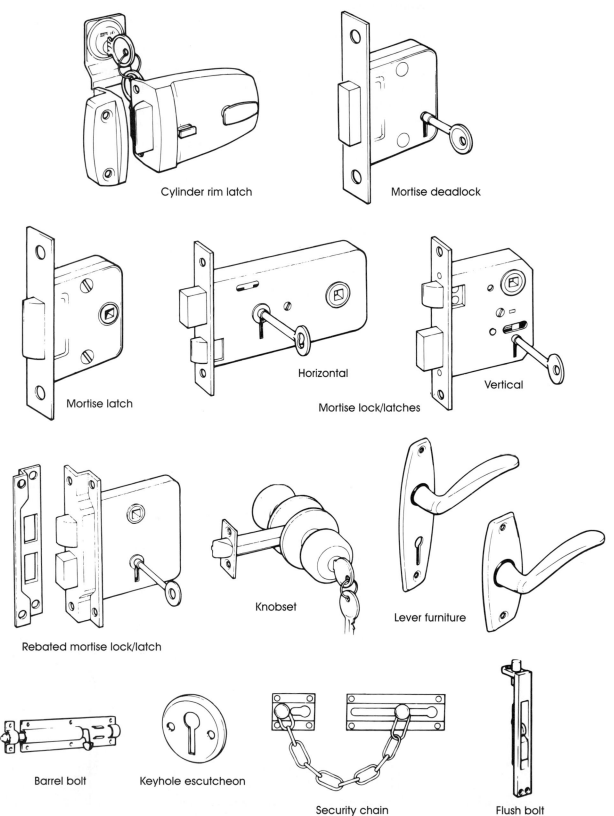

Cylinder rim latch

Mortise deadlock

Mortise latch

Mortise lock/latches

Horizontal

Vertical

Rebated mortise lock/latch

Knobset

Lever furniture

Barrel bolt

Keyhole escutcheon

Security chain

Flush bolt

Figure 4.71 *Door locks and furniture*

Knobset – consists of a small mortise latch and a pair of knob handles that can be locked with a key, so that it can be used as a lock/latch in most situations both internally and externally. Knobsets can also be obtained without the lock in the knob for use as a latch only.

Knob furniture – is for use with the horizontal mortise lock/latch. It should not be used with the vertical type as hand injuries will result.

Keyhole escutcheon plates – are used to provide a neat finish to the keyhole of both deadlocks and horizontal mortise lock/latches.

Lever furniture – is available in a wide range of patterns, for use with the mortise latches and mortise lock/latches.

Barrel bolts – are used on external doors and gates to lock them from the inside. Two bolts are normally used, one at the top of the door and the other at the bottom.

Flush bolt – is flush fitting and therefore requires recessing into the timber. It is used for better quality work on the inside of external doors to provide additional security and also on double doors and French windows to bolt one door in the closed position. Two bolts are normally used, one at the top of the door and the other at the bottom.

Security chains – can be fixed on front entrance doors, the slide to the door and the chain to the frame. When the chain is inserted into the slide, the door will only open a limited amount until the identity of the caller is checked.

Ironmongery positioning

Hinge positions – are shown in Figure 4.72. Lightweight internal doors are normally hung on one pair of 75 mm hinges; glazed, half-hour fire resistant and other heavy doors need one pair of 100 mm hinges. All external doors and one-hour fire resistant doors need one and a half pairs of 100 mm hinges. The standard hinge positions for flush doors are 150 mm down from the top, 225 mm up from the bottom and the third hinge where required, positioned centrally to prevent warping, or towards the top for maximum weight capacity. On panelled and glazed doors the hinges are often fixed in line with the rails to produce a more balanced look.

Other furniture positions – will depend on the type of door construction, the specification and the door manufacturer's instructions.

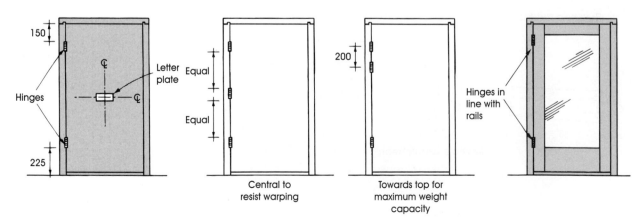

Figure 4.72 *Position of door hardware*

The standard position for mortise locks and latches, shown in Figure 4.73, is 990 mm from the bottom of the door to the centre line of the lever or knob furniture spindle. However, on a panelled door with a middle rail, locks/latches may be positioned centrally in the rail's width. Cylinder rim latches are positioned in the door's style between 1200 mm and 1500 mm from the bottom of the door and the centre line of the cylinder. Before fitting any locks/latches the width of the door stile should be measured to ensure the lock/latch length is shorter than the stile's width, otherwise a narrow stile lock may be required.

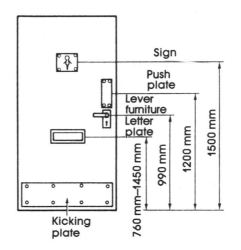

Figure 4.73 *Fixing heights*

Letter plates are normally positioned centrally in a door's width and between 760 mm and 1450 mm from the bottom of the door to the centre line of the plate. Again on panelled doors letter plates may be positioned centrally in a rail and sometimes even vertically in a stile.

- Always read the job specification as exact furniture positions may be stated.
- Always read both the door manufacturer's instructions and the ironmongery manufacturer's instructions to ensure the intended position is suitable to receive the item, e.g. the positioning of the lock block on a flush door, and the item is fixed correctly.

Door and ironmongery schedules

Schedules are used to record repetitive design information, see Figure 4.74. Read with a range drawing and floor plans, they may be used to identify a type of door, its size, the number required, the door opening in which it fits, the hinges it will swing on and details of other furniture to be fitted to it.

Details relevant to a particular door opening are indicated in the schedules by a dot or cross, a Figure is also included where more than one item is required. Extracting details from a schedule is called 'taking off'.

The following information concerning the WC door D2 has been taken off the schedules: One polished plywood internal flush door type B2 762 mm × 1981 mm × 35 mm, hung on one pair of 75 mm brass butts and fitted with one mortise lock/latch, one brass mortise lock/latch furniture and two brass coat hooks.

119

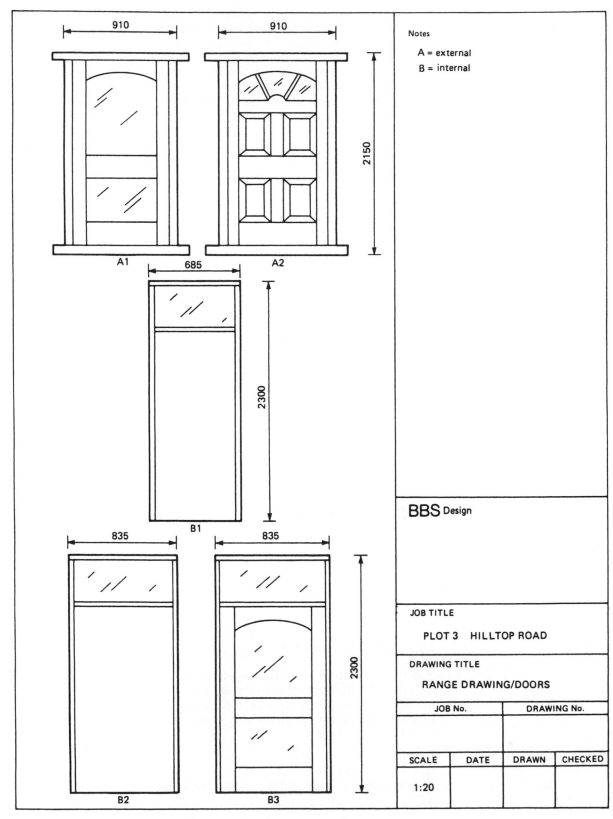

Figure 4.74 (a) *Door range drawing*

Ground-floor plan   First-floor plan

Figure 4.74 (b) *Floor plans*

Description	D1	D2	D3	D4	D5	D6	D7	D8	D9	D10			NOTES
Type (see range)													
External glazed A1					●								
External panelled A2	●												
Internal flush B1									●				
Internal flush B2		●				●	●	●		●			
Internal glazed B3			●	●									
Size													
813 mm × 2032 mm × 44 mm	●				●								
762 mm × 1981 mm × 35 mm		●	●	●		●	●	●		●			
610 mm × 1981 mm × 35 mm									●				
Material													**BBS** DESIGN
Hardwood	●												
Softwood			●	●	●								
Plywood/polished		●											JOB TITLE
plywood/painted						●	●	●	●	●			PLOT 3 Hilltop Road
Infill													DRAWING TITLE
6 mm tempered safety glass													Door Schedule/doors
clear			●	●	●								JOB NO. / DRAWING NO.
obscured	●												
													SCALE / DATE / DRAWN / CHECKED

Figure 4.74 (c) *Door schedules*

121

4 *Manufacture of joinery products*

Description	D1	D2	D3	D4	D5	D6	D7	D8	D9	D10			NOTES
Frames													
75 mm × 100 mm (outward opening)					●								
75 mm × 100 mm (inward opening)	●												
Linings													
38 mm × 125 mm		●	●	●									
38 mm × 100 mm						●	●	●	●	●			
Shape													
Rebated stop	●				●								
Planted stop		●	●	●		●	●	●	●	●			
Transom		●	●	●		●	●	●	●	●			
Sill	●				●								
Material													
Hardwood	●												
Softwood		●	●	●	●	●	●	●	●	●			**BBS** DESIGN
Fanlight infill													JOB TITLE
6 mm tempered safety glass													PLOT 3 Hilltop Road
clear													DRAWING TITLE
													Door Schedule/frames/lining
obscured		●							●				JOB NO. · DRAWING NO.
6 mm plywood									●				SCALE · DATE · DRAWN · CHECKED

Description	D1	D2	D3	D4	D5	D6	D7	D8	D9	D10			NOTES
Hanging													
Pair 100 mm pressed steel butt hinges			●	●	●[1.5]								
Pair 100 mm brass butt hinges	●[1.5]												
Pair 75 mm pressed steel butt hinges						●	●	●	●[1.5]	●			
Pair 75 mm brass butt hinges		●											
Fastening													
Rim night latch	●												
Mortise deadlock	●												
Mortise lock/latch		●			●				●				
Mortise latch			●	●		●	●	●					
100 mm brass bolts	●[2]				●[2]								**BBS** DESIGN
Miscellaneous													
Brass lock/latch furniture		●			●				●				
Brass latch furniture			●	●		●	●	●					JOB TITLE
Brass letterplate	●												PLOT 3 Hilltop Road
Brass knocker	●												DRAWING TITLE
													Ironmongery schedule/doors
Brass coat hook		●[2]								●[2]			JOB NO. · DRAWING NO.
Brass escutcheon	●[2]												
													SCALE · DATE · DRAWN · CHECKED

Figure 4.74 (d) *Door schedules*

READ THE INSTRUCTIONS AND COMPLETE THE TASK

━━━━━━━ **Learning task** ━━━━━━━

Take off the following information from the schedules:

How many type B2 painted doors are required?

_____

Produce a list of locks and bolts required for the whole house.

State the size and type of door for opening D5.

_____

_____

Door frames and linings

The main difference between door frames and door linings is that linings cover the full width of the reveal in which they are fixed, from wall surface to wall surface whereas frames do not, as illustrated in Figure 4.75.

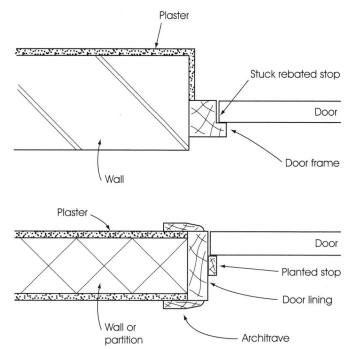

Figure 4.75 *Door frames and linings*

Door frames

The surround on which an external door or internal door is hung, consists of a head, two jambs, and where required for external use a threshold, normally with stuck-on solid stops rather than planted ones and of a bigger section than door linings, see Figure 4.76.

The component parts of a door frame are jointed using draw-pinned mortise and tenon joints see Figure 4.77. Draw pins are used in preference to wedges, as they will hold the joint even if the horns are cut off on-site prior to fixing. In addition the use of draw pins has the advantage of not requiring cramps to pull up the joint during assembly. As with the assembly of window frames, by off-setting the hole in the tenon slightly towards the shoulder, the joint will be drawn up tight as

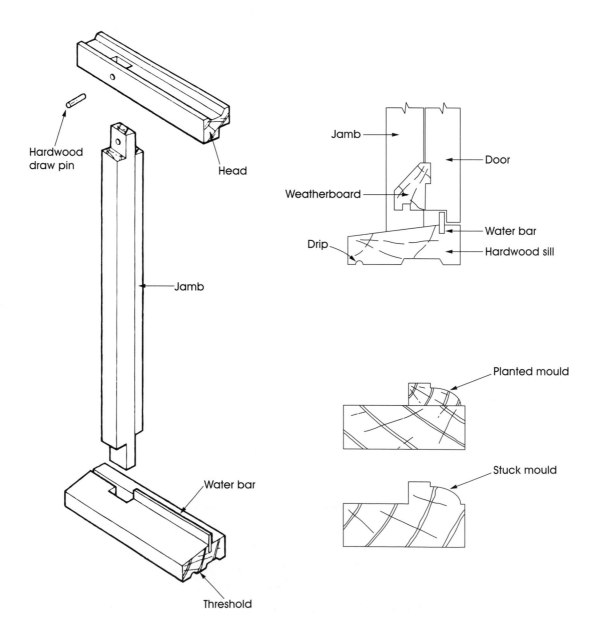

Figure 4.76 *Door frame and details*

the pin is driven in. The draw pin can be simply cut-off flush with the frame after driving in, or alternatively it may in addition be wedged.

Storey-height frames – Figure 4.78 shows these are used for door openings in thin non-loadbearing blockwork partitions. The jambs and head which make up the frame are grooved out on their back face to receive the building blocks. The jambs above the head are cut back to finish flush with the blockwork wall. A mortise and tenon joint is used between the head and the jambs (see Figure 4.79). This frame is designed to be fixed in position, at the bottom to the wall plate and at the top to the joists, before the blocks are built up (see Figure 4.80).

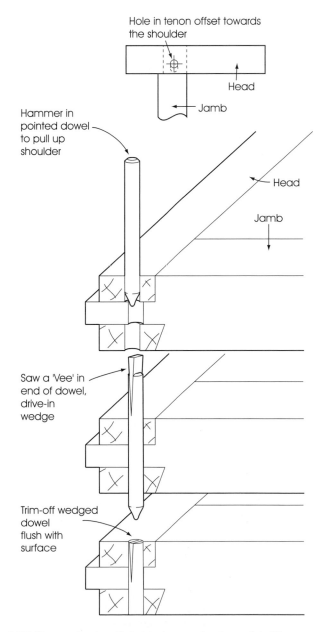

Hole in tenon offset towards the shoulder

Head

Jamb

Hammer in pointed dowel to pull up shoulder

Head

Jamb

Saw a 'Vee' in end of dowel, drive-in wedge

Trim-off wedged dowel flush with surface

Figure 4.77 *Draw pinning (joint cut away to show detail)*

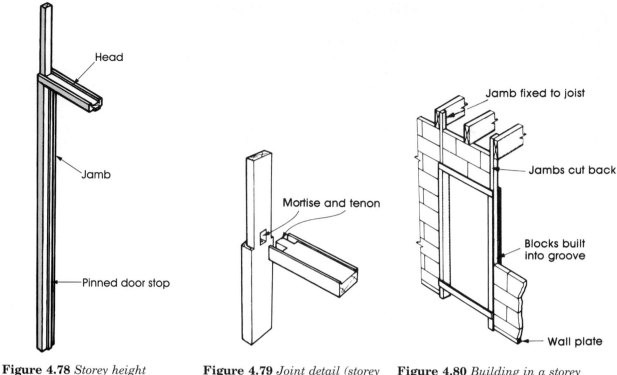

Figure 4.78 *Storey height frames*

Figure 4.79 *Joint detail (storey height frame)*

Figure 4.80 *Building in a storey height frame*

Storey height frames with fanlights – Figure 4.81 shows a frame for internal use and Figure 4.82 a frame for external use. Both types consist of two jambs, a head and a transom, the external frame also has a threshold.

For a plain internal frame the joint between the transom and the jamb can be a single mortise and tenon but where a rebated frame is used, the joint should be a double mortise and tenon as shown in Figure 4.83.

On external storey height frames where the transom extends beyond the face, the joint will be a mortise and tenon and the overhanging edge of the transom should be housed across the face of the jambs (see Figure 4.84).

Door linings – the surrounds on which mainly internal doors are hung, normally of a thinner section than door frames.

Plain linings – consist of two plain jambs and a plain head joined together using a housing or a bare-faced tongue and housing for better quality work. The planted stop is fixed around the lining after the door has been hung. (See Figure 4.85.)

Rebated linings – are used for better quality work. They consist of two rebated jambs and a rebated head. The rebate must be the correct width so that when the door is hung it finishes flush with the edges of the lining. (See Figure 4.86.)

Skeleton linings – are used for deeper reveals, where the brickwork is too thick for a normal lining to be used. They consist of a basic framework which is stub tenoned together. A stopped bare-faced tongue and housing is used between the head and the jambs. A ply or solid timber lining is used to cover the framework and form the rebate to receive the door. (See Figure 4.87.)

Door frames and linings

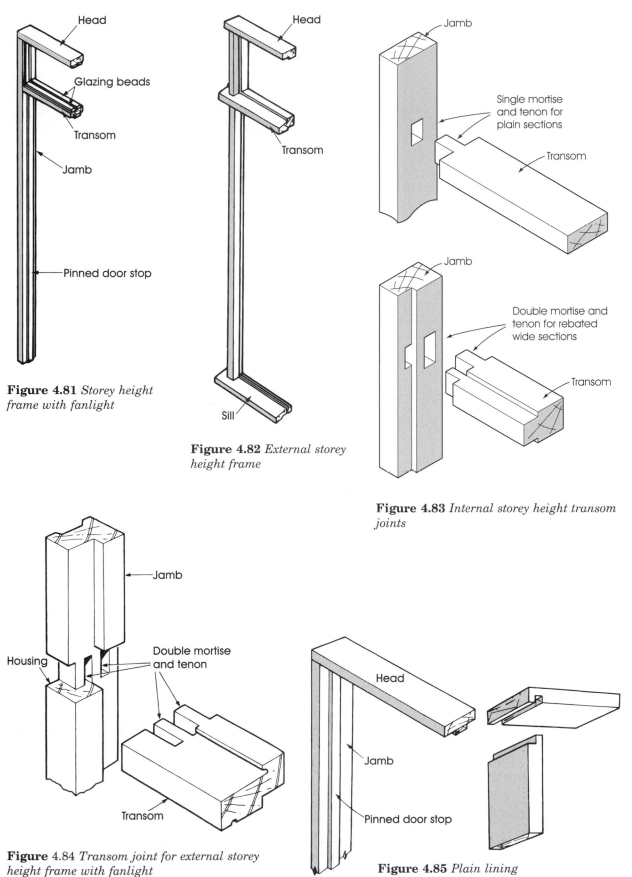

Figure 4.81 *Storey height frame with fanlight*

Figure 4.82 *External storey height frame*

Figure 4.83 *Internal storey height transom joints*

Figure 4.84 *Transom joint for external storey height frame with fanlight*

Figure 4.85 *Plain lining*

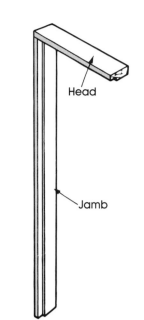

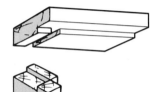

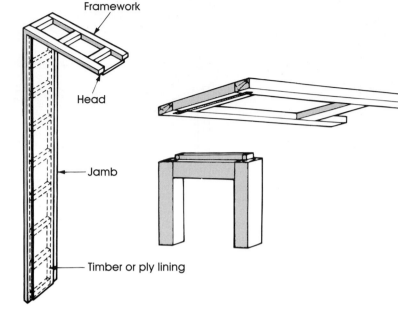

Figure 4.87 *Skeleton lining*

Figure 4.86 *Rebated lining*

Assembly of door frames and linings

It is standard practice to assemble door frames in the joiners shop, whereas linings are normally sent to site in flat-pack form, to be assembled by the carpenter.

Frames without a threshold are assembled with a temporary distance piece and braces to hold the jambs parallel and square. Frames with a threshold may be assembled with temporary braces for squaring purposes. Both are illustrated in Figure 4.88.

Door sets

A door-set consist of a pre-hung door and frame or lining, complete with all ironmongery. Architraves are normally fixed to one side of the set and loose pinned on the other. All work is undertaken in the joinery shop and supplied to site ready for fixing into its opening. The main advantages of using door-sets is the 'joiners shop quality' and the considerable saving in on-site time to install. See Figure 4.89

Door hanging

Speed and confidence in door hanging can be achieved by following the procedure illustrated in Figure 4.90 and outlined below:

- Measure height and width of door opening.
- Locate and mark the top and hanging side of the opening and door.
- Cut off the horns.

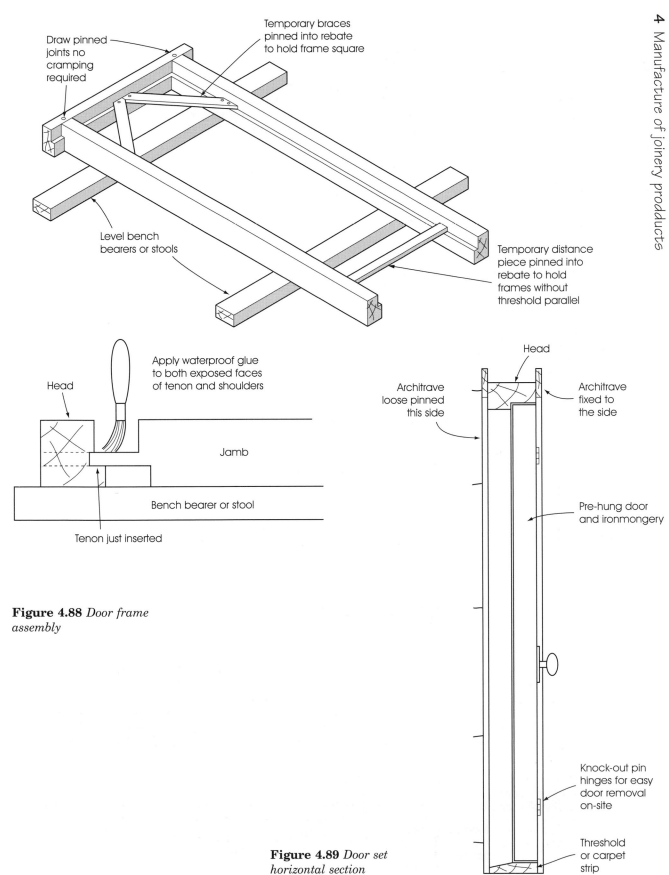

Draw pinned joints no cramping required

Temporary braces pinned into rebate to hold frame square

Level bench bearers or stools

Temporary distance piece pinned into rebate to hold frames without threshold parallel

Apply waterproof glue to both exposed faces of tenon and shoulders

Head

Jamb

Bench bearer or stool

Tenon just inserted

Figure 4.88 *Door frame assembly*

Head

Architrave loose pinned this side

Architrave fixed to the side

Pre-hung door and ironmongery

Knock-out pin hinges for easy door removal on-site

Threshold or carpet strip

Figure 4.89 *Door set horizontal section*

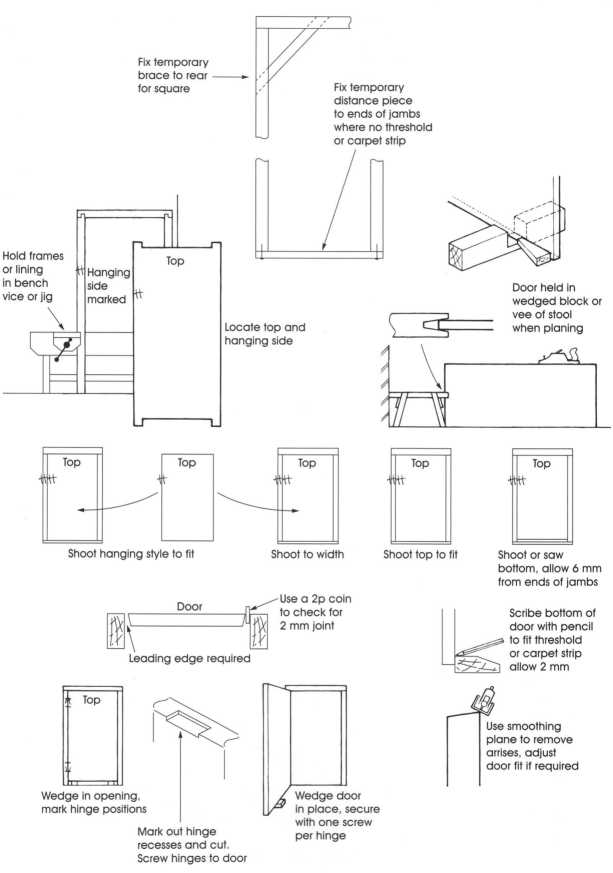

Fix temporary brace to rear for square

Fix temporary distance piece to ends of jambs where no threshold or carpet strip

Door held in wedged block or vee of stool when planing

Hold frames or lining in bench vice or jig

Hanging side marked

Top

Locate top and hanging side

Top

Shoot hanging style to fit

Top

Top

Shoot to width

Top

Shoot top to fit

Top

Shoot or saw bottom, allow 6 mm from ends of jambs

Door

Use a 2p coin to check for 2 mm joint

Leading edge required

Scribe bottom of door with pencil to fit threshold or carpet strip allow 2 mm

Use smoothing plane to remove arrises, adjust door fit if required

Top

Wedge in opening, mark hinge positions

Mark out hinge recesses and cut. Screw hinges to door

Wedge door in place, secure with one screw per hinge

Figure 4.90 *Typical door hanging procedure*

- 'Shoot' (plane to fit) in the hanging stile of door to fit the hanging side of the opening. A leading edge will be required to prevent binding.
- 'Shoot' the door to width. Allow a 2 mm joint all around between door and frame or lining. Use a two pence coin to check. The closing side will require planing to a slight angle to allow it to close.
- 'Shoot' the top of the door (if required) to fit the head of the opening, allow a 2 mm joint. Saw or shoot the bottom of the door (if required) to give a 6 mm gap at floor level or a 2 mm gap at a threshold.
- Mark out and cut in the hinges. Screw one leaf of each hinge to the door.
- Offer up the door to the opening and screw the other leaf of each hinge to the frame.
- Adjust fit as required. Remove all arrises (sharp edges) to soften the corners and provide a better surface for the subsequent paint finish. If the closing edge rubs the frame, the hinges may be proud and require the recesses being cut deeper. If the recesses are too deep, the door will not close fully and tend to spring open, which is known as 'hinge bound'. In this case a thin cardboard strip can be placed in the recess to pack out the hinge.
- Fit and fix the lock.
- Fit any other ironmongery, e.g. bolts, letter plates, handles, etc.

Mortise dead lock – fitting procedure is shown in Figure 4.91.

Cylinder rim night latch- fitting procedure is shown in Figure 4.92.

Letter plate – fitting procedure is shown in Figure 4.93.

Mortise deadlock, latch or lock/latch

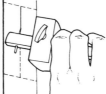
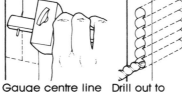

Mark position on door edge | Gauge centre line on door edge | Drill out to width and depth of lock | Pare sides to form mortise | Mark lock face plate | Let-in face plate

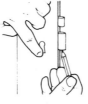
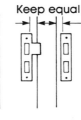
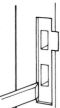

Mark spindle and keyhole centres as required | Drill holes, cut keyhole to guide key | Mark bolt position on frame/lining | Keep equal — Mark position of striking plate | Let–in striking plate, cut mortise for bolts

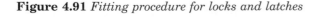

Figure 4.91 *Fitting procedure for locks and latches*

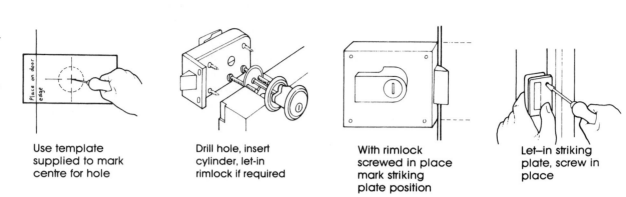

Use template supplied to mark centre for hole

Drill hole, insert cylinder, let-in rimlock if required

With rimlock screwed in place mark striking plate position

Let–in striking plate, screw in place

figure 4.92 *Fitting procedure for a cylinder rim night latch*

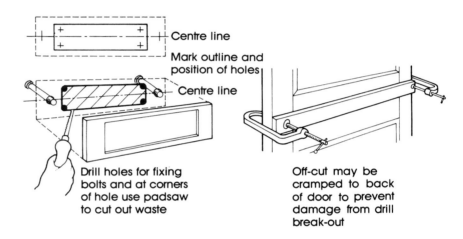

Centre line

Mark outline and position of holes

Centre line

Drill holes for fixing bolts and at corners of hole use padsaw to cut out waste

Off-cut may be cramped to back of door to prevent damage from drill break-out

Figure 4.93 *Fitting procedure for a letter plate*

Fixing architrave

READ THIS PAGE

Architrave is the decorative trim that is placed internally around door openings to mask the joint between wall and timber and conceal any subsequent shrinkage and expansion.

Figure 4.94 shows that a set of architraves consist of a horizontal head and two vertical jambs or legs. A 6 mm to 9 mm margin is normally left between the frame or lining edge and the architrave see Figure 4.95. This margin provides a neat appearance to an opening: an unsightly joint line would result if architraves were to be kept flush with the edge of the opening.

The return corners of a set of architraves are mitred. For right-angled returns (90 degrees) the mitre will be 45 degrees (half the total angle) and can be cut using a mitre box or block as shown in Figure 4.96.

Mitres for corners other than right angles will be half the angle of intersection. They can be practically found by marking the outline of the intersecting trim on the frame/lining or wall, and joining the inside

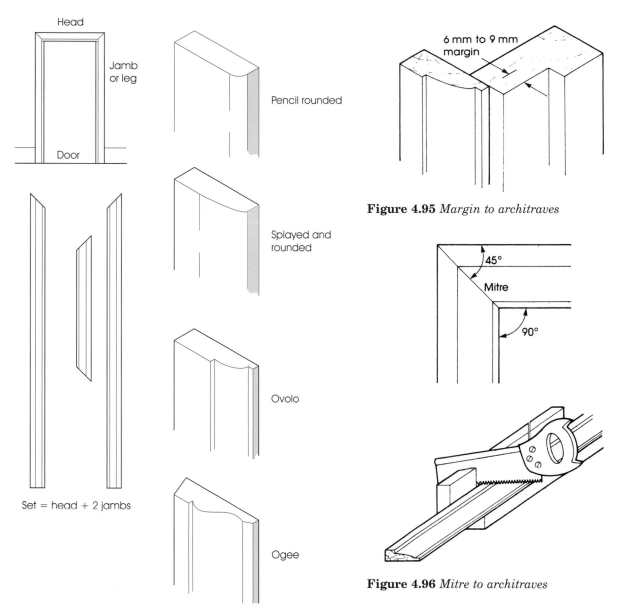

Head

Jamb or leg

Door

Set = head + 2 jambs

Figure 4.94 *Architrave*

Pencil rounded

Splayed and rounded

Ovolo

Ogee

6 mm to 9 mm margin

Figure 4.95 *Margin to architraves*

45°

Mitre

90°

Figure 4.96 *Mitre to architraves*

and outside corners to give the mitre line (see Figure 4.97). Mouldings can be marked directly from this or alternatively an adjustable bevel can be set up for use.

The head is normally marked, cut and temporarily fixed in position first as shown in Figure 4.98. The jambs can then be marked, cut, eased if required and subsequently fixed.

Where the corner is not square or you have been less than accurate in cutting the mitre, it will require easing, either with a block plane or by running a tenon saw through the mitre.

Fixing is normally direct to the door frame/lining at between 200 mm and 300 mm centres using typically 38 mm or 50 mm long oval or lost-head nails. These should be positioned in the fillets or quirks (flat surface or groove in moulding) and punched in, see Figure 4.99.

Mitres should be nailed through their top edge to reinforce the joint and ensure both faces are kept flush (see Figure 4.100). 38 mm oval or lost-head nails are suitable for this purpose.

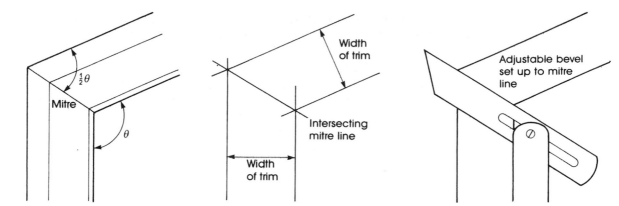

Figure 4.97 *Determining mitre for corners other than right angles*

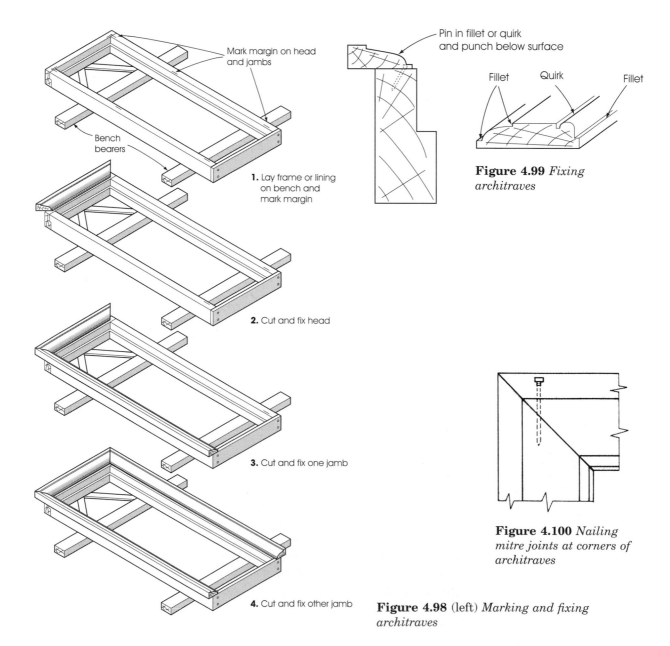

1. Lay frame or lining on bench and mark margin

2. Cut and fix head

3. Cut and fix one jamb

4. Cut and fix other jamb

Mark margin on head and jambs

Bench bearers

Pin in fillet or quirk and punch below surface

Fillet   Quirk   Fillet

Figure 4.99 *Fixing architraves*

Figure 4.100 *Nailing mitre joints at corners of architraves*

Figure 4.98 (left) *Marking and fixing architraves*

Plinth block – A plinth block was traditionally fixed at the base of an architrave to take the knocks and abrasions at floor level (see Figure 4.101). It is also used to ease fixing problems which occur when skirtings are thicker than the architrave.

In current practice plinth blocks will rarely be found except in restoration work, new high quality work in traditional style or where the skirting is thicker than the architrave.

Architraves may be butt jointed to the plinth block, but traditionally they were joined using bare-faced tenon and screws as illustrated in Figure 4.102.

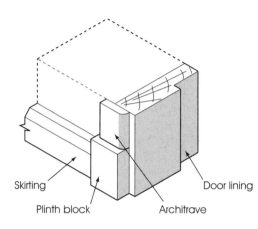

Figure 4.101 *Use of a plinth block*

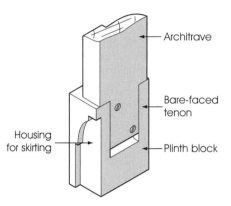

Figure 4.102 *Traditional jointing of architrave plinth block (rear view)*

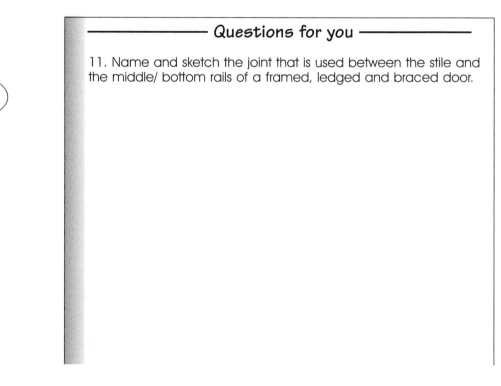

TRY TO ANSWER THESE

Questions for you

11. Name and sketch the joint that is used between the stile and the middle/ bottom rails of a framed, ledged and braced door.

12. State the purpose of door and ironmongery schedules.

_____

_____

13. Produce a sketch to show the typical positions of the hinges and mortise lock/latch to an external plywood flush door.

14. State why manufacturer's instructions should be followed when fitting ironmongery.

_____

_____

_____

15. Define 'arris' and state why it should be removed from joinery.

_____

_____

_____

_____

16. Explain the treatment required to the top edge of a door head when hung using rising butts.

_____

_____

17. List the sequence of operations for hanging a door in a joiners shop as part of a door set.

_____

_____

_____

_____

_____

18. Braces are incorporated into matchboarded doors in order to:

    (a) provide a fixing for the hinges
    (b) prevent the door from sagging
    (c) joint matchboarding together
    (d) protect the door from weather.

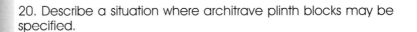

19. Produce a sketch to show the jointing arrangement between the jamb and head of a rebated door lining.

20. Describe a situation where architrave plinth blocks may be specified.

_____

_____

WELL, HOW DID YOU DO?

WORK THROUGH THE SECTION AGAIN IF YOU HAD ANY PROBLEMS

4 Manufacture of joinery products

COMPLETE THE
WORD SQUARE

WORD-SQUARE SEARCH

Hidden in the word square are the following 20 words associated with *'doors and ironmongery'*. You may find the words written forwards, backwards, up, down or diagonally.

DOOR	MORTISE	EXTERNAL
CYLINDER	PANELLED	KNOBSET
FLUSH	LEVER	FOLDING
SECURITY	KNUCKLE	BOLT
HINGE	LETTER	LOCK
SCHEDULE	LATCH	HANGING
HAND	SHOOT	

Draw a ring around the words, or line in using a highlight pen thus:

EXAMPLE

EXAMPLE

WELL, HOW
MANY DID YOU
GET?

```
E X T E R N A L F K D E L L E N A P
E G H F F G H J M N O Q S U W Y A B
H S U L F E I K M H P R T V X Z C T
C A C E O F K G B E I G I K N H O E
T B R H L T G J C F H N J M L A P S
A C E K T E N C F G K D G A G N E B
L A V G I E I K J I O H G E F D C O
C B E C N I G Z X O Y C O P E D I N
Y B L I G N N G H O S S L O W E D K
T D O O K C A S E F I R O O D O G O
I C I H E R H I A C O M C I C B E R
R O E A M O R L A Y H O K K O T X E
U B A C O B R T S L C O V E L R O T
C A H T R S F E G I E D A O L E M T
E C I M T X Y Z A N A M B K T L H E
S F J O I R P Q S D G N C F U O Y L
B G K P S W T U V E H O E V O L I E
E L U D E H C S E R M K N U C K L E
```

138

Stairs

READ THIS PAGE

A stairway can be defined as a series of steps (combination of tread and riser) giving floor-to-floor access. Each continuous set of steps is called a **flight**. **Landings** are introduced between floor levels either to break up a long flight, giving a rest point, or to change the direction of the stair.

Straight flight stairs

These run in one direction for the entire length. Figure 4.103 shows there are three different variations.

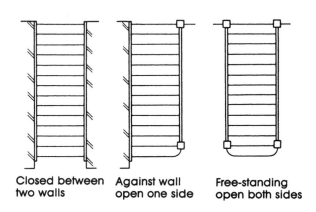

Closed between two walls | Against wall open one side | Free-standing open both sides

Figure 4.103 *Straight flight of stairs*

The flight which is closed between two walls (also known as a cottage stair) is the simplest and most economical to make. Its handrail is usually a simple section fixed either directly on to the wall or on brackets.

The flight fixed against one wall is said to be open on one side. This open or outer string is normally terminated and supported at either end by a newel post. A balustrade must be fixed to this side to provide protection. The infilling of this can be either open or closed and is usually capped by a handrail. Where the width of the flight exceeds one metre, a wall handrail will also be required.

Where the flight is freestanding, neither side being against a wall, it is said to be open both sides. The open sides are treated in the same way as the previous flight.

Stair terminology (Figure 4.104)

Apron lining – the boards used to finish the edge of a trimmed opening in the floor.

Balustrade – the handrail and the infilling between it and the string, landing or floor. This can be called either an open or closed balustrade, depending on the infilling.

Baluster – the short vertical infilling members of an open balustrade.

Bull nose step – the quarter-rounded end step at the bottom of a flight of stairs.

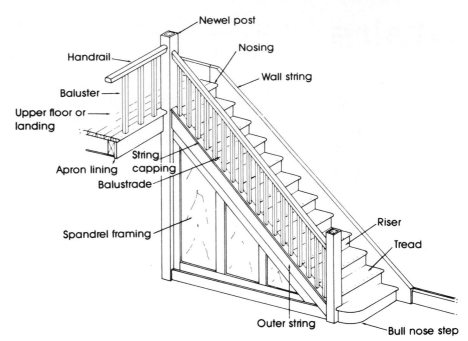

Figure 4.104 *Stairway terminology*

Carriage – This is a raking timber fixed under wide stairs to support the centre of the treads and risers. Brackets are fixed to the side of the carriage to provide further support across the width of the treads.

Commode step – a step with a curved tread and riser normally occurring at the bottom of a flight.

Curtail step – the half-rounded or scroll-end step at the bottom of a flight.

Newel – the large sectioned vertical member at each end of the string. Where an upper newel does not continue down to the floor level below it is known as a pendant or drop newel.

Nosing – the front edge of a tread or the finish to the floorboards around a stairwell opening.

Riser – the vertical member of a step.

Spandrel – the triangular area formed under the stairs. This can be left open or closed in with spandrel framing to form a cupboard.

String – the board into which the treads and risers are housed or cut. They are also named according to their type, for example, wall string, outer string, close string, cut string, and wreathed string.

Tread – the horizontal member of a step. It can be called a parallel tread or a tapered tread, etc., depending on its shape.

Stair regulations

The design and construction of stairs is closely controlled by the Building Regulations. These set out different requirements for stairs, depending on the use of the building in which they are located. Figure 4.105 summarizes these requirements.

REFER TO THESE REGULATIONS

Type of building where stairs are located			
Requirement	**Private (domestic use)**	**Industrial/assembly**	**Other**
Pitch 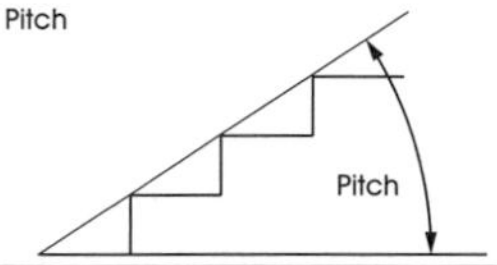	Maximum 42°	Governed by tread and riser requirements	Governed by tread and riser requirements
Number of risers	Good practice not to exceed 16 Consecutive flights of more than 36 risers, must change direction between flights by at least 30 degrees	Maximum 16 for shop and assembly buildings	As for private
Rise of step 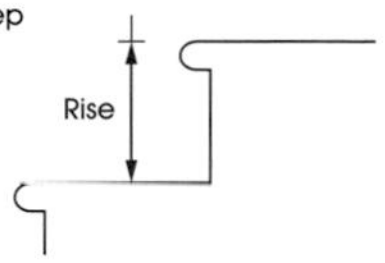	Maximum 220 mm	Maximum 180 mm	Maximum 190 mm
Going of step 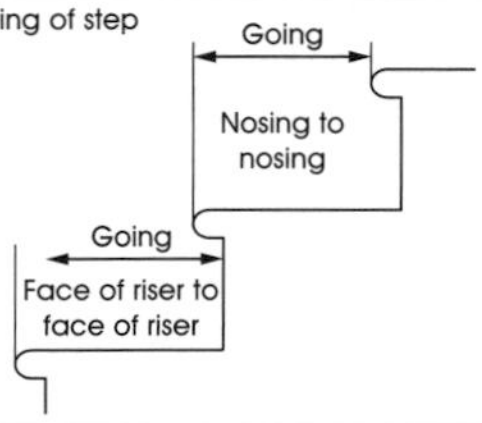	Minimum 220 mm (provided pitch does not exceed 42°)	Minimum 280 mm	Minimum 250 mm
Combined rise and going	Twice the rise plus going to fall between 550 mm and 700 mm	Twice the rise plus going to fall between 550 mm and 700 mm	Twice the rise plus going to fall between 550 mm and 700 mm
Headroom stair 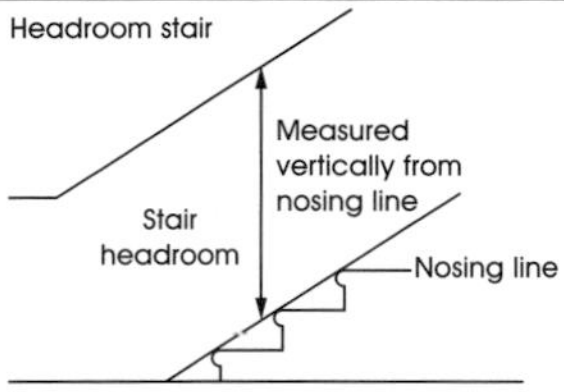	Minimum 2 m (may be reduced for loft conversion)	Not less than 2 m	Not less than 2 m
Headroom Landing 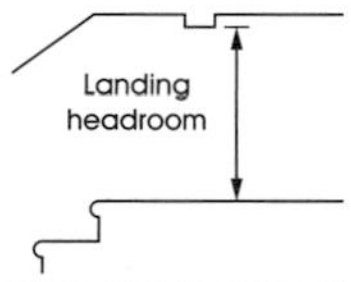	Minimum 2 m (may be reduced for loft conversion)	Not less than 2 m	Not less than 2 m
Guarding	Guarding to be provided on open side of stairs and landing with a drop of 600 mm or more	Guarding required for 2 or more risers	Guarding required for 2 or more risers
Handrail height and provision 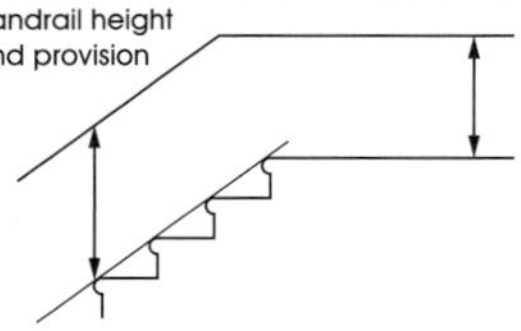	900 m on stair and open landing Handrail required on both sides for stairs over 1 m wide	900 mm on stair 1000 mm on landing. Stairs wider than 1.8 m too be divided by a central handrail	900 mm on stair 1000 mm on landing
Balustrading 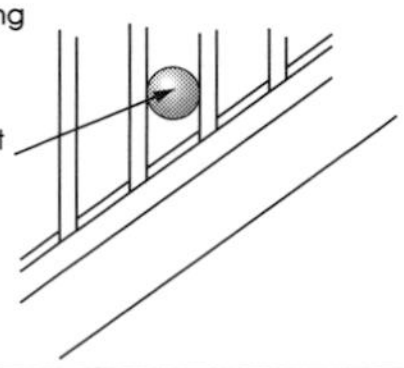	Not easily climbed by children under 5. Maximum gap between members must not permit passage of 100 mm sphere		
Open riser stairs 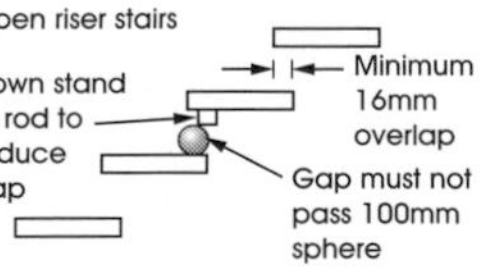	Gap between treads must not permit passage of 100 mm sphere. Front of tread must overlap back of tread below by at least 16 mm		

Figure 4.105 *Stair requirements*

141

Stair construction and assembly

The construction of any staircase with closed strings follows the same basic procedure, with slight variations depending on the particular type of stair.

The housings in the string, can be cut out on a spindle moulder or by using a portable router and a stair housing template (see Figure 4.106). Where neither of these is available, they can be cut by hand using the sequence of operations shown in Figure 4.107.

- Bore out at nosing end with brace and bit.
- Clean out nosing and cut edges of housing with a tenon saw.
- Clean out waste with a chisel and hand router.

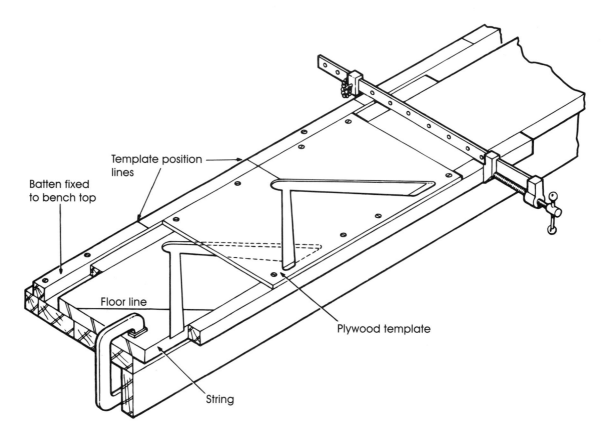

Figure 4.106 *Portable router stair housing template*

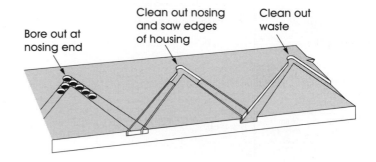

Figure 4.107 *Sequence of operations*

A method of forming a bull-nose step is shown in Figure 4.108. The curved section of the riser is reduced to a 2 mm thickness and bent around a laminated block. The wedges tighten the riser around the block and hold it there until the glue has set. The reduced section of the riser should be steamed before bending. It can then be bent around the block fairly easily without risk of breaking. Splayed end steps are sometimes used in cheaper quality work with the riser mitred and tongued at the joints (see Figure 4.109).

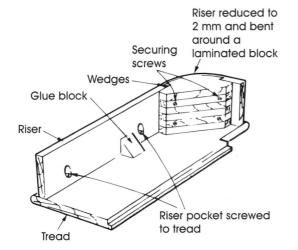

Figure 4.108 *Forming a bull-nose step*

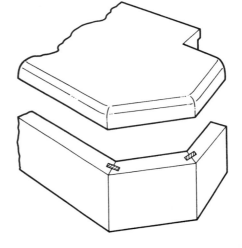

Figure 4.109 *Splayed end step*

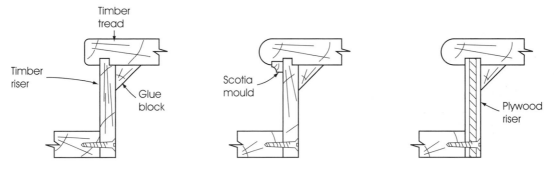

Figure 4.110 *Tread and riser details*

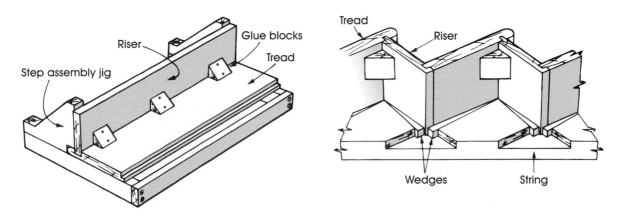

Figure 4.111 *Step assembly jig*

Figure 4.112 *Fixing of steps into string*

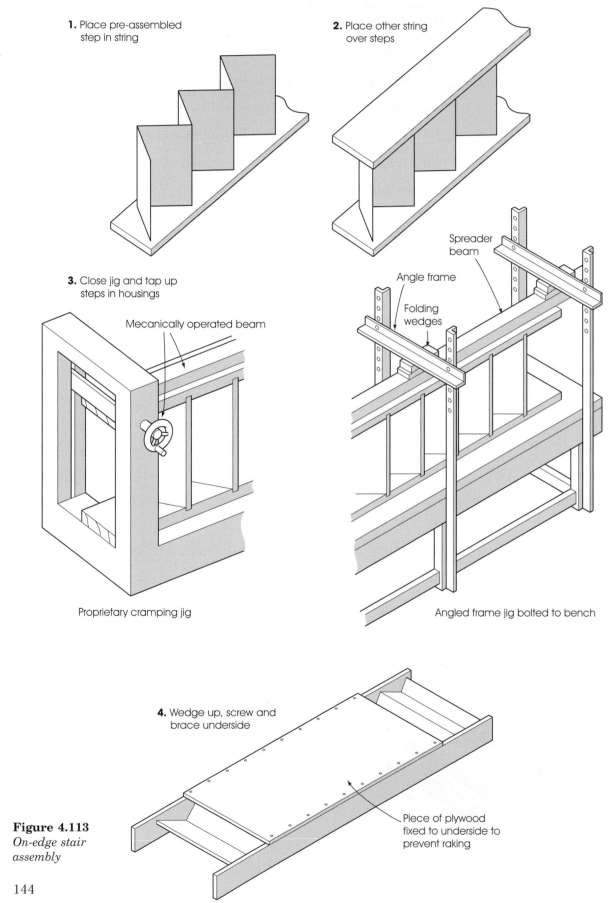

1. Place pre-assembled step in string

2. Place other string over steps

3. Close jig and tap up steps in housings

Mecanically operated beam

Proprietary cramping jig

Spreader beam

Angle frame

Folding wedges

Angled frame jig bolted to bench

4. Wedge up, screw and brace underside

Piece of plywood fixed to underside to prevent raking

Figure 4.113
On-edge stair assembly

Figure 4.110 shows three alternatives for tread and riser details. The tread can be made from 25 mm timber and the riser traditionally from 19 mm timber or, as is now standard practice, 9 mm or 12 mm plywood is used for the risers.

Figure 4.111 shows how each step (tread and riser) is made up in a jig before being fixed to the strings. Glue blocks strengthen the joint between the tread and the riser. The absence or loosening of these often results in squeaky stairs.

A part view of the steps fixed into a string is illustrated in 4.112. The treads and risers are glued and securely wedged into their positions in the string housing.

This on-edge assemble employs a cramping jig to cramp up the strings and hold the staircase square. The following procedure is illustrated in Figure 4.113.

- Clean up the inner housed faces of the string, the upper face and edge of tread and exposed face of the risers.
- Pre-assemble the treads and risers including glue blocks.
- Position one string on base of the cramping up frame.
- Apply glue to the string housings and tread riser intersections of the pre-assembled steps. Place the steps in position.
- Apply glue to the housings of the other string and place in position over the steps.
- Close the cramping frame and tap up all the treads and risers, making sure they are all fully home in their housings.
- Glue and drive the wedges for the treads. Trim off any surplus length, with a chisel, so that they clear the riser housings.
- Glue and drive the wedges for the risers.
- Screw bottom edge of risers to back edge of treads at about 225 mm centres.
- Temporarily brace underside of stair, with diagonal braces or a piece of sheet material to prevent it raking out of square before installation.
- Finally remove any squeezed out surplus glue from seen faces with a damp cloth. Clean up outer face and top edge of string. Remove any sharp arrises.

It is normal practice to assemble the flight of stairs to this stage only, for ease of handling and installation. Each flight will be separate, with the bottom bullnose step, top nosing, newels, handrail and balustrade supplied loose, ready for on-site completion.

Units and fitments

Units fall into two distinct categories.

Purpose made – a unit made in a joiners shop for a specific job. Most will be fully assembled prior to their arrival on site.

Proprietary – a unit or range of units mass-produced to standard designs by a manufacturer. Budget-priced units are often sent in knock-down form (known as flat packs) ready for on-site assembly. Better quality units are often ready assembled (known as rigid units) in the factory.

Unit terminology

Cupboard – historically derived from the name given to the simple open boards or shelves which were used to display cups, silverplate and other items (cup board).

Carcass – the main assembly or frames of a cupboard, excluding doors and drawers.

Potboard – the lower shelf or base of a cupboard. Again historically derived from the name given to a low board or shelf, raised just off the floor on which heavy cooking pots were stored.

Plinth – the recessed base of a cupboard, which supports the potboard. It also provides a footspace for those standing in front of the cupboard and is often called a kickboard.

Standards – The vertical end frames or panels and intermediate divisions of a cupboard.

The two main methods of carcass construction for both proprietary and purpose-made units, shown in Figure 4.114, are box construction and framed construction.

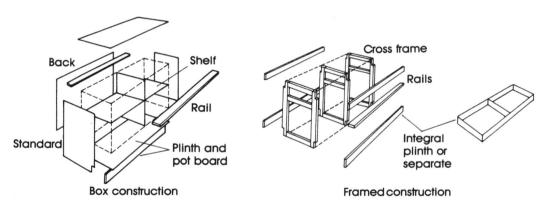

Figure 4.114 *Unit construction*

Box construction

This is also known as **slab construction**. It uses vertical standards and rails and horizontal shelves.

A back holds the unit square and rigid. The plinth and potboard are often integral with the unit.

Proprietary units are almost exclusively made from 15 mm to 19 mm thick melamine-faced chipboard (MFC) or medium density fibre board (MDF).

Purpose-made units may be constructed using MFC, MDF, blockboard, plywood or, more rarely, solid timber.

Flat packs use knock down fittings or screws to join the panels. Assembly is a simple process of following the manufacturer's instructions and drawings, coupled with the ability to use a screwdriver. See Figure 4.115

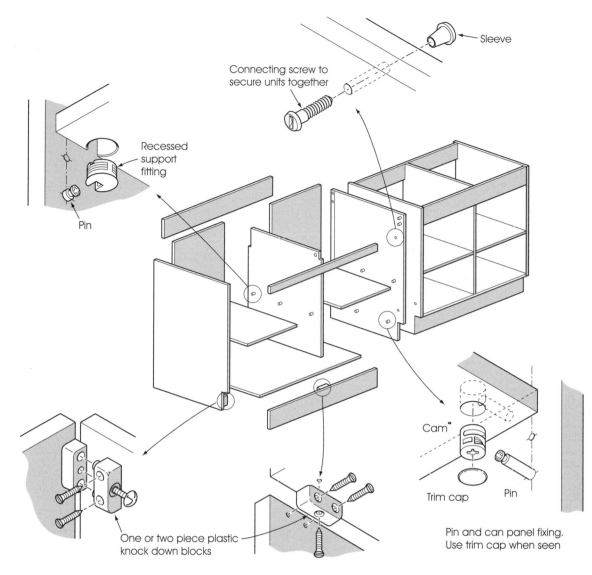

Figure 4.115 *Box construction unit typical knock-down fittings*

Rigid and purpose-made units may be either dowelled or housed and screwed together. Glue is used on assembly to form a rigid carcass. Typical carcass construction details are illustrated in Figure 4.116.

Framed construction

This is also known as **skeleton construction**. This uses frames either front and back joined by rails or standards, or cross frames joined by rails. The plinth and potboard are normally separate items.

The frames of proprietary units are normally dowelled, whereas purpose-made ones would be mortised and tenoned together. Typical carcass construction details are illustrated in Figure 4.117.

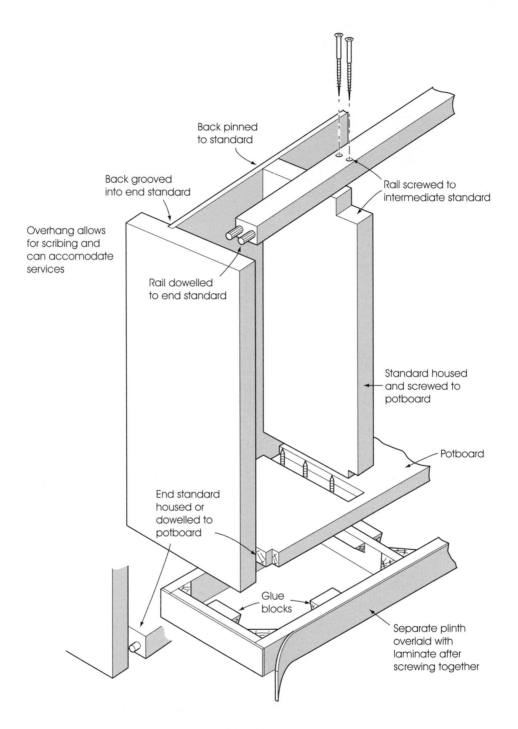

Back pinned
to standard

Back grooved
into end standard

Rail screwed to
intermediate standard

Overhang allows
for scribing and
can accomodate
services

Rail dowelled
to end standard

Standard housed
and screwed to
potboard

Potboard

End standard
housed or
dowelled to
potboard

Glue
blocks

Separate plinth
overlaid with
laminate after
screwing together

Figure 4.116 *Rigid box construction*

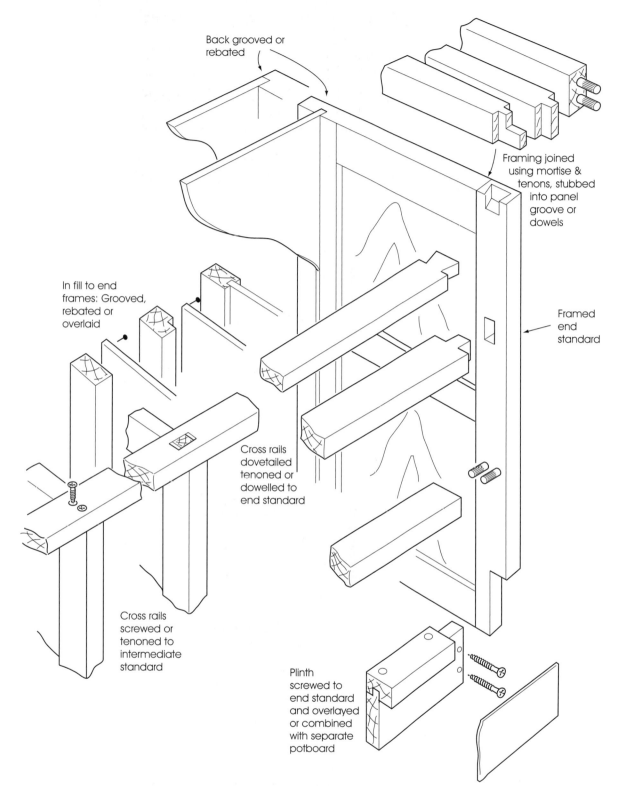

Back grooved or rebated

Framing joined using mortise & tenons, stubbed into panel groove or dowels

In fill to end frames: Grooved, rebated or overlaid

Framed end standard

Cross rails dovetailed tenoned or dowelled to end standard

Cross rails screwed or tenoned to intermediate standard

Plinth screwed to end standard and overlayed or combined with separate potboard

Figure 4.117 *Framed unit construction details*

Adjustable shelves

In situations where the sizes of the items to be stored are not known or where they are subject to change, some form of shelf adjustment must be incorporated.

Illustrated in Figure 4.118 are three of the many methods used:

● The traditional solution was the use of saw tooth supports and splayed end push-in shelf bearers, that can be fitted at any desired height.

● A very popular and efficient method is the use of 'tonks': bookcase strips and studs, which allow height adjustment in 25 mm units.

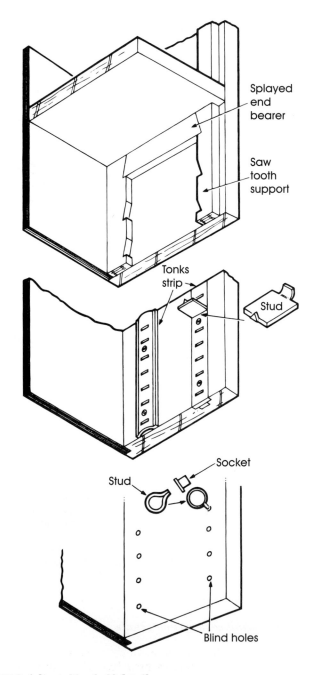

Figure 4.118 *Adjustable shelf details*

The flush strip is designed to be recessed into the standards and a smaller, deeper groove must also be run to give clearance for inserting the tongues of the studs. Alternatively, a surface-fixed strip can be used. This overcomes the need for grooving out and weakening members, but results in an inferior finish.

- Sockets tapped into blind holes which have been drilled at intervals down the standards, and used with push-in studs, are suitable for a lighter range of applications.

Drawers

Drawers may be incorporated into units in order to provide storage and security (when fitted with a lock) for smaller items. The size of a drawer will be related to the items it is intended to store, but in general will range between 100 mm and 200 mm in depth. When they are vertically stacked in one unit the deeper drawers should be located at the bottom.

Figure 4.119 illustrates a traditional method of drawer construction which uses through dovetails at the back and lapped dovetails at the front. The plywood bottom is grooved into the front and sides and is pinned to the bottom of the drawer back. Small glue blocks are positioned under the bottom to provided additional rigidity and assist sliding. Rounded machine-made dovetails, produced on a router or spindle moulder, are a more economic alternative for better quality work where repetitive production is required.

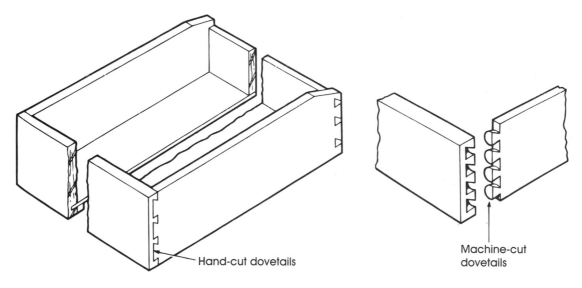

Hand-cut dovetails

Machine-cut dovetails

Figure 4.119 *Draw construction*

Modern mass-produced drawers are made in MFC or MDF. The corner joints can be housed and pinned, butted and screwed, dowelled or biscuited. The bottom of the drawer is typically either nailed or screwed directly to the underside of the drawer sides. A separate false slab front is secured to the drawer by screws from the inside as illustrated in Figure 4.120.

Various methods can be used to suspend and slide drawers. Figure 4.121 shows how traditionally rails may be incorporated into a unit for this purpose. The dustboard shown grooved into the rails is mainly used on

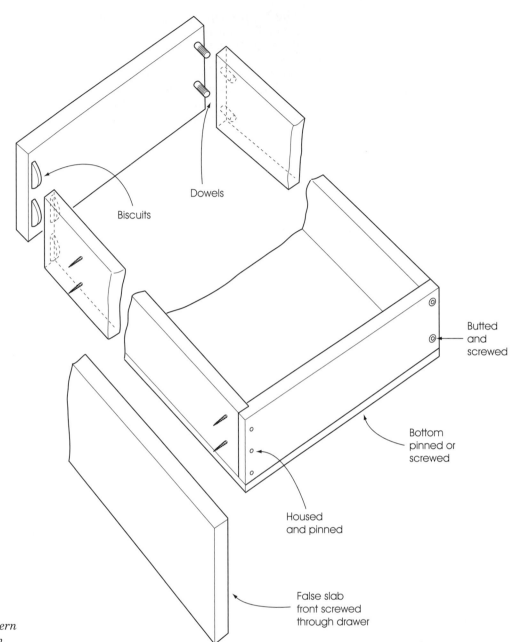

Dowels

Biscuits

Butted
and
screwed

Bottom
pinned or
screwed

Housed
and pinned

False slab
front screwed
through drawer

Figure 4.120 *Modern
drawer construction*

better quality work. Its purpose is to separate the drawer and cupboard spaces. A drawer kicker is fitted between the top rails to prevent the front of the drawer falling downwards as it is pulled out. When closed, the drawer front should finish flush with the unit. This can be achieved by pinning small plywood drawer stops to the front of the drawer rail.

Another traditional method of suspending and sliding drawers is shown in Figure 4.122. This uses grooved drawer sides, preferably of a hardwood with good wearing qualities, which slide on hardwood runners glued and screwed to the unit's sides or standards. Where this method is used, the drawer is often fitted with a false slab front screwed from the inside of the drawer. This front has projecting ends to conceal the runner from view. Alternatively, fibre drawer slides may be used (see Figure 4.123). One part fixed to the side of the drawer and the other to the unit.

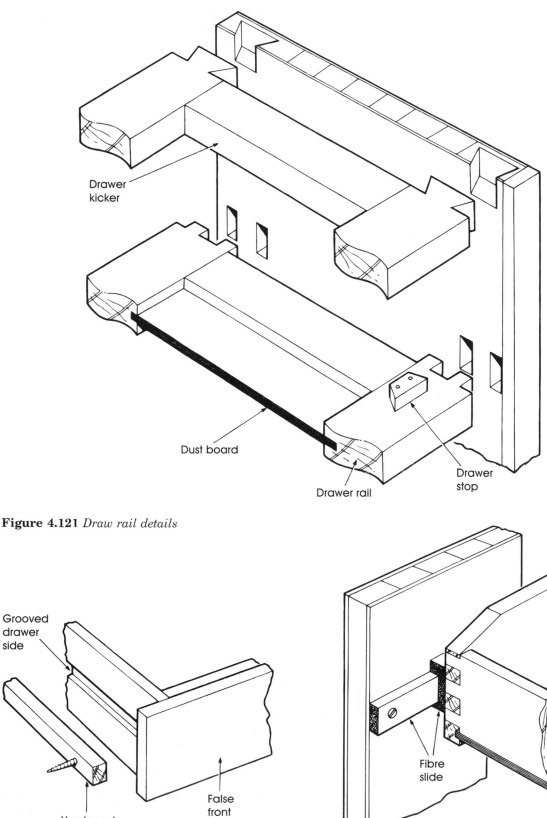

Figure 4.121 *Draw rail details*

Figure 4.122 *Draw slide detail*

Figure 4.123 *Fibre draw slides*

Modern methods of suspending and sliding drawers, shown in Figure 4.124, employ the use of metal, side or bottom mounted runners. These incorporate a ball race or plastic rollers to ensure ease of operation.

Doors

Doors can be incorporated to close the front of open units for reasons of tidiness, protection or security. They may be either side-hung or

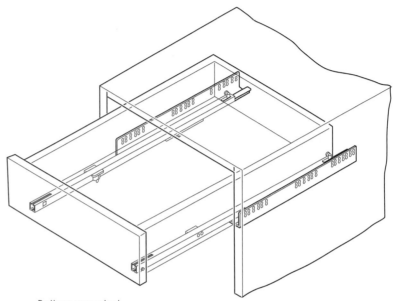

Bottom mounted

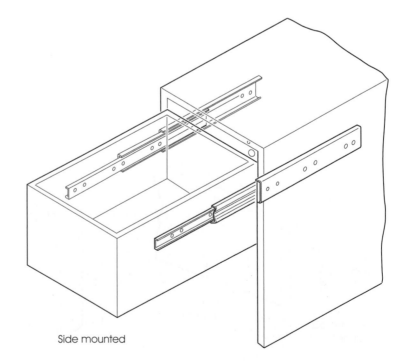

Side mounted

Figure 4.124 *Metal drawer runners*

sliding doors. Side-hung doors allow maximum access but when they are open, they project into the room, which can be restrictive and even hazardous in confined spaces. Figure 4.125 illustrates various methods of side hanging cupboard doors:

A) The door is set flush within the unit and hung on butt hinges. The use of flush hinges avoids the need for recessing and provides the necessary clearance joint.

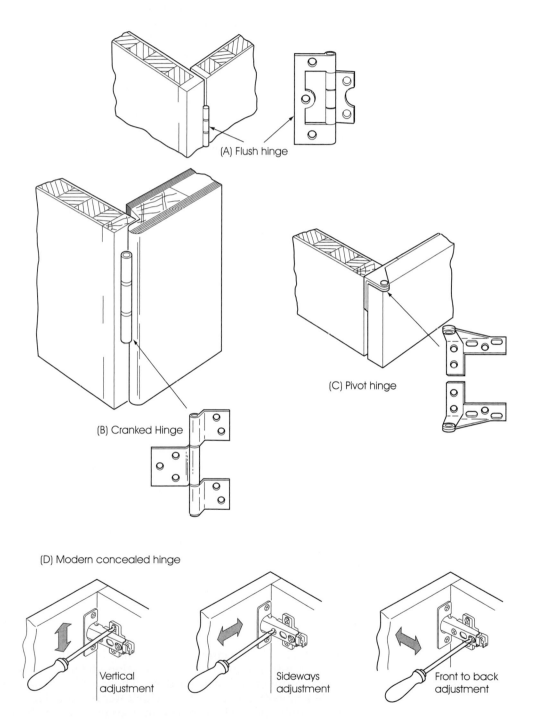

(A) Flush hinge

(B) Cranked Hinge

(C) Pivot hinge

(D) Modern concealed hinge

Vertical adjustment

Sideways adjustment

Front to back adjustment

Figure 4.125 *Side-hung cupboard doors*

B) Rebated doors hung on cranked hinges were at one time popular for mass produced units. These doors do not require any individual fitting as the rebate, which laps over the face of the unit, conceals the very large clearance joint.

C) Doors hung on the face of a unit are probably the simplest to make and fit. Although this arrangement is possible with standard butt hinges, the use of cranked or special extended pivot hinges permits the door to open within the width of the unit.

D) Doors are again face hung. A **concealed cabinet hinge** is bored into the rear face of the door and its mounting plate fixed to the inside of the standard. This type which is extensively used in modern kitchen units, allows the door to be adjusted in height, sideways, backwards and forward. They include a degree of self-closing in the final stage of swing and do not require a catch.

There are various methods available for making cupboard doors slide. Glass, thin plywood or MDF doors are often made to slide in nylon or fibre tracks (see Figure 4.126). The deeper channel track is used at the top, so the doors can be inserted and removed by pushing them up into the top track, clearing the bottom one.

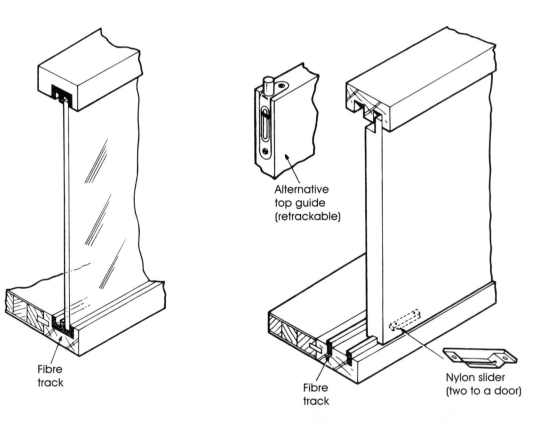

Fibre
track

Alternative
top guide
(retrackable)

Fibre
track

Nylon slider
(two to a door)

Figure 4.126 *Glass sliding doors*   **Figure 4.127** *Sliding cupboard doors*

Figure 4.127 shows how a cupboard door may be made to slide on fibre tracks grooved into the pot board. Two nylon sliders are recessed and screwed to the underside of each door. These run on the fibre track and provide a smooth sliding action which wears well. The top edge of the door is usually rebated to engage in a groove run in the underside of the top rail. Sufficient clearance for insertion and removal must be made at this point to allow the bottom of the door to clear the pot board when pushed up into the top groove. Retractable top guides similar to flush bolts can be used instead of rebating the top edges of the doors.

Heavyweight cupboard doors are best top hung to achieve a smooth running action.

Figure 4.128 illustrates one of the simplest types of top-hung cupboard door sliding track. It consists of a surface fixed aluminium top track and bottom guide. The door is suspended by two nylon hangers/sliders fixed to its top edge.

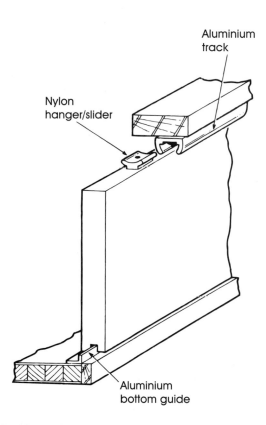

Figure 4.128 *Top-hung door*

The handle position of bottom-sliding doors is best kept nearer the bottom of the door for smooth sliding action. There will be a tendency for the door to tip and judder if the handle is positioned higher than a distance equal to the doors width. The best action is achieved with top-hung doors when the handle position is kept as high as possible.

Worktops

The main types which are in common use are illustrated in Figure 4.129.

Solid timber – made up from narrow-edge jointed boards. Provision for moisture movement needs to be considered when fixing them to a carcass. Mitred return ends may be specified; these serve to hold the top flat and also cover the exposed end grain.

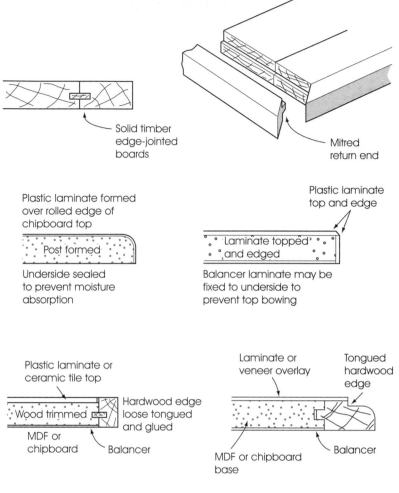

Figure 4.129 *Worktop details*

Post-formed – a chipboard base covered with a plastic laminate which has been formed over a rolled edge. The most popular type of worktop for kitchen units, it is ready finished and simply requires fixing in place.

Edged sheet material – a chipboard or MDF base covered with either a melamine face, plastic laminate or wood veneer. Matching edging is applied to the seen edges. The undersides of sheet material tops should be the same as the topface or be sealed to prevent distortion. It is good practice to use a double faced, melamine or wood veneer board. On good quality work a balancer laminate is applied to the underside of laminate faced tops to relieve the stresses which would result from facing one side only. A cheaper alternative is to seal the underside with an application of varnish or adhesive.

Wood trimmed – a chipboard or MDF base covered with either melamine face, plastic laminate or wood veneer. A hardwood lipping or edging is simply glued; rebated, glued and screwed; or tongued and glued to the seen edges, providing a neat finish. Return corners are better mitred than butted.

Wood trimmed and over-laid – a chipboard or MDF base edged in hardwood and overlaid with either laminate or wood veneer. The laminate is trimmed off on the spindle moulder or by use of a hand-held power router. Often a decorative edge feature is incorporated in the trimming process.

Built-in fitments

These normally use the wall, floor and/or ceiling as part of the construction.

Cupboards – Figure 4.130 shows details of a cupboard that is built into a reveal at the side of a fireplace. It has been framed up using 38 mm × 75 mm framing. The skirting is continued across the front of the frame to match in with the existing timber work. The doors, which have rebated meeting stiles are also framed up and a 9 mm plywood is used for the panels. The top, base, shelf and front framework are fixed to 25 mm × 50 mm battens that have been plugged and screwed to the walls.

Wardrobes – Shown in Figure 4.131 is a plan, elevation and section of a 'built-in' wardrobe. This can be made up using 18 or 25 mm MFC or MDF for the base, partitions, shelves and doors.

To provide a good finish, the exposed edges should be either lipped with 10 mm timber edging or be taped with an iron-on edging. See Figure 4.132.

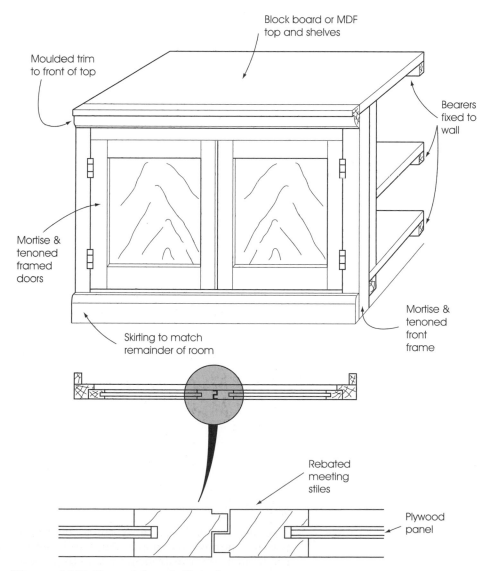

Figure 4.130 *Framed front built-in fitment*

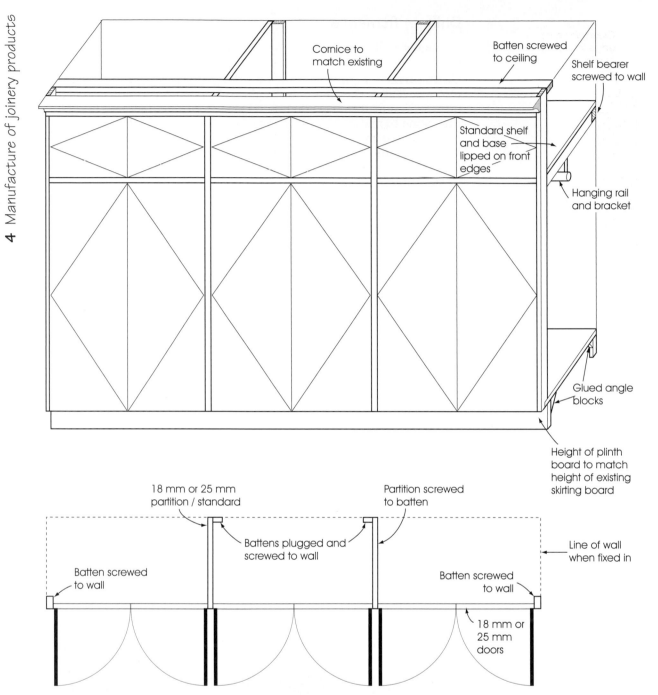

Cornice to match existing

Batten screwed to ceiling

Shelf bearer screwed to wall

Standard shelf and base lipped on front edges

Hanging rail and bracket

Glued angle blocks

Height of plinth board to match height of existing skirting board

18 mm or 25 mm partition / standard

Partition screwed to batten

Battens plugged and screwed to wall

Line of wall when fixed in

Batten screwed to wall

Batten screwed to wall

18 mm or 25 mm doors

Figure 4.131 *Built-in wardrobe*

The outside doors are hung on 25 mm × 50 mm battens which have been fixed to the walls, while all the remaining doors are hung on the partitions. These can be hung inside the opening using flush hinges, or on the face using concealed cabinet hinges.

The base is made up on a plinth board to match the height of the existing skirting as shown. An in-fill piece is used at the top to drop the head of the wardrobe down, so that a cornice to match the existing one can be fixed along the ceiling line if required.

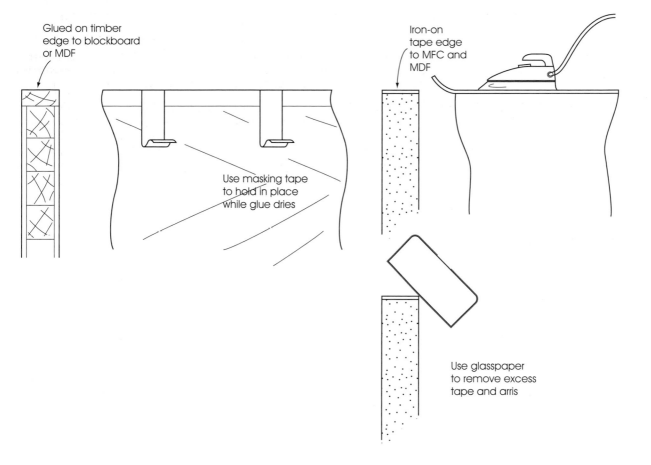

Glued on timber
edge to blockboard
or MDF

Use masking tape
to hold in place
while glue dries

Iron-on
tape edge
to MFC and
MDF

Use glasspaper
to remove excess
tape and arris

Figure 4.132 *Edging sheet material*

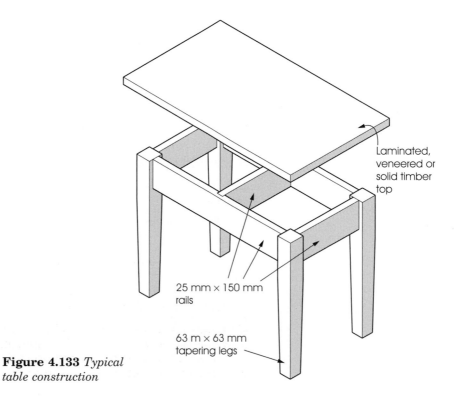

Laminated,
veneered or
solid timber
top

25 mm × 150 mm
rails

63 m × 63 mm
tapering legs

Figure 4.133 *Typical
table construction*

Table construction

Details of a typical table suitable for use in most situations is illustrated in Figure 4.133. The table consists of four legs which are joined by four rails. The joint shown in Figure 4.134 between the rails and legs is a table haunched mortise and tenon.

The tenon is bare-faced and is mitred on its end to allow for the tenon of the other rail. Alternatively dowels, biscuits or proprietary brackets may be used for the leg to rail joints. Also illustrated are different methods, which can be used for fixing the table top to the framework. Pocket screwing and plastic blocks are suitable for sheet material whereas the other methods allow for moisture movement when solid timber tops are used.

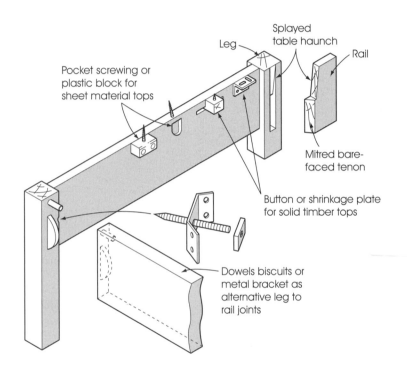

Figure 4.134 *Table jointing details*

Assembly procedure for units and fitments

The assembly of framed items follows closely that of other framed joinery items.

The following procedure is illustrated in Figure 4.135:

● Dry assemble to check fit of joints, overall sizes, square and winding.
● Clean up inside edges of all framing components and both faces of infill panels, etc.
● Glue, assemble, cramp up and wedge each individual frame. Re-check for square and winding.
● Clean up internal faces of individual frames.
● Clean up any rails, shelves, top and potboard, etc.
● Glue, assemble and cramp up individual frames and other members to form the unit carcass. Check for square.
● Clean up external surfaces and prepare for finishing.

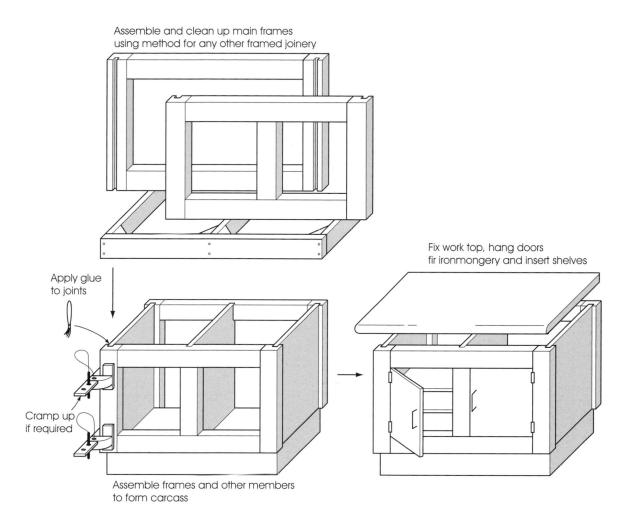

Figure 4.135 *Assembly of framed units*

- Fix worktop if separate.
- Install drawers, hang doors and fix any ironmongery.

The assembly of box construction units can be carried out using the following procedure shown in Figure 4.136.

- Check measurement of panels.
- Carry out any necessary handwork, such as squaring out corners, iron-on edging, fittings for shelves and drawers, etc.
- Where proprietary knock-down fittings are being used, these should be pre-fitted to each panel at this stage.
- Assemble panels, use glue and cramps if required.
- Fix worktop if separate.
- Install drawers, hang doors, fix any ironmongery and insert any shelving.

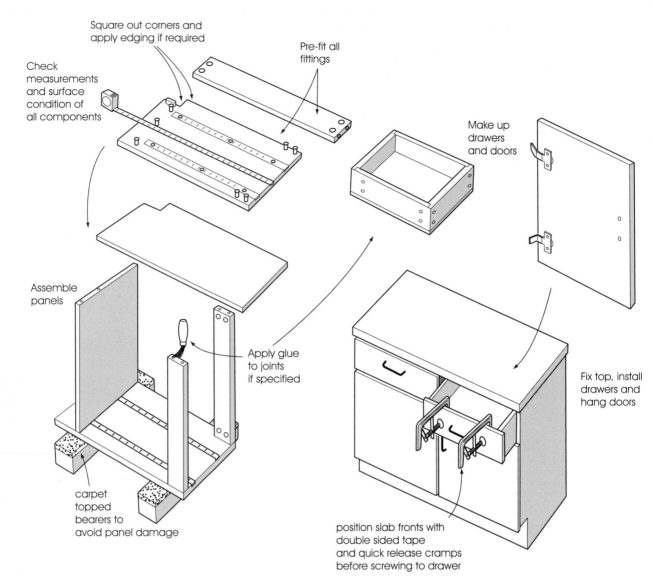

Check measurements and surface condition of all components

Square out corners and apply edging if required

Pre-fit all fittings

Make up drawers and doors

Assemble panels

Apply glue to joints if specified

carpet topped bearers to avoid panel damage

Fix top, install drawers and hang doors

position slab fronts with double sided tape and quick release cramps before screwing to drawer

Figure 4.136 *Assembly of box construction*

READ THE INSTRUCTIONS
AND COMPLETE
THE TASK

— **Learning tasks** —

Study the method statement and data sheet shown in Figure 4.137 for any irregularities.

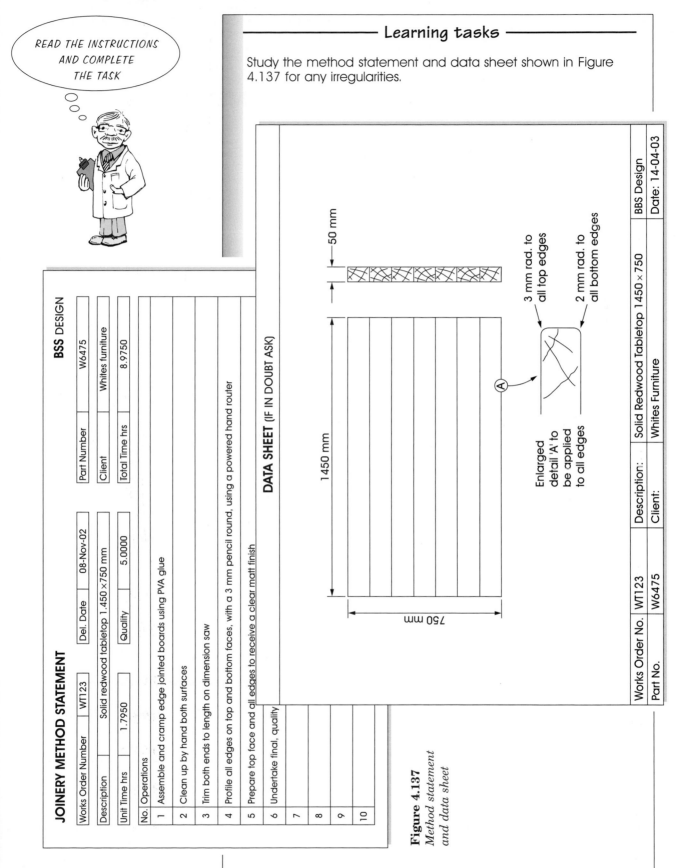

JOINERY METHOD STATEMENT

BSS DESIGN

Works Order Number	WT123	Del. Date	08-Nov-02	Part Number	W6475
Description	Solid redwood tabletop 1.450 × 750 mm			Client	Whites furniture
Unit Time hrs	1.7950	Quality	5.0000	Total Time hrs	8.9750

No.	Operations
1	Assemble and cramp edge jointed boards using PVA glue
2	Clean up by hand both surfaces
3	Trim both ends to length on dimension saw
4	Profile all edges on top and bottom faces, with a 3 mm pencil round, using a powered hand router
5	Prepare top face and all edges to receive a clear matt finish
6	Undertake final, quality
7	
8	
9	
10	

DATA SHEET (IF IN DOUBT ASK)

50 mm

1450 mm

750 mm

Enlarged detail 'A' to be applied to all edges

(A)

3 mm rad. to all top edges

2 mm rad. to all bottom edges

Works Order No.	WT123	Description:	Solid Redwood Tabletop 1450 × 750	BBS Design
Part No.	W6475	Client:	Whites Furniture	Date: 14-04-03

Figure 4.137
Method statement and data sheet

Complete the blank memo or telephone conversation call-out, seeking clarification if required, from Mark Wood, the setter/marker-out responsible for the job.

BBS CONSTRUCTION   **MEMO**

From _____ To _____

Subject _____ Date _____

Message

Figure 4.138

READ THE INSTRUCTIONS
AND COMPLETE
THE TASK

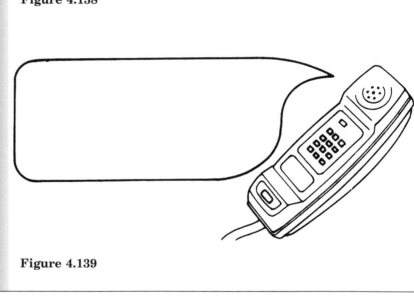

Figure 4.139

—— **Questions for you** ——

21. Describe or sketch the difference between, box and frame unit construction.

_____

_____

TRY TO
ANSWER THESE

22. Produce a sketch to show the following **THREE** worktop edge details:
a) post-formed
b) wood trimmed
c) wood trimmed with laminate overlay

23. Explain the purpose of a balancer, when laminating sheet material.

_____

_____

24. The vertical member used to form a step is a:
a)   tread
b)   string
c)   riser
d)   newel

a	b	c	d
⌸	⌸	⌸	⌸

25. Explain the term 'going' when applied to stairs.

_____

_____

26. Define the abbreviations MFC & MDF.

_____

_____

27. Produce sketches to show the difference between traditional and modern methods of drawer construction.

28. List the main sequence of operation for assembling a straight flight of stairs, 'closed' on both sides.

_____

_____

_____

_____

_____

_____

29. Glass sliding doors are to be fitted in a book display unit, using a plastic channel track. Explain why the channels for the top and bottom are of a different section.

_____

_____

_____

_____

30. Sketch or describe **TWO** methods of providing, adjustable height shelf supports.

_____

_____

_____

_____

WELL, HOW DID YOU DO?

WORK THROUGH THE SECTION AGAIN IF YOU HAD ANY PROBLEMS

COMPLETE THE
WORD SQUARE

WORD-SQUARE SEARCH

Hidden in the word-square are the following 20 words associated with
'*Joinery*'. You may find the words written forwards, backwards, up, down
or diagonally.

JOINERY	LIGHT	CASEMENT
BAREFACED	SASH	ROD
TRADITIONAL	WORKSHOP	MATCHBOARD
CUTTING LIST	STORMPROOF	WINDOW
STILE	DOOR	RAIL
SQUARING	MULLION	WINDING
JAMB	ALLOWANCE	

Draw a ring around the words, or line in using a highlight pen thus:

EXAMPLE

```
L A N O I T I D A R T K B G E W C M
R C K B C D R H L C D E F N G O X A
C D P E C C E A L I A R D I Y D Z T
U X O A A B L K O D E H A R K N W C
T A H C S E I B W O Q B O A A I B H
T R S B E K T C A E H D A U E W O B
I C K D M E S F N G I J L Q K M L O
N B R O E M C U C D P V S S X J P A
G D O K N K T E E F W K C E O F P R
L E W M T B V C G I G X Z I F E Y D
I F I L S C A Z N P A C N B J F J K
S G J N S F O D K Q C E R B N A M L
T H H P E A I P O O R S T E F G M C
B C S R T N P D L Y D H I L K N B B
A D A O G E W E I E F B B C L R A C
E B S R H G Y F G F M U L L I O N B
G F H Q A F X J H C E M W A T O F E
F O O R P M R O T S G B J I V D H G
```

WELL, HOW
MANY DID YOU
GET?

5 Woodworking machining

READ THIS CHAPTER, WORKING THROUGH THE 'QUESTIONS FOR YOU'

In undertaking this chapter you will be required to demonstrate your skill and knowledge of:

● Using and maintaining a hand fed circular rip saw.

You will be required practically to:

● Use a hand fed circular rip saw complying with current regulations to produce sawn components: square, rectangular, bevelled, angled, wedged and tapered.

Hand fed circular rip saw

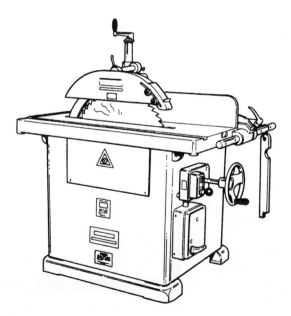

Figure 5.1 *Rip saw*

The main purpose of a rip saw (Figure 5.1) is to resaw timber from its marketable sectional size into the required section.

This may involve (Figures 5.2 to 5.4):

- cutting the timber to the required width, known as *flatting*.
- cutting the timber to the required thickness, known as *deeping*.
- cutting the timber to the appropriate angle or bevel. Machine operators will make their own bed pieces and saddles that enable them safely to carry out angle and bevel ripping.
- cutting the timber to the appropriate taper or wedge shape. Machine operators will make their own push blocks having the required taper or wedge shape on their edge which enable them safely to carry out tapered ripping or wedge cutting.

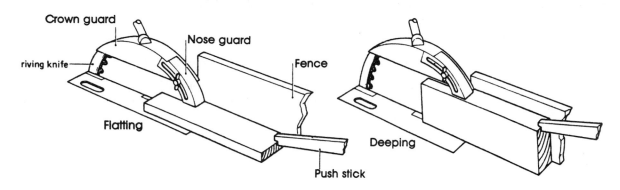

Figure 5.2 *Flatting and deeping*

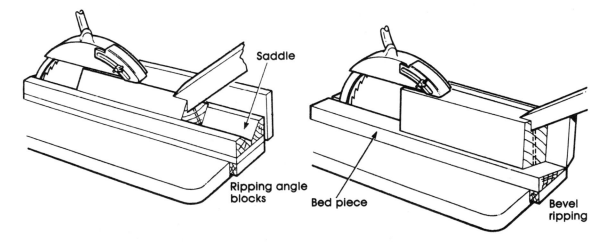

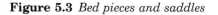

Figure 5.3 *Bed pieces and saddles*

Figure 5.5 shows the following parts of the rip saw:

- The *crown guard* (A) is vertically adjustable and when set up for sawing, it must completely cover the gullets of the top teeth.
- The *nose guard* (B) should be adjusted for each cutting operation so that the gap between the nose guard and the material being cut is as close as practicably possible. A maximum of 12 mm is permissible.
- The *pillar* (C) and adjusting handle for the crown guard.
- The *riving knife* (D) rises and falls along with the saw when the depth of cut is altered. Whenever a saw blade is changed, the riving

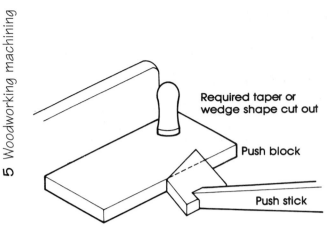

Figure 5.4 *Use of push block to cut wedges*

Figure 5.5 *Parts of the rip saw*

ENSURE MACHINE IS ISOLATED FROM POWER SUPPLY BEFORE MAKING ANY ADJUSTMENTS TO GUARDS OR CLEANING DOWN

knife must be adjusted so that it is as close as practicably possible to the saw blade and, in any case, the distance between the riving knife and the teeth of the saw blade should not exceed 12 mm. It should be thicker than the saw blade as its purpose is to stop the material binding on the saw blade while being cut and also to guard the back edge of the saw blade.

- The *fence* (E) is adjusted by slackening the hand lever and moving the fence on its slide to give the required width of cut. The fence should be set so that the arc at the end of the fence is in line with the gullets of the saw teeth at table level. This helps to prevent the timber binding on the saw blade.
- The *knurled adjusting knob* (F), by rotation, gives a fine adjustment of the fence. The measurement between the saw blade and fence is indicated on the graduated scale above the slide.
- The *rise and fall handle* (G) raises or lowers the blade.
- *Start* and *stop* controls (H).
- The *table groove* (I) enables a cross-cut guide or mitre fence to be used.
- The *access cover* (J) is removed to give access to the spindle when changing saw blades.
- The *finger plate* (K) is removed to give access to the spindle when changing saw blades. Some saws have a recess on each side of the blade where it enters the table. These recesses are to receive felt packings, a hardwood mouthpiece and a hardwood backfilling. The packings and backfillings prevent the saw being deflected and keep it cutting in a true line (Figure 5.6). The mouthpiece protects the packing from damage by the saw teeth and prevents the underside of the timber breaking out or 'spelching'. The backfilling also prevents damage to the saw teeth should it run out of true.

Figure 5.6 *Saw packings and mouthpiece.*

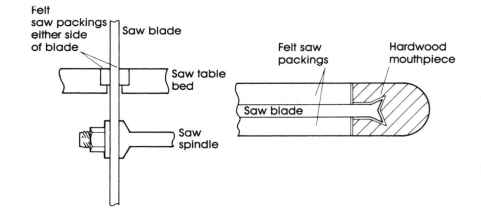

Safety in operation

The safeguarding of woodworking machines is covered by the British Standard Code of Practice BS 6854. This standard takes into account both the practical aspects of safeguarding and the legal requirements contained in the Health and Safety at Work Act, the Woodworking Machine Regulations (now revoked) and the Provision and use of Work Equipment Regulations.

The main points to be considered wherever woodworking machines are in use may be summarized as follows (Figure 5.7 refers):

1) The cutters of every machine must be enclosed by a substantial guard to the maximum possible extent.
2) In general no adjustment should be made to the guards or any other part of the machine while the cutters are in motion.
3) Every machine must have an effective starting and stopping device. This should be located so that it is easily used by the operator especially in the case of an emergency.
4) The working area around a machine must be kept free from obstruction, offcuts, shavings, etc.
5) The floor surface of the work area must be level, non-slip and maintained in good condition.
6) A reasonable temperature must be maintained in the workplace and in any case must not fall below 13°C or 10°C in a saw mill. Where this is not possible because the machine is situated in the open air, radiant heaters must be provided near or adjacent to the work area, to enable operators to warm themselves periodically.
7) No person must use any woodworking machine unless he/she has been properly trained for the work being carried out or he/she is under close supervision as part of the training.
8) Machine operators must:
   (a) Use correctly all guards and safety devices required by the regulations.
   (b) Report to the supervisor or employer any faults or contraventions of the regulations.
9) Any person who sells or hires a woodworking machine must ensure it complies with the regulations.

REFER TO THESE REGULATIONS

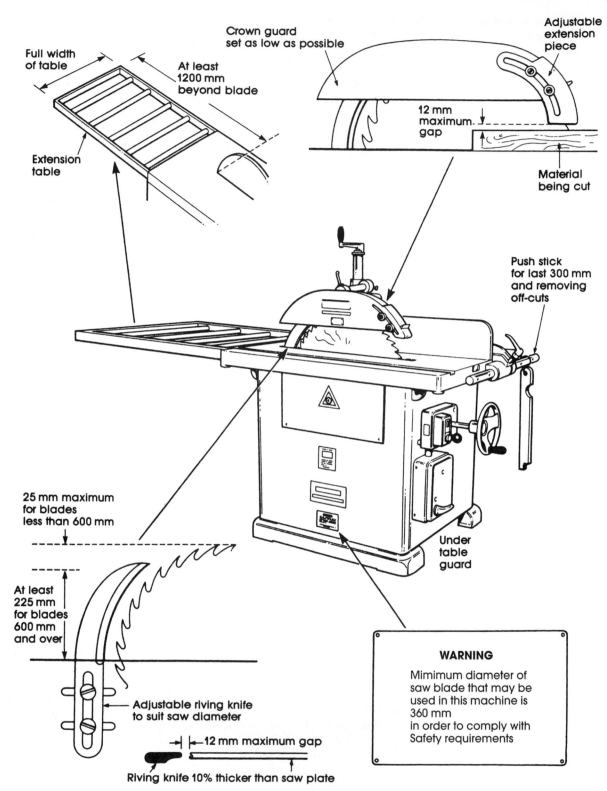

Full width of table

At least 1200 mm beyond blade

Extension table

Crown guard set as low as possible

Adjustable extension piece

12 mm maximum gap

Material being cut

Push stick for last 300 mm and removing off-cuts

Under table guard

25 mm maximum for blades less than 600 mm

At least 225 mm for blades 600 mm and over

Adjustable riving knife to suit saw diameter

12 mm maximum gap

Riving knife 10% thicker than saw plate

WARNING

Mimimum diameter of saw blade that may be used in this machine is 360 mm in order to comply with Safety requirements

Figure 5.7 *Circular saw safety requirements*

174

The safety requirements applicable to circular saws are:

1) The part of the saw blade which is below the saw table must be enclosed to the maximum possible extent.

2) A strong, adjustable riving knife must be fitted directly behind the saw blade. Its purpose is to part the timber as it proceeds through the saw and thus prevents it jamming on the blade and being thrown back towards the operator.

3) The upper part of the saw blade must be fitted with a strong adjustable crown guard which has flanges that cover the full depth of the saw teeth. The adjustable extension piece should be positioned to within 12 mm of the surface of the material being cut.

4) The diameter of the saw blade must never be less than ⁶⁄₁₀ (60%) of the largest saw blade for which the machine is designed. In the case of a multi-speed machine the diameter of the saw blade must never be less than 60% of the largest saw blade which can be properly used at the highest speed. A notice must always be fixed to each machine clearly stating the minimum diameter of the saw blade that may be used.

5) Circular saws must not:

    (a) Be used for cutting tenons, grooves, and rebates or moulding unless effectively guarded. These normally take the form of Shaw 'tunnel type' guards which, in addition to enclosing the blade, apply pressure to the work piece, keeping it in place.

    (b) Be used for ripping unless the saw teeth project above the timber, i.e. deeping large sectioned material in two cuts is not permissible.

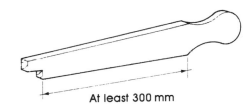

Figure 5.8 *Push stick*

At least 300 mm

6) A suitable push stick (Figure 5.8) must be provided and kept readily available at all times. It must be used for:

    (a) Feeding material where the cut is 300 mm or less.

    (b) Feeding material over the last 300 mm of the cut.

    (c) Removing cut pieces from between the saw blade and fence.

A push block may be used in conjunction with a push stick for cutting short sections.

7) Anyone working at the machine, except the operator, must stand at the delivery end. A full-width table extension must be fitted so that the distance between the nearest part of the saw blade and the end of the table is at least 1200 mm (except in the case of a portable saw bench having a saw blade of 450 mm or less in diameter). See Figure 5.9.

8) The safe working position for the operator is at the feed end offset away from the fence and out of the blade line.

9) It is recommended that operators wear personal protection (Figure 5.10): ear protection to reduce the risk of hearing loss; dust mask, particularly when cutting hardwood to reduce the risk of respiratory problems.

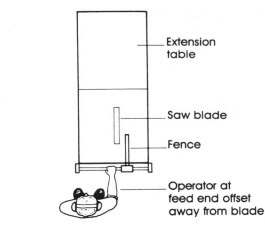

Figure 5.9 *Saw operator position*

Figure 5.10 *Use personal protection when machining*

Tooling

The teeth and their terminology for a circular saw blade used for most ripping operations is illustrated in Figure 5.11.

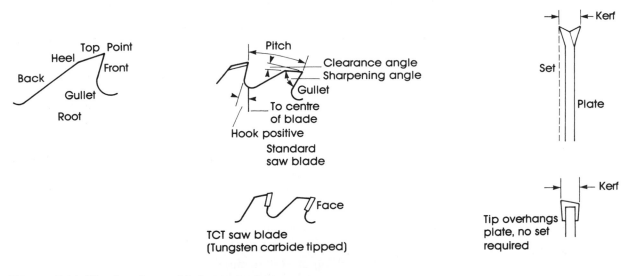

Figure 5.11 *Circular rip saw blade terminology*

Pitch – is the distance between two teeth.

Hook – is the angle of the front of the tooth. Positive hook is required for ripping. (The teeth incline towards the timber.) An angle of 20 to 25 degrees is normally used for softwoods and 10 to 15 degrees for hardwoods.

Clearance angle – ensures the heel clears the timber when cutting. An angle of 15 degrees is normally used for softwoods and 5 to 10 degrees for hardwoods.

Top bevel – is the angle across the top of the tooth. An angle of 15 degrees is normally used for softwood and 5 to 10 degrees for hardwoods.

Gullet – is the space between two teeth. It carries away the sawdust.

Kerf – is the total width of the saw cut in the timber made by the blade. It equals twice the set plus the thickness of the saw plate or twice the overhang plus the thickness of the saw plate on tungsten carbide tipped saws (TCT).

Set – is the amount each tooth is bent or sprung out to give a clearance on the sawplate. The cutting edge of sprung set blades quickly dull when ripping abrasive timbers. Many sawmills now use tungsten carbide tipped (TCT) saws. These stay sharper much longer and don't require a set as they overhang the sawplate.

Maintenance

ENSURE MACHINE IS ISOLATED FROM POWER SUPPLY BEFORE MAKING ANY ADJUSTMENTS TO GUARDS OR CLEANING DOWN

Saw blade maintenance

After a period of use, saw blades will start to dull (lose their cutting edge). This will progressively cause a poor finish to the saw cut including burning of both the timber and the blade and possibly cause blade wobble due to overheating. In addition, it will require excessive pressure by the operator to force the timber through the saw.

The sharpening of circular ripsaw blades is normally carried out on a saw sharpening machine or by hand filing. However, neither of these operations is within the scope of this Unit of Competence.

To ensure true running of a saw blade, it should be fitted in the same position on the saw spindle each time it is used. This can be achieved by always mounting the blades on the spindle with the location/driving peg uppermost and, before tightening, pulling the saw blade back onto the peg.

Resin deposits on saw blades should be cleaned off periodically. They can be softened by brushing with an oil/paraffin mixture and scraped off. A wood scraper is preferable as it will avoid scratching the saw blade.

Machine maintenance

Routine periodic maintenance of the machine will:

- prolong its serviceable life
- ensure all moving parts work freely
- ensure the machine operates safely.

The manufacturer's maintenance schedule supplied with each machine, gives the operator information regarding routine maintenance procedures. The schedule will detail the parts to be lubricated, the location of grease nipples and the type, frequency and amount of grease.

A typical procedure might be:

- Remove all rust spots with fine wire wool.
- Clean off resin deposits and other dirt, using an oil/paraffin mixture and wooden scraper.

- Wipe over entire machine using clean rag.
- Apply a coat of light grade oil to all screws and slides. Excess should be wiped off using a clean rag.
- Clean off grease nipples and apply correct grade and amount of grease using the correct gun. Parts can be rotated manually during this operation.
- Check freeness of all moving parts.

READ THE INSTRUCTIONS
AND COMPLETE
THE TASK

Learning task

Consult BS 6854 Safe Guarding of Woodworking Machines. Answer the following questions.

Define a circular sawing machine in accordance with the Standard.

_____

_____

_____

Name the part that covers circular sawing machines.

_____

What paragraph relates to the thickness of a riving knife?

_____

Describe what the Standard says about training.

_____

_____

TRY TO
ANSWER THESE

Questions for you

1. Produce sketches to show the difference between deeping and flatting.

2. Name a type of saw blade that is most suitable for ripping abrasive timber.

_____

3. Describe the safe working position that the operator of a circular hand fed saw bench should take.

_____

_____

4. The riving knife fitted to a circular saw must have a maximum clearance between itself and the blade of:
(a)   6 mm
(b)   10 mm
(c)   12 mm
(d)   20 mm

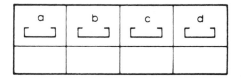

5. The guard on a circular saw that covers the top of a saw blade is known as the:
(a)   shaw guard
(b)   top guard
(c)   crown guard
(d)   bridge guard

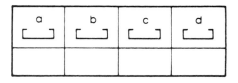

6. List **FOUR** general requirements for the safe use of woodworking machines.

_____

_____

_____

_____

7. State one piece of information that must be fixed to every circular saw machine.

_____

_____

8. State the purposes of packings to circular saw blades.

_____

_____

9. State **TWO** reasons for using a hardwood mouthpiece.

_____

_____

10. Label the illustration that shows a portion of a circular saw blade.

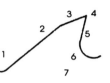

11. State **TWO** reasons for undertaking routine periodic maintenance of woodworking machines.

_____

_____

12. State **TWO** situations where a push stick must be used.

_____

_____

13. List **FIVE** tasks that may be included in the periodic maintenance of a circular saw.

_____

_____

_____

_____

_____

14. Explain why a riving knife thicker than the saw blade should be used.

_____

_____

15. Describe how you would ensure that a saw blade is refitted in exactly the same position after each time it has been taken off for sharpening.

_____

_____

WELL, HOW DID YOU DO?

WORK THROUGH THE SECTION AGAIN IF YOU HAD ANY PROBLEMS

WORD PUZZLE

Solve the clues to complete the word puzzle. All the answers are associated with 'Woodworking Machining'. The number of letters in each word is shown in brackets e.g. (6) indicates a six-letter word and (4, 3) indicates two words having four and three letters each.

COMPLETE THE
WORD PUZZLE

Across

  3. Covers top of saw blade (5, 5)
  6. To cut out of vertical (5)
  7. Sideways projection of saw teeth (3)
  9. Not flat (4)
10. Fitted behind saw blade (5) (second word)
11. Fitted to top of saw tooth (3)
13. Sawing with the grain (7)
14. A component being machined (4, 5)

Down

  1. Abbreviation for type of saw (3)
  2. Used to provide protection (5)
  4. Prevents binding (6) (first word)
  5. Cutting timber to the required thickness (7)
  7. Not required by tipped saws (3)
  8. The width of a saw cut (4)
12. Used to rip timber (3)

WELL, HOW
MANY DID YOU
GET?

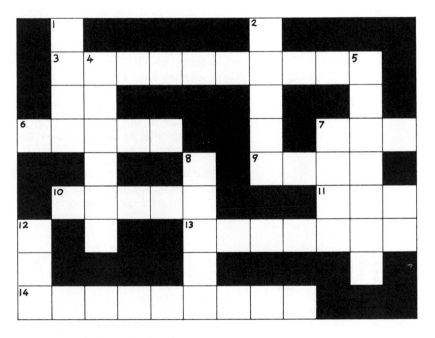

6 Maintenance of buildings

READ THIS CHAPTER, WORKING THROUGH THE 'QUESTIONS FOR YOU'

In undertaking this chapter you will be required to demonstrate your skill and knowledge of maintaining internal and external timber components along with the associated trade skills of painting, plastering, brickwork, glazing and ceramic tiling.

You will be required practically to:

- Repair timber by splicing
- Remove and replace timber frames
- Remove and replace structural timber
- Replace sash cords
- Paint timber and plaster
- Re-lay brickwork
- Make good plasterwork and rendering
- Cut glass and install glazing with beads and putty
- Re-fix ceramic tiles.

It is an accepted fact that all buildings will deteriorate (develop faults and defects which if not rectified may lead on to failures) to some extent as they age. This deterioration may even start as the individual components are incorporated into the building elements during the construction process. In certain circumstances the deterioration of the components may have started either prior to their delivery to the building site or during the storage, before the commencement of construction operations.

The rate and extent to which a building deteriorates is dependent on one or more of the following main factors: maintenance; the environment; design and construction.

Defining maintenance

This is taken to mean the keeping, holding, sustaining, or preserving of a building and its services to an acceptable standard. This may take one of two forms: planned maintenance or unplanned maintenance.

Planned or routine maintenance

This is a definite programme of work aimed at reducing to a minimum the need for often costly unplanned work. It includes:

- the annual inspection and servicing of general plumbing, heating equipment, electrical and other services, etc.
- the periodic inspection and cleaning out of gutters, gullies, rainwater pipes and airbricks, etc.

- the periodic redecoration, both internally and externally;
- the routine general inspection/observation of the building fabric and moving parts.

Preventative maintenance – Finally, also included under this heading, is what is known as preventative maintenance. Basically this is any work carried out as a result of any of the previous inspections in anticipation of a failure, e.g. the early replacement of an item, on the assumption that minor faults almost certainly lead onto bigger and more costly faults unless preventative work is carried out.

Unplanned emergency or corrective maintenance

This is work that is left until the efficiency of the element or service falls well below the acceptable level or even fails altogether. This is the most expensive form of maintenance, making inefficient use of both labour and materials and often also creating serious health/safety risks, and is the type most often carried out. This is because the allocation of money to enable maintenance work to be planned is often given low priority.

Environmental factors

These include:

- the deterioration of components and finishes owing to chemical pollution in the atmosphere;
- the effect of the elements (weather) on the structure, e.g. frost, rain, snow, sun and the wind;
- the effect of these elements when allowed to penetrate into the building;
- the deterioration of components owing to biological attack (fungal decay and insect attack).

Design and construction factors

Faulty design and construction methods can lead to rapid deterioration of a building. In fact over 30% of all maintenance/repair could be avoided if sufficient care is taken at the design and construction stages.

Faulty design

This results from inadequate knowledge or attention to detail on the part of the architect or designer leading to, for example, poor specification of materials/components, structural movement, moisture penetration, biological attack and the inefficient operation of the building services.

Faulty construction

Inadequate supervision during the construction process can result in poor workmanship, the use of inferior materials and the lack of attention to details/specifications. These can all lead to the same problems as those stated for faulty design, resulting in subsequent problems and expense for the building owner.

Agents of deterioration

Apart from the natural ageing process of all buildings during their anticipated life (however well maintained), deterioration of buildings can be attributed directly to one or often a combination of the following agents:

- dampness
- movement
- chemical attack
- biological attack
- infestation.

Dampness

Dampness in buildings is the biggest single source of trouble. It causes the rapid deterioration of most building materials, can assist chemical attack and creates conditions which are favourable for biological attack. Dampness can arise from three main external sources: rain penetration, rising damp and condensation. In addition, leaking plumbing and heating systems and spillage of water in use are also significant causes of dampness.

Rain penetration – This is rain penetrating the external structure either through the walls or the roof and appearing on the inside of the building as damp patches. After periods of heavy rain these patches will tend to spread and then dry out during prolonged periods of dry weather. They will, however, never completely disappear, as a moisture stain and in some cases even efflorescence (crystallised mineral salts) will be left on the surface.

Mould growth (fungi resulting in dark-green or black patchy spots) may occur in damp areas particularly behind furniture, in corners and other poorly ventilated locations. The main causes of rain penetration are shown in Figures 6.1 and 6.2. It can be seen that penetration takes place through gaps, cracks, holes and joints either in, around or between components and elements.

Roofs – Loose or missing tiles or slates including the hip and ridge capping tiles will allow rainwater to run down rafters, causing damp patches on the ceilings and tops of walls. These patches may appear some distance away from the defective area as the water spreads along timbers and across the ceiling, etc. This dampness will also saturate any thermal insulation material making it ineffective. If left unrepaired, saturation of the roof timbers will occur leading to fungal decay in due course. Another major area of penetration is around the chimney stack and other roof-to-wall junctions; this may be due to cracked chimney pots, cracked or deteriorating flaunchings (the sloping mortar into which the pots are set), or corroded or pitted metal flashings (these cover the joint between the stack or wall and the roof) which may be cracked or deteriorated. Poor pointing to the stack can also be a cause of penetration. Any of these defects can cause large patches of damp on the internal wall.

Walls – Clearly rainwater travels downwards and when assisted by high winds it will travel sideways through gaps. But depending on the nature of the material, it can often move unassisted both sideways or upwards because of capillary attraction (the phenomenon whereby water can

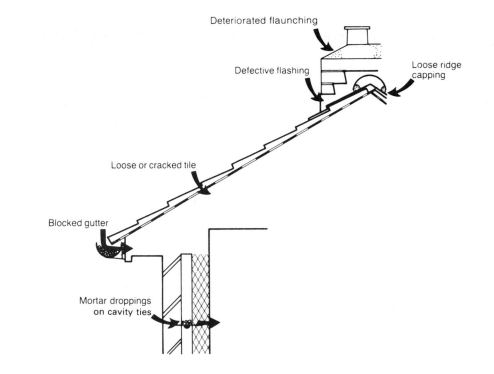

Figure 6.1 *Rain penetration*

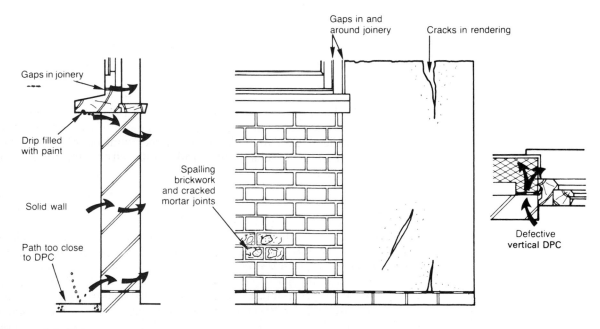

Figure 6.2 *Rain penetration*

travel against the force of gravity in fine spaces or between two surfaces which are close together; the smaller the space the greater the attraction (see Figure 6.3).

There are two main conditions that promote **capillarity** in the external envelope. The fine cellular structure of some materials provides the interconnecting pores through which water can travel. Also

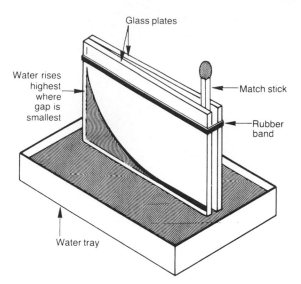

Figure 6.3 *Experiment to show capillarity*

the fine joints between components, e.g. wall and door or window frame, mortar joints between brickwork, close joints between overlapping components. The risk of capillarity is reduced or avoided by either:

- Physically separating the inside and outside surface by introducing a gap (e.g. cavity wall construction).
- Introducing an impervious (waterproof) barrier between components (e.g. mastic pointing, DPCs, DPMs, moisture barriers and flashing, etc.).

Over time, the water resistance of brick/stonework and their mortar joints will deteriorate. This deterioration can be accelerated by the action of frost. Rainwater may accumulate below the surface and freeze. Ice expands causing the brickwork/stonework and their mortar joints to spall (crumble away). The wall then offers little resistance to the weather and should be replaced. This entails either:

- Cutting the surface of the spalled components back and replacing with matching thin components (half bricks) and finally repointing the whole wall.
- The entire wall may be 'hacked off' (cut back to remove spalling) and covered with one of the standard wall finishes, cement rendering, rough cast, pebble dash, Tyrolean or silicone-nylon fibre.

Cracks in cement rendering and other wall finishes can be caused by shrinkage on drying, building movement or chemical attack. Once opened up, deterioration is accelerated by frost action. Small cracks may be enlarged and filled with a cement slurry. Large areas which may have 'blown' (come away) from the surface will require hacking back to sound (firmly adhering) work and replaced. With cavity wall construction, rainwater that does penetrate the outer leaf should simply run down inside the cavity and not reach the internal leaf. The vertical mortar joints of the outer leaf are sometimes raked out at intervals along the bottom of the cavity to provide weep holes through which the water can escape.

However, when the cavity is bridged by a porous material (e.g. the collection of mortar droppings on the wall ties during construction), the water will reach the inner leaf causing small isolated damp patches on the internal wall surface. The remedy for this fault is to remove one or two bricks of the outer leaf near the suspected bridge and either clean out or replace the tie as necessary.

Dampness around door and window frames is likely to be caused by wind-assisted rain entering the joint between the wall and frame, by the action of capillarity or by a defective vertical DPC used around openings in cavity walls, where the inner and outer leaf join. An exterior mastic can be used to seal the joints but where DPCs are defective they will require cutting out and replacing. A check should be made at the sill level of frames. Cracked sills allow water to penetrate and therefore should be filled. The drip groove on the underside of the sill should be cleaned out as it often collects dirt/dust and is filled by repeated painting. The purpose of the drip groove is to break the under surface of the sill making the water drip off at this point and not run back underneath into the building.

Blocked or cracked gutters and down-pipes, dripping outside taps and constantly running overflows can cause an excessive concentration of water in one place which will be almost permanently damp. This will result in an accelerated deterioration of the wall and subsequent internal damp patches etc. The immediate fault can be easily rectified by repairing or replacing the defective component. But if left unattended the resulting damage to the building structure has most serious and costly implications.

Rising damp – This is normally moisture from below ground level rising and spreading up walls and through floors by capillarity. This most often occurs in older buildings. Many of these were built without DPCs and DPMs, or, where they were incorporated have broken down possibly with age (e.g. slate, a one time popular DPC material cracks with building movement, thus allowing capillarity). The visual result on the walls is a band of dampness and staining spreading up from the skirting level; wallpaper peeling from the surface and signs of efflorescence. The skirting, joists and floorboards adjacent to the missing or failed DPC are almost certain to be subject to fungal attack. Solid floors may be almost permanently damp causing considerable damage to floor coverings and adjacent timber/furniture etc. Rising damp can still occur in buildings that have been equipped with DPCs and DPMs (see Figure 6.4).

One of the main reasons for this is the bridging of DPCs; in the case of cavity walls, builders' mortar droppings or rubble may have collected at the bottom of the cavity, allowing moisture to rise above the DPC level; or earth in a flower bed being too high above the DPC. **Note:** DPCs are normally located at least two courses of brickwork (150 mm) above the adjacent ground level. This is because even very heavy rain is unlikely to bounce up and splash the walls much more than 100 mm from the surrounding surface. Thus the splashed rainwater is still prevented from rising above the DPC. Where the surrounding surface is later raised these splashes might bypass the DPC and result in rising damp. Weak porous rendering which has been continued over the DPC is another means by which the DPC may be bypassed.

In solid floors with a DPM, rising damp can only occur if this is defective (see Figure 6.5). For example, it may have been penetrated by jagged hardcore during the pouring of the concrete or may have been inadequately lapped (permitting capillarity between the lapped joint) or finally it may not have been linked in with the DPC in the surrounding walls (allowing moisture to bypass at this point).

The remedy to rising damp faults will of course vary; bridged or bypassed DPCs can be rectified by simply removing the cause, e.g. lowering the ground level or removing mortar and rubble from the cavity etc. Where

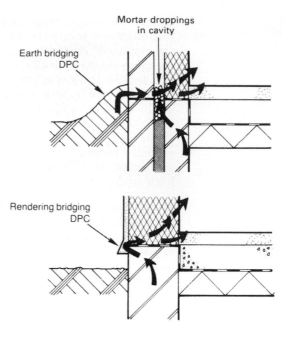

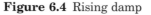

Figure 6.4 Rising damp

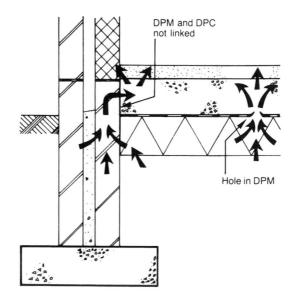

Figure 6.5 Rising damp

the DPC itself is faulty or missing altogether, one can be inserted by either cutting out a few bricks at a time to allow the positioning of a new DPC, sawing away the mortar joint a section at a time and inserting a new one.

Alternatively, liquid silicone may be injected near the bottom of the wall. This soaks into the lower courses which then acts as a moisture barrier preventing capillarity.

Localised faults in DPMs can be remedied by cutting out a section of the floor larger than the damp patch, down to the DPM, taking care not to cut through it. This should reveal the holed or badly lapped portion which can be repaired with a self-adhesive DPM. An alternative method which can also be used in floors without any DPM, is to cover the existing concrete floor with a liquid bituminous membrane or a sheet of heavy-duty polythene sheeting before laying a new floor finish, although, to be effective it should be joined into the DPC.

Condensation – The results of this form of dampness are often mistakenly attributed to rain penetration or rising damp, as they can all cause damp patches, staining, mould growth, peeling wallpaper, efflorescence, the fungal attack of timber and generally damp, unhealthy living conditions. The water or moisture for condensation actually comes from within the building. People breathing, kettles boiling, food cooking, clothes washing and drying, bath water running, etc. Each of these processes adds more moisture to the air in the form of vapour.

Air is always capable of holding a certain amount of water vapour. The warmer the air, the more vapour it can hold, but when air cools the excess vapour will revert to water. This process is known as condensation. Thus whenever warm moist air meets a cool surface condensation will occur (see Figure 6.6). This can only be controlled effectively by achieving a proper balance between heating, ventilation and insulation. The building should be kept well heated but windows should be opened or mechanical ventilators used especially in kitchens and bathrooms to allow the vapour-laden air escape outside and not spread through the building. External walls need thermally insulating to remove their cold surfaces. Both cavity wall insulation and lining the walls with a thin polystyrene veneer help a great deal. Double glazed windows also help reduce condensation by preventing the warm moist air coming into direct contact with the cold outside pane of glass.

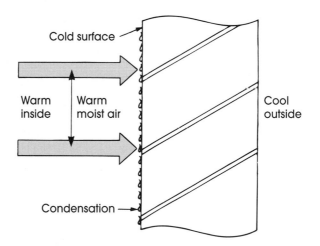

Figure 6.6 *Surface condensation*

In addition to this surface condensation, there is another condensation problem that occurs when wall surfaces are warm. This is known as interstitial or internal condensation. This is illustrated in Figure 6.7. It is caused by the warm moist air passing into the permeable structure until it cools, at which point it condenses, thus leading to the same problems associated with penetrated and rising dampness.

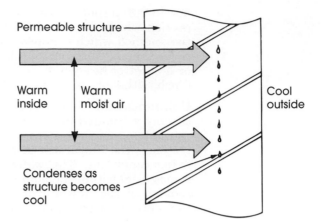

Figure 6.7 *Interstitial condensation*

Interstitial condensation can be dealt with either:

- by the use of a vapour barrier (this prevents the passage of water vapour) on the warm inside of the wall, e.g. a polythene sheet or foil backed plasterboard; or
- by allowing this water vapour to pass through the structure into a cavity where it can be dispersed by ventilation.

Movement

The visual effects of movement (Figure 6.8) in buildings may apparently be of a minor nature, e.g. windows and doors that jamb or bind in their frames; fine cracks externally along mortar joints and rendering; fine cracks internally in plastered walls and along the ceiling line etc. They can however be the first signs of serious structural weakness. Movement in buildings takes two main forms these being: ground movement and movement of materials.

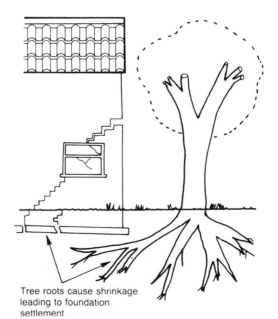

Figure 6.8 *Ground movement*

190

Ground movement – Any movement in the ground will cause settlement in the building. When it is slight and spread evenly over the building it may be acceptable, although when more than slight or is differential (more in one area than another), it can have serious consequences for the building's foundations and load-bearing members, requiring expensive temporary support (shoring) and subsequently, permanent underpinning (new foundations constructed under existing ones).

Ground movement is caused mainly by its expansion and shrinkage near the surface, owing to wet and dry conditions. Compact granular ground suffers little movement, whereas clay ground is at high risk. Tree roots cause ground shrinkage owing to the considerable amounts of water they extract from it. Tree roots can extend out in all directions from its base, greater than its height. In addition, overloading of the structure beyond its original design load can also result in ground movement.

Frost also causes ground movement. Water in the ground on freezing expands. Where this is allowed to expand on the undersides of foundations it has a tendency to lift the building (known as **frost heave**) and drop it again on thawing. This repeated action often results in serious cracking. Freezing of ground water is limited in the UK to about the top 600 mm in depth.

Movement in materials – All building materials will move to some extent owing to one or more of the following reasons: temperature changes, moisture-content changes and chemical changes. Provided the building is designed and constructed to accommodate these movements or steps are taken to prevent them, they should not lead to serious defects.

Temperature changes – These cause expansion on heating and shrinkage on cooling; particularly affected are metals and plastics, although concrete, stonework, brickwork and timber can be affected also.

Moisture changes – Many materials expand when wetted and shrink on drying. This is known as moisture movement. The greatest amount of moisture movement takes place in timber, which should be painted or treated to seal its surface. Brickwork, cement rendering and concrete can also be affected by moisture movement. Rapid drying of wetted brickwork in the hot sun can result in cracks, particularly around window and door openings.

Chemical and fungal attack

Corrosion – These consist of the corrosion of metals and the sulphate attack of cement. Corrosion causes metals to expand and lose strength. Corrosion of steel beams can lift brickwork causing cracks in the mortar joint. Bulges in cavity brickwork may be caused by corroded wall ties. The sulphate attack of cement is either in the ground or from products of combustion in chimneys. The sulphate mixes with water and causes cement to expand. Sulphate-Resisting Portland Cement (SRPC) should be used in conditions where high levels of sulphate are expected.

Smoke containing chemicals is given off into the atmosphere as a result of many manufacturing processes. This mixes with water vapour and rainwater to form dilute or weak acid solutions. These solutions corrode iron and steel, break down paint films and erode the surfaces of brickwork, stonework and tiles. The useful life of materials in these environments can be prolonged by regular cleaning to remove the contamination.

Ageing – Exposure to sunlight can cause bleaching, colour fading of materials and even decomposition owing to solar radiation. Particularly affected are bituminous products, plastics and painted surfaces.

Biological attack – Timber, including structural, non-structural and timber-based manufactured items are the targets for biological attack. The agents of this are fungi and wood-boring insects. Given the right conditions an attack by one or both agents is almost inevitable.

There are two main types of fungi that cause decay in building timbers, these being dry rot and wet rot.

Dry rot – This is the more serious and is more difficult to eradicate than wet rot. It is caused by a fungus that feeds on the cellulose found mainly in sapwood (outer layers of a growing tree). This causes timber to lose strength and weight, develop cracks in brick-shape patterns and finally to become so dry and powdery that it can easily be crumbled in the hand. The appearance of a piece of timber after an attack of dry rot is shown in Figure 6.9. Two initial factors for an attack are damp timber in excess of about 20% moisture content (MC) and bad or non-existent ventilation.

Figure 6.9 *Timber after dry rot attack*

As the fungus is a living plant, an attack commences with the germination of its microscopic spores (seeds) that send out into the timber hyphae (roots) to feed on the cellulose. Once established, these hyphae branch out and spread through and over the timber forming a matt of cottonwool-like threads called mycelia. At this stage, the hyphae can penetrate plaster and brickwork in search of further timber supplies to feed on. This further timber supply need not be damp as the developed hyphae can conduct their own water supply, thus adjusting the moisture content as required. Finally the fruiting body like a fleshy pancake with an orange brown centre, will start to ripen and eject into the air millions of the rust-red spores, to begin the process elsewhere. Very often in the early stages, apart from a damp musty mushroomy smell, there is little evidence of an attack. It is not until the wall panelling, skirting or floorboards are removed that the full effects are realised, as Figure 6.10 shows.

Eradication and treatment – To eradicate an attack of dry rot, firstly rectify sources of dampness and bad ventilation:

- Remove all traces of decayed timber and at least 600 mm of apparently sound timber beyond the last signs of attack.
- All affected timber including swept-up dust, dirt and old wood shavings etc. must be sealed in airtight polythene bags and arrangements made for their incineration (contact your local authority for information). This prevents spreading and kills hyphae and spores.
- Strip plaster from walls, wire brush brickwork, heat up brickwork with a blow lamp to sterilise, and brush or spray wall with a dry-rot fungicide (this kills any hyphae and spores in the walls).
- Finally, work may be reinstated with preservative treated timber. (**Note:** The idea behind preservative treatment is to poison the food supply of fungi and wood-boring insects, by applying a toxic liquid to the timber.)

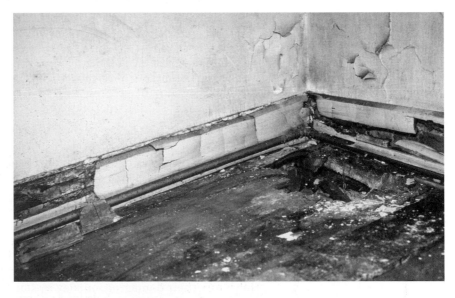

Figure 6.10 *Advanced dry rot*

Wet rot – This is also caused by a fungus, but it does not normally involve such drastic eradication treatment, as it does not spread to the same extent as dry rot. It feeds on wet timber (30% to 50% MC) and is most often found in cellars, neglected external joinery, ends of rafters, under leaking sinks or baths and under impervious (waterproof) floor coverings. During an attack, the timber becomes soft, darkens to a blackish colour and develops cracks along the grain. Very often timber decays internally with a fairly thin skin of apparently sound timber remaining on the surface. The hyphae when apparent are dark brown or black; internally hyphae may be white and form

Figure 6.11 *Wet rot in rafters*

into sheets. Its fruiting body, which is rarely found, is of an irregular shape and normally olive green in colour, as are the spores. Figure 6.11 shows the appearance after an attack of wet rot in the rafters of a roof.

Timber treatment – To eradicate an attack of wet rot all that is normally required is to cure the source of wetness and allow the timber to dry out. Replacement of soft timber may be required after an extensive attack particularly where structural timber is concerned. Non-structural timber may be treated with a wet rot wood hardening fluid.

Infestation

Wood-boring insects – This is also known as **woodworm**, after the larvae which are able to feed on, and digest, the substance of wood. The majority of the damage done to building timber in the UK can be attributed to five species illustrated in Table 6.1, which also includes their identifying characteristics.

The female adult beetle lays eggs during the summer months, usually in the end grain, open joints, or cracks in the timber. This affords the eggs a certain amount of protection until the larvae hatch. The larvae then start their damaging journey by boring into the timber, consuming it and then excreting it as fine dust. The duration of this stage varies between six months and ten years depending on the species. During the early spring, at the close of this stage, the larvae bore out a pupal chamber near the timber surface, where they undergo the transformation into adult beetles. This takes a short period after which the beetles bite out of the timber leaving characteristic flight holes. The presence of flight holes is often the first external sign of an attack. After emerging from the timber the beetle's instinct is to mate, lay eggs and then die, thus completing one life cycle and starting another.

Timber treatment – To eradicate an attack of wood-boring insects open up the affected area (take up floorboards etc.) remove all affected timber and replace with new preservative-treated timber. **Note:** again all removed timber and swept up dust and old wood shavings etc. must

Table 6.1 *Wood-boring insects*

Name	Actual size	Location and timber attacked
Furniture beetle	beetle flight holes	Softwoods and the sapwood of hardwoods; causes considerable damage to timber, flooring and furniture
Death-watch beetle		Mainly hardwoods in old damp buildings (churches); often in association with fungal attack
Lyctus beetle (powder post)		Sapwood of freshly-cut hardwoods; normally in timber yards before use
House long-horn beetle		Sapwood of softwoods; mainly roof timbers
Weevils		Damp or decayed hardwoods and softwoods; often found around sinks, baths, toilets and in cellars

STUDY THIS TABLE

be sealed in airtight polythene bags and arrangements made for their incineration. Brush timber to remove dust, strip off surface coating, e.g. paint, varnish, etc. (wood-worm fluid will not penetrate surface coatings). Apply two coats of a proprietary woodworm killer by brush or spray to all timber, even apparently unaffected timber. Pay particular attention to cracks, joints, end grain and flight holes. Inspections for fresh flight holes should be carried out for several successive summers. A further treatment of fluid will be required if any are found. (Fresh bore dust around the affected area indicates fresh flight holes.)

TRY TO
ANSWER THESE

— **Questions for you** —

1. Define the term 'building maintenance'.

_____

_____

2. Name two factors that affect the rate and extent to which a building deteriorates.

_____

_____

3. Name three agents to which deterioration in buildings can be directly attributed.

_____

_____

_____

4. Produce a sketch to show two methods by which moisture may bypass DPCs.

5. Define the term 'capillary attraction'.

_____

_____

6. Name two causes of movement in buildings and identify their likely effect.

_____

_____

_____

7. State the purpose of treating timber with preservative.

_____

_____

8. Identify two causes of rising damp and suggest a remedy for each.

_____

_____

9. List two defects under each of the following headings that can lead to the rapid deterioration of a building:

(a) movement

_____

_____

(b) biological attack.

_____

_____

10. Identify the probable causes of the following defects:

(a) small isolated damp patches at intervals on the internal leaf of an external cavity wall;

_____

(b) small holes in the surface of timber with fine dust around them;

_____

(c) damp patch in the centre of a solid ground floor.

_____

WELL, HOW DID YOU DO?

WORK THROUGH THE SECTION AGAIN IF YOU HAD ANY PROBLEMS

Undertaking repairs and maintenance work

Building firms who specialise in maintenance work, will often tend to employ or give preference to operatives, who possess multi-skills, as they will be expected to carry out in conjunction with their main craft skill, a range of basic skills of the other crafts e.g.

- After hanging a replacement door you may be expected to paint it.
- When replacing a window you may be expected to glaze it, re-lay the brickwork under the sill and patch in the plasterwork. If this was in a bathroom or kitchen it may also involve replacing ceramic tiles.

Inspections and repair surveys

Whenever a building firm undertakes major repairs or maintenance it is desirable to undertake a survey of the building. The extent of the measurements, sketches and details taken, will depend on the nature and extent of the work. Clearly a survey prior to replacing windows in a house will be very different to that of one involving structural movement.

Existing information – In many cases, there will already be in existence information that can assist you when carrying out a survey:

- *Drawings* – Make enquiries to the buildings owner to determine whether there are any existing drawings of the building. These may be in their possession from when the building was new or from when an extension was added some time in the past. Figure 6.12 illustrates the typical general location plans from when the house was built, which might be available. If so these can simplify your task by forming the basis of the survey sketches.
- *Previous survey reports* – Often there are existing reports, made by building society surveyors for mortgage purposes, or structural reports made for insurance purposes when a claim is being made. Figure 6.13 shows extracts from a typical schedule of remedial works made following a structural survey of a house, as part of an

READ THIS PAGE

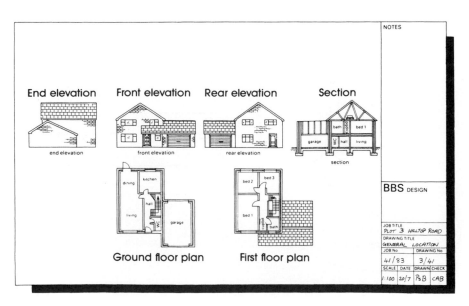

Figure 6.12 *General location plans*

198

Figure 6.13 *Schedule of remedial work*

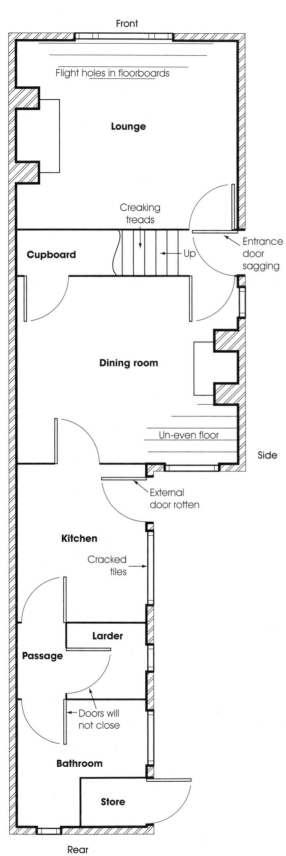

Figure 6.14a *Ground floor plan showing defects*

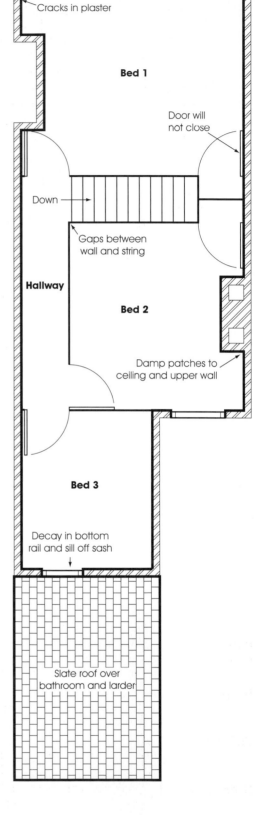

Figure 6.14b *First floor plan showing defects*

STUDY
THIS
TABLE

insurance claim. This identifies the main areas of concern. You would concentrate on these points to estimate the precise amount of work involved.

Undertaking the survey – Before you start the actual survey you should provisionally look the building over, both internally and externally, to determine its general layout and any likely difficulties. This will involve making notes and sketches to create a true record of the building's existing condition, including work/defects outside your craft.

Internal survey

Sketch plans are made of each floor or room, starting at ground floor level. You may be guided to the apparent major problem by the building's occupants, or another survey report etc. (e.g. schedule of remedial work). This can be the starting point for adding details to your sketches. Doors, windows, stairs and fitments should be added along with any defects you come across. This work may involve lifting floorboards, partial removal of skirting, panelling or casings and gaining access to the roof space. Figure 6.14 illustrates a typical set of internal survey sketches for an early 1900's built semi-detached house.

Where a lot of detail is required an accompanying list of defects should be made. Table 6.2 shows details of the defects found in the form of a tabled schedule.

Table 6.2 *Internal defects schedule*

Location	Defect	Possible cause	Remedial action
Lounge	● Flight holes in floorboards	● Woodworm	● Expose under-floor space and check remainder of house to determine the extent of attack, then rectify
Dining room	● Uneven floor	● Possible structural movement (subsidence) or fungal attack	● Consult structural engineer ● Expose under-floor space to determine extent, then rectify
Lower hall	● Entrance door sagging	● Joints failed	● Dismantle and re-assemble door using external WBP adhesive
Stairs	● Creaking treads ● Gap between wall and string	● Shrinkage between tread and riser, glue blocks loose ● Moisture movement and/or failure of fixing	● Screw treads to risers. Re-fix glue blocks ● Re fix string , cover gap with decorative moulding
Kitchen	● External door rotten ● Cracked tiling	● Wet rot ● Movement or accidental	● Replace with new door ● Replace tiles
Bathroom/larder	● Doors will not close	● Door twisted ● Hinge bound ● Defective ironmongery	● Ease rebates or replace door ● Scrape off paint, pack out hinge ● Adjust or replace tiles
Bedroom 1	● Cracks in plaster ● Door will not close	● Structural movement/ shrinkage ● As above	● Consult structural engineer ● Cut out and repair ● As above
Bedroom 2	● Damp patches to ceiling and upper wall	● Condensation ● Defective slates ● Deflective flashing	● Provide roof space ventilation ● Replace ● Replace
Bedroom 3	● Decayed window	● Wet rot due to lack of repainting	● Replace window

Where joinery items are to be repaired or replaced, full size details of the sections and mouldings must be made to enable them to be matched up. This task can be eased by the use of a **moulding template** see Figure 6.15. The pins of the template are pressed into the contours of the moulding. It can be placed on the sketch pad, drawn around and dimensions added. The location of where the moulding was taken should be noted as they may vary from room to room.

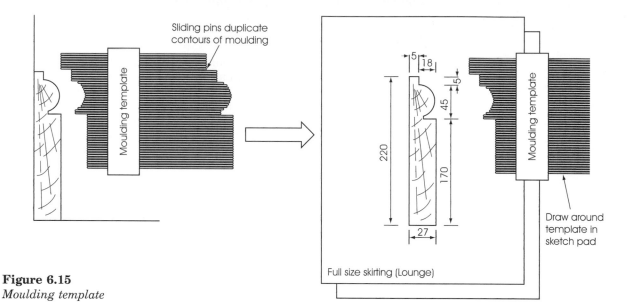

Figure 6.15
Moulding template

External survey

Sketch outline elevations of the building and add any defects found. Photographs of the elevation may be taken as a backup to your sketches, especially where intricate details have to be replaced. Often defects found on the internal survey are a result of external defects. These should be your starting point. As an example a damp mouldy patch in the corner of a kitchen might be the result of surface condensation, due to poor ventilation. Alternatively it may be due to a leaking rainwater gutter or down pipe. Binoculars are useful for viewing higher levels of a building; closer observation might involve the use of a ladder or the erection of a scaffold. Figure 6.16 illustrates a typical set of external survey sketches used for the inspection of an early 1900's semi-detached house.

Your focus of attention when carrying out the external survey should include the following points.

Walls:

- Signs of structural movement: cracks in brickwork joints, rendering and missing pointing.
- Staining: particularly just below the roof eaves, above the damp proof course (DPC) and behind rainwater down pipes.
- Height of DPC above ground level: this should be a minimum of 150 mm.
- Air bricks: ensure they are clear and not blocked by overgrown vegetation.

Window and doors:

- Condition of woodwork: look out for poor fitting doors and casements.

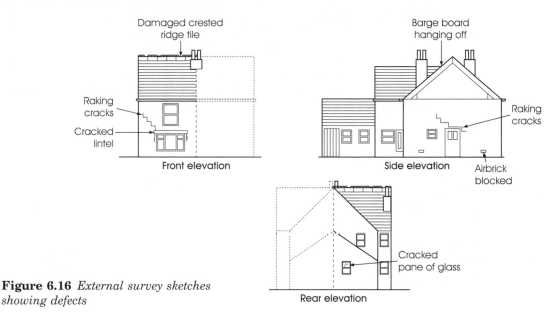

Figure 6.16 *External survey sketches showing defects*

- Condition of paintwork: cracked paintwork at joints will allow water penetration and may lead to wet rot. The easy insertion of a penknife or bradawl may confirm your suspicions.
- Condition and operation of ironmongery.
- Condition of glass, putty and glazing beads.

Roofs:

- Missing, displaced or damaged tiles, slates and flat roof coverings.
- Missing, displaced or damaged flaunching, flashings, valley gutters and verges.
- Barge boards, fascia and soffits: condition of paintwork; look out for signs of decay and distortion. Also check soffits for the presence of any ventilation gaps or grills (these may require cleaning, collected debris or repeated painting may block them).

Guttering, down pipes and drains:

- Check joints are sealed; look out for signs of water staining and moss growth.
- Feel behind cast iron down pipes for corrosion damage due to lack of paint protection.
- Check all brackets and clips are secure.
- Check drain gullies are clear. Look out for signs of them discharging water over their edges onto a path or house wall.
- Check drain gullies are retaining their water seal. If no water is seen in the 'U' bend, it may be cracked or broken and discharging water to undermine the foundations and also causing dampness.

Outside areas:

- Check condition of garden walls, paths and driveways. Look out for signs of structural movement.
- Wooden fences, post and gates: look out for signs of decay. They are particularly susceptible at ground level and joints, where water can be retained.
- Note position of trees and other large plants.

Table 6.3 shows the results of the external survey in schedule form.

Table 6.3 *External defects schedule (Figure 6.16 refers)*

Location	Defect	Possible cause	Remedial action
Front elevation	• Ridge tile damaged • Cracking to ground floor lintel and raking cracks above	• Wind damage/uncertain • Structural movement	• Replace and make good • Consult structural engineer
Side elevation	• Air bricks blocked • Raking cracks above entrance door • Barge board hanging off	• Build up of dirt, soil and vegetation • Structural movement • Fixings failed	• Clean out, reduce ground level to at least 150 mm below DPC • Consult structural engineer • Re-fix and make good slates if required
Rear elevation	• Cracked pane of glass to bathroom	• Accidental/unknown	• Re-glaze window
Outbuildings and structures		(Not viewed)	

Timber repairs

READ THIS PAGE

When considering timber repairs a great deal of judgement and nego-tiation with the client is often required. Can it be repaired cost effectively or is it cheaper in the long run to replace it? Each job being considered on its own merits, cost against future service life being the main consideration.

Doors

There are many defects associated with doors. Remedial action will depend on the type and location and may range from a simple adjust-ment through to complete replacement. Table 6.4 and Figure 6.17 cover the most common defects, causes and recommend remedial action.

In all but minor cases consider/discuss with clients the possibility of renewing the door.

Note: Always wear a dust mask when rubbing down paintwork and eye protection goggles when scraping off. Surfaces painted prior to the 1960's may contain harmful lead within the paint. In these circum-stances, rub down using a wet process (with wet and dry paper) to minimise the potential risks.

Door frames – Defects to external door frames can normally be attrib-uted to either wet rot to the lower end of the jambs or breakout damage in the lock striking plate area as a result of an attempt to force the door. Both of these can normally be resolved by splicing in new timber to the area of damage. See Figure 6.18. In the worst cases a new frame may be required. However, this option will cause the most disturbance to the internal plasterwork and decoration.

Table 6.4 *Door defects*

Defect	Sketch	Causes	*Remedial action*
Will not close, door sticking at head, sill or stile	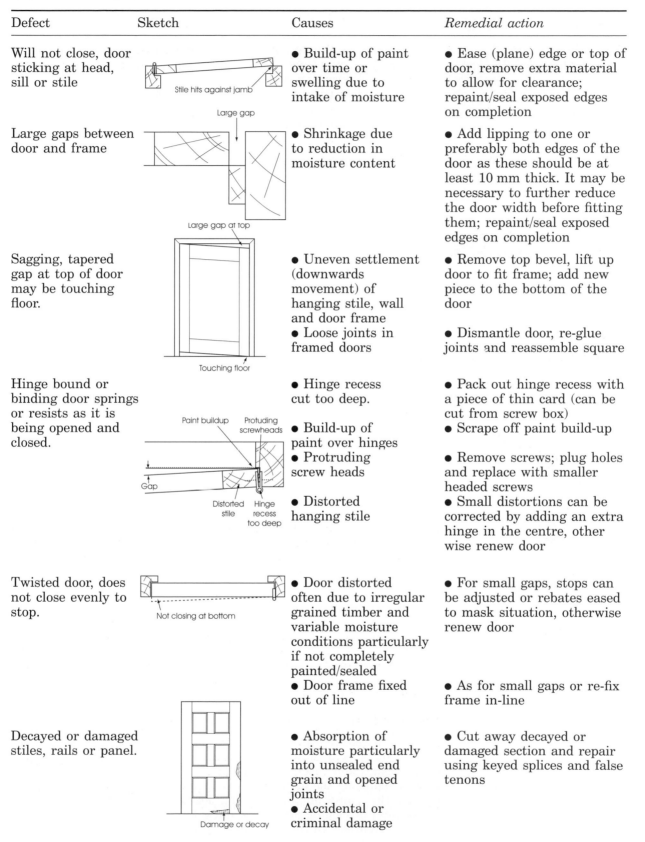	● Build-up of paint over time or swelling due to intake of moisture	● Ease (plane) edge or top of door, remove extra material to allow for clearance; repaint/seal exposed edges on completion
Large gaps between door and frame		● Shrinkage due to reduction in moisture content	● Add lipping to one or preferably both edges of the door as these should be at least 10 mm thick. It may be necessary to further reduce the door width before fitting them; repaint/seal exposed edges on completion
Sagging, tapered gap at top of door may be touching floor.		● Uneven settlement (downwards movement) of hanging stile, wall and door frame	● Remove top bevel, lift up door to fit frame; add new piece to the bottom of the door
		● Loose joints in framed doors	● Dismantle door, re-glue joints and reassemble square
Hinge bound or binding door springs or resists as it is being opened and closed.		● Hinge recess cut too deep.	● Pack out hinge recess with a piece of thin card (can be cut from screw box)
		● Build-up of paint over hinges	● Scrape off paint build-up
		● Protruding screw heads	● Remove screws; plug holes and replace with smaller headed screws
		● Distorted hanging stile	● Small distortions can be corrected by adding an extra hinge in the centre, other wise renew door
Twisted door, does not close evenly to stop.		● Door distorted often due to irregular grained timber and variable moisture conditions particularly if not completely painted/sealed	● For small gaps, stops can be adjusted or rebates eased to mask situation, otherwise renew door
		● Door frame fixed out of line	● As for small gaps or re-fix frame in-line
Decayed or damaged stiles, rails or panel.		● Absorption of moisture particularly into unsealed end grain and opened joints	● Cut away decayed or damaged section and repair using keyed splices and false tenons
		● Accidental or criminal damage	

Table 6.4 *Door defects (continued)*

Defect	Sketch	Causes	*Remedial action*
Door does not stay latched when closed.	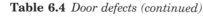 Paint buildup / Latch does not engage	• Build-up of paint over time to the stops or rebate • Distorted door • Defective lock/latch	• Ease stops/scrape off paint build up; adjust striking plate • Rectify distortion and adjust striking plate • Replace lock/latch
Damaged panel	Split in panel	• Shrinkage; accidental or criminal damage	• Cut out panel and stuck (moulded on solid) beads to form new rebate in place of panel groove; fit new panel and secure with planted beads.

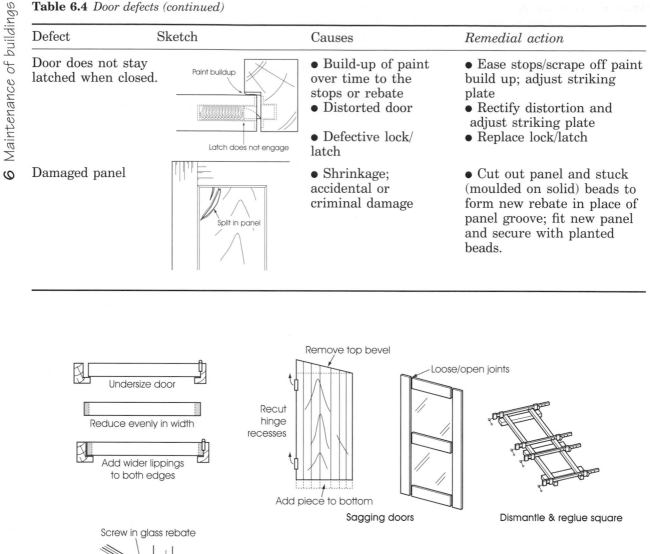

Figure 6.17 *Remedial treatment to doors*

Window frames

Defects to wooden windows are similar to those of doors and door-frames. They will either be associated with poorly fitting opening parts (sashes and casements) or decayed/damaged frames. These can be rectified using the methods previously outlined for doors e.g. scraping off the paint build-up, easing leading edges, dismantling and re-assembly of sagging casements and splicing of new timber to decayed or damaged areas. In the worst cases the installation of a new window should be considered.

Figure 6.18 *Repairs to door and window frames*

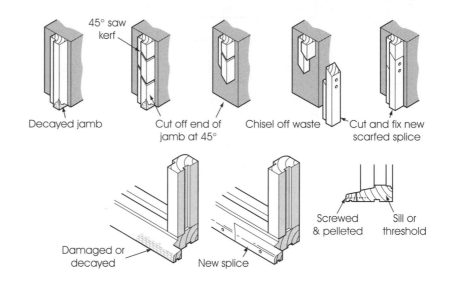

Boxed frame sash windows – This type of window is the traditional pattern of sliding sashes and for many years has been superseded by casements and solid frame sash windows. This was mainly due to the high manufacturing and assembly costs of the large number of component parts. An understanding of their construction and operation is essential as they will be met with frequently in renovation and maintenance work.

The double-hung boxed window consists of two sliding sashes suspended on cords that run over pulleys and are attached to counter-balanced weights inside the boxed frame.

Figure 6.19 shows an elevation, horizontal and vertical section of a boxed frame sliding sash window. It shows the make-up of this type of window and names the component parts.

Re-cording sashes – The maintenance carpenter is often called upon to renew a broken sash cord (Figure 6.20). It is good practice to renew all four cords at the same time, for the remaining old cords will be liable to break in the near future.

Figure 6.19 *Boxed frame sliding sash window details*

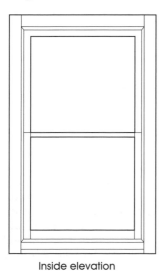

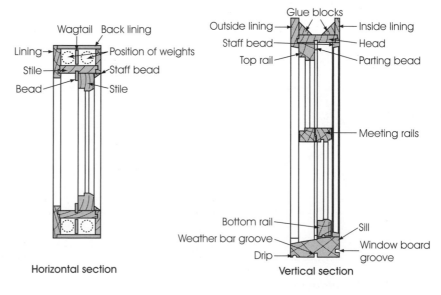

Inside elevation   Horizontal section   Vertical section

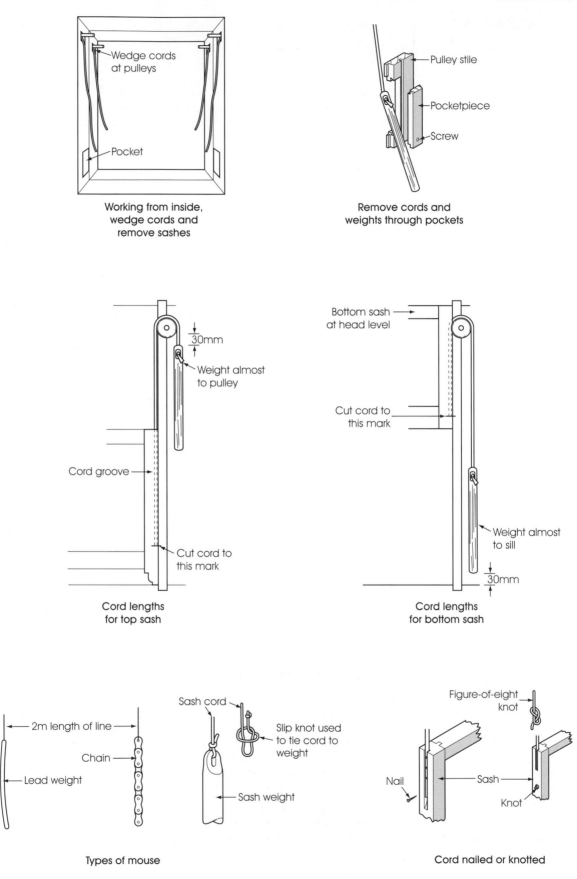

Working from inside, wedge cords and remove sashes

Remove cords and weights through pockets

Cord lengths for top sash

Cord lengths for bottom sash

Types of mouse

Cord nailed or knotted

Figure 6.20 *Re-cording sashes*

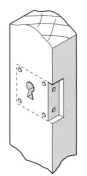

Old lock removed

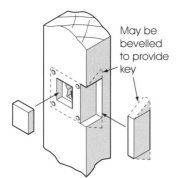

May be bevelled to provide key

Filling pieces cut, holes and recesses enlarged

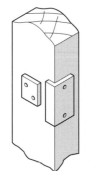

Oversize filling pieces glued and pinned in place

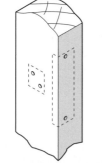

Filling pieces planed off flush, pin holes filled and sanded off flush

Figure 6.21 *Making good holes and recesses*

The sequence of operations for renewing sash cords is as follows:

- Carefully remove staff beads.
- Carefully remove pockets, (access pieces cut towards the bottom of pulley stiles).
- Take out bottom sash. The sash cords should be wedged at the pulley and removed from the groove in the sash.
- Carefully remove parting beads. Break paint joints first and carefully prise out with a chisel.
- Take out top sash in a similar manner to the bottom sash.
- Remove the weights and cords through the pockets. The wagtail will move to one side to give access to the outside weights.

Note: the weights may not all be the same, so ensure they are returned to their original positions.

- Thread new cords over pulleys and down to the pockets. A 'mouse' can be used to thread the cords easily. A 'mouse' is a small lead weight that is attached to a 2 m length of string that in turn is tied to the cord. The mouse is inserted over the pulley and drops to the bottom of the frame. The sash cord can now be pulled through. Many carpenters use a length of small chain instead of a mouse.
- Fasten sash cords to weights. To obtain the length of cord for the top sash, rest the sash on the sill and mark on the pulley stile the end of the sash cord groove. Pull the weight up to almost the top and cut the cord to the position marked on the pulley stile. Wedge the cord in the pulley to prevent the weight from dropping. To obtain the length of cord for the bottom sash, place the sash up against the head of the frame and mark on the pulley stile the end of the sash cord groove. With the weight just clearing the bottom of the frame cut the cord to the position marked on the pulley stile. Wedge the cord in the pulley.
- Fix sash cords to the top sash and insert the sash into the frame. The cords are normally attached to the sashes by nailing them into the cord grooves. Alternatively the cord can pass through a closed groove and end in a knot.
- Replace the parting beads. Where these have been damaged new ones should be used.
- Fix the sash cords to the bottom sash and insert the sash into the frame.
- Replace the staff beads and check the window for ease of operation. Candle wax can be applied to the pulley stiles and beads to assist smooth operation.

Door and window hardware

The moving parts of locks, latches, bolts and hinges require regular lubrication and need to be kept free from paint build-up, in order to ensure their trouble-free operation. Inevitably they will eventually begin to wear and require replacement. In general these should be replaced with like for like or the nearest alternative. However proposed replacement does provide the opportunity to upgrade hardware, particularly locks for increased security.

When replacing or upgrading hardware it is often necessary to make good holes and recesses. Figure 6.21 illustrates a typical situation. In general all follow the same procedure:

- Cut oversize filling pieces of a similar material. These are often bevelled to provide a key.

- Mark and cut out enlarged hole and recesses to receive filling pieces.
- Glue and pin filling pieces in place.
- Punch in pins, plane off flush, fill pinholes with wood filler, sand off smooth and repaint or seal the area.

Frame replacement – When extensive repairs are required it is often more cost effective in the long run to consider a complete replacement. This should be discussed with the building owner. It should be emphasised that although the replacement may be more expensive than the repair initially, the replacement would last a lot longer and also provide the opportunity of upgrading fittings, etc. and modification to suit their requirements.

Before removing frames, always check the wall above for signs of support. See Figure 6.22. Newer building may have a concrete or steel lintel, older properties a stone lintel, brick arch, or soldier course or sometimes none at all apart from the frame. Also look out for cracks in the brickwork mortar joints above the opening, which could be indications of structural movement, possibly leading to collapse on removing the frame.

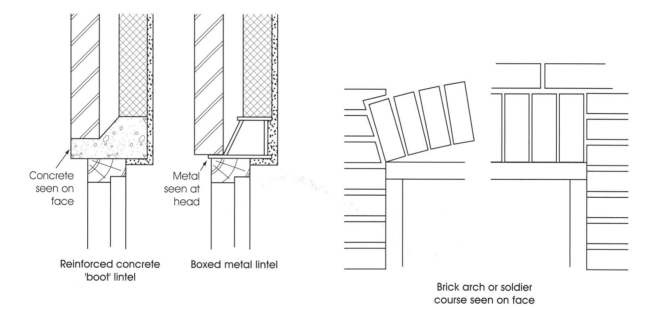

Concrete seen on face

Metal seen at head

Reinforced concrete 'boot' lintel

Boxed metal lintel

Brick arch or soldier course seen on face

Figure 6.22 *Means of support over openings*

Do not proceed if a means of support is not evident or there are signs of movement. Seek the advice of a structural expert, as arrangements may have to be made for temporary support, the insertion of a lintel and structural repairs to be carried out by others before the frame replacement itself.

Once you are sure the opening is correctly supported, the frame can be cut out and removed in sections in sequence as shown in Figure 6.23. When the frame has been removed, clean off any projecting mortar and previous fixings. Make good any damaged brickwork and holes previously occupied by 'built-in' horn fixings. Finally fix in position the new frame. See Figure 6.24.

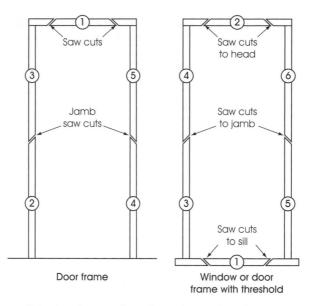

Figure 6.23 *Frame replacement*

Cut out and remove in sections using numbered sequence

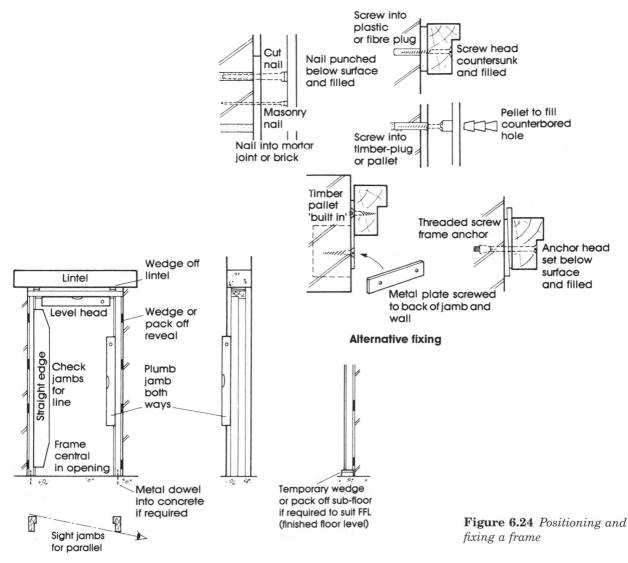

Alternative fixing

Positioning frame

Figure 6.24 *Positioning and fixing a frame*

- Cut off horns and seal cut ends (paint or preservative).
- Place frame in the opening, temporarily holding with wedges at head or sill if required.
- Check head and sill with a level and adjust wedges as required.
- Check jambs for line with a straight edge, plumb one jamb with level, 'sight in' the other, adjust position and wedge as required.

Floors and roofs

If the defect is the result of fungal decay or wood boring insect damage, the procedure outlined previously should be adopted. Use Figures 6.25

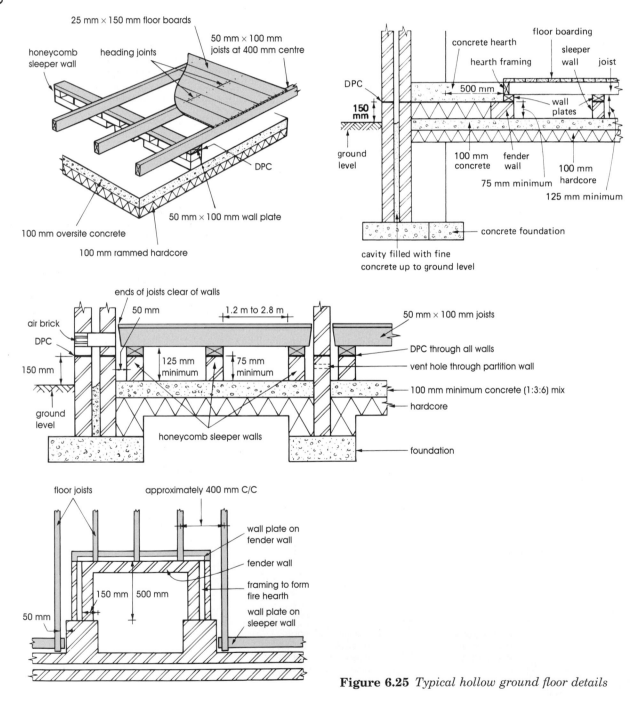

Figure 6.25 *Typical hollow ground floor details*

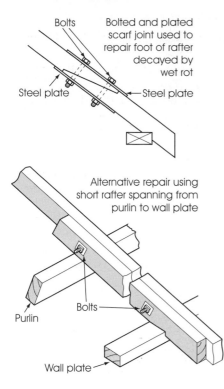

Bolts

Bolted and plated scarf joint used to repair foot of rafter decayed by wet rot

Steel plate — Steel plate

Alternative repair using short rafter spanning from purlin to wall plate

Purlin

Bolts

Wall plate

Figure 6.26 *Typical roof details*

and 6.26 as a guide to replacing timber components like for like. However, where the work is extensive, especially in circumstances where structural timber is affected, e.g. upper floor joists, rafters and purlins, etc. it is often wiser and more cost effective to have this work referred to a specialist contractor who will be fully equipped and experienced to undertake it.

Floorboards – Again where the defect is the result of fungal attack or wood boring insects, the procedure explained before should be adopted. If due to movement (loose fixings), wear or damage, one or more boards can simply be re-fixed or replaced.

Note: Care must be taken when re-fixing or replacing floorboards as there is always the possibility of services (water, gas and electricity) running below.

The surface of the area to be worked on can be scanned before starting work, with a metal/live electric circuit detector. As an added precaution it is wise to turn off all service supplies at their meter/stop valve before any re-fixing or cutting out operations commence.

Loose boards are best re-fixed by screwing down into the joists rather than nailing, especially at upper floor levels in older properties, where significant amounts of nailing causing vibration, may damage the lath and plaster ceiling.

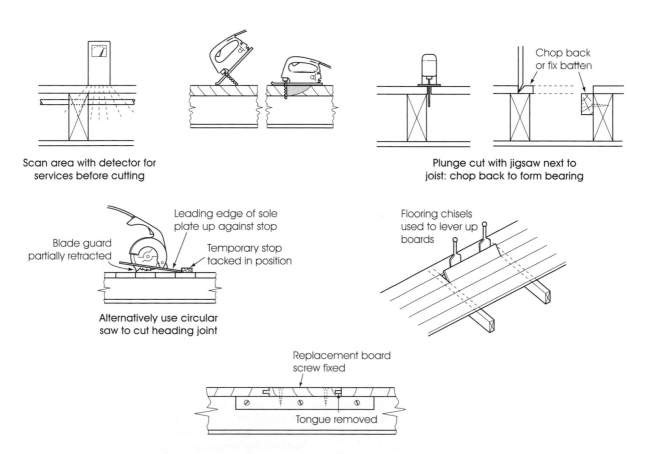

Scan area with detector for services before cutting

Plunge cut with jigsaw next to joist: chop back to form bearing

Chop back or fix batten

Blade guard partially retracted

Leading edge of sole plate up against stop

Temporary stop tacked in position

Alternatively use circular saw to cut heading joint

Flooring chisels used to lever up boards

Replacement board screw fixed

Tongue removed

Figure 6.27 *Removing and replacing floorboards*

Removing a floorboard:

- A jigsaw can be used to cut the ends of a floorboard next to a joist. The ends can then be chopped back to form a bearing (for heading joints) using a wood chisel, or fix a batten to the edge of the joist.
- Alternatively a small circular saw may be used to cut the heading joints over the joists. The blade should be set to the floorboard thickness.
- A sharp knife, padsaw or jigsaw can be used along the length of the board to separate the tongue.
- Punch the fixing nails through the board. Insert two wide blade flooring chisels in one of the edge joints and lever up the board.
- Where more than one adjacent boards are to be replaced the heading joints should be staggered over different joists.
- Finally, cut the new boards to length and re-fix in place. Where more than one board wide a folding technique should be used.

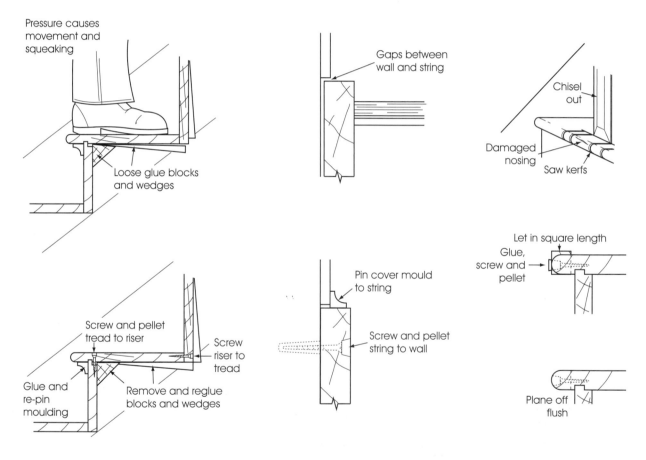

Figure 6.28 *Common stair defects*

Stairs – The most common defects encountered are illustrated in Figure 6.28.

- *Creaking treads* – This results from movement between the tread and riser joint when walked on. Where access to the underside of the flight is possible (in cases where it has not been plastered over) the creaking can be remedied by renewing the glue blocks at the tread to riser junction and re-gluing/re-wedging the treads and risers in their string housings. Where access to the underside is not possible, the problem can be remedied by gluing and screwing the tread down into the top of the riser. Small gaps, normally the result of shrinkage, may be apparent at the tread-to-string housing. These should be filled by gluing in thin strips of timber veneer.

- *Gaps between the wall and string* – This may be the result of either shrinkage or movement, or a combination of both. Shrinkage gaps can be masked by the application of a cover mould. Movement gaps are normally the result of the fixings between the wall and string becoming loose or failing, causing the string to move away from the wall when using the stairs. Re-fix the string back to the wall by plugging and screwing. Any gap or damage between the string and plasterwork can again be masked by a cover mould.

- *Damaged nosings* – These can be repaired by cutting out the damaged section and splicing in a new piece. A square length should be 'let-in'. Cut at 45° at either end for additional support and glue line. This is fixed by gluing and screwing. Finally planing and rubbing down to match the nosing profile. Where a scotia mould is used at the underside of the tread to riser junction, it is best to renew the whole length, gluing and pinning the new one in place.

Brickwork, plastering and tiles

READ THIS PAGE

You may be required to replace one or two bricks which have been removed or damaged during other work, or even lay several courses to fill in, say under the sill of a reduced height replacement window.

Replacing bricks

The first task is to attempt to match the pattern, size and make of the original. Measure the brick size and take a small piece to the brick supplier for them to identify. Brick sizes vary slightly due to the way they are made. New metric size bricks are a little smaller than the old imperial ones. When working on older property matching bricks may be difficult to obtain. Try suppliers who specialise in reclaimed building materials. If imperial bricks cannot be obtained, matching metric ones can be bonded into the existing work by slightly increasing the mortar joints.

Figure 6.29 illustrates the procedure to follow when replacing a single brick. In this case the brick previously cut around is the built-in horn of a sill or threshold.

- Using a bolster and club hammer (do not forget to wear eye protection goggles) cut out the old brick and clean away the old mortar joints. Brush out all dust particles, taking care in modern buildings to ensure nothing is allowed to enter the cavity.
- Cut the brick to size if required. First gently score a line around the brick using a bolster and club hammer, finally use a heavier blow on the lines to sever it.

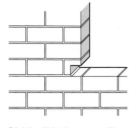

Old 'built in' horn position

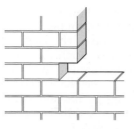

Cut out to nearest joint

Cut replacement brick
to size

Lay bed joint, 'butter' up
end and top edge of brick

Place brick in position and
clean off excess mortar

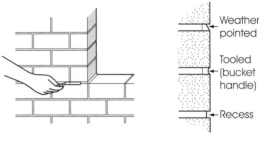

Rake out adjacent mortar
joints and point up to match
existing pointing

Weather
pointed

Tooled
(bucket
handle)

Recess

Figure 6.29 *Replacing a brick*

- Prepare a mortar mix, typically 1:6 (1 part Portland Cement to 6 parts bricklaying sand). Sufficient water is added so that the mix has the consistency of soft butter (firm enough not to collapse when heaped, but easily compressed with a shovel). One part lime or a mortar plasticiser may be included in the mix for improved workability. Alternatively, pre-packed bricklaying mortar mixes are available. **Note:** The colour of the sand used should match the existing mortar joints. Red and yellow sands are commonly available.
- Lay the bed of mortar into the prepared hole.
- Butter up (apply mortar) to the end and the top edge of the brick. Place it in position and then remove the surplus mortar.
- Fill any gaps in the mortar joint. When it has started to go off, rake the joints out below the brick surface.
- After about 24 hours rake out the adjacent mortar joints.
- Re-point the joints with a mortar mix that matches the original in colour and finish.

Repointing – The most common methods are:

- weather pointed, which is done with a pointing trowel;
- tooled, a concave finish (bucket handle) created by working along the drying mortar with a special jointing tool, or alternatively a metal bucket handle (hence the name) or a piece of 15 mm copper pipe may be used;
- recessed, created by brushing out the drying mortar with a stiff bristle hand brush; alternatively a more consistent depth can be achieved by working the joint with a piece of timber having a protruding countersunk head screw.

Area to be bricked up

Cut out bricks at either end to form a bond

Avoid straight vertical joints

Lay bed mortar, butter up and lay bricks. Remove surplus mortar

Periodically check for line and level

Figure 6.30 *Laying brick courses*

Re-laying brick courses – Figure 6.30 illustrates the procedure to follow when relaying or building whole courses of bricks. Refers in this case to under the sill of a reduced replacement window.

- Cut out bricks at either end to form the bond between the adjacent vertical joints. Clean away any old mortar and dust particles.
- Dry lay the bricks to determine the pattern. Cut the bricks to size if required.
- Prepare a mortar mix as before, using a 10 mm joint. Approximately 1 kg of mix is required for each brick.
- Apply a bed of mortar to the existing brick course, approximately 10 mm thick. Furrow the surface to a 'V' shaped groove with the point of a trowel. Butter up and lay bricks, removing surplus mortar as you go.
- Repeat the process to lay the subsequent brick courses. Periodically check the bricks are being laid horizontal and in line with a spirit level. Use the end of the trowel to tap the bricks into place if required.
- Complete the job by raking out the mortar joints and finally pointing them as before.

Repairs to plasterwork

Modern buildings – The internal brick and blockwork walls, will have a hard plastered finish. This is normally applied in two layers, a 9 to 12 mm thick backing coat and a 2 to 3 mm thick finishing coat. Ceilings and stud partition walls are surfaced with sheets of plasterboard. These may be finished by a 2 to 3 mm coat of board finishing plaster applied on to the plasterboard, which acts as the backing. Alternatively the plasterboard joints may be taped up and filled to provide a 'dry lined' finish, ready for decoration. Ceilings which have been 'dry lined' were often decorated using a textured coating, worked to create a repeating pattern or stipple finish.

Older buildings – The wall plaster may be much softer. This is still normally two coats. A thick lime-based backing coat followed by a thin finishing coat. Ceilings and stud partition walls were then finished using 'lath and plaster'.

This is a system using thin timber laths nailed to the undersides of joists and faces of studs. Wet plaster was pressed up against them and allowed to squeeze between the gaps in the laths forming a key to hold this backing plaster in place. This was finally finished using again a thin coat of finishing plaster.

External walls – The external walls of both modern and older buildings may be covered in rendering. This is a surface coat of sand and cement mortar applied to a wall for decorative and/or waterproofing purposes.

All of these finishes may crack due to structural movement, damage by accidental impact or be disturbed during renovation work, therefore requiring repairs that the maintenance carpenter and joiner may be asked to undertake.

Patching plasterwork – The first thing to do when patching plasterwork on any background is to protect the floor, by covering with a dustsheet. Figure 6.31 shows the procedure to follow when patching a 'blown' or damaged area of plasterwork to a brick or blockwork wall.

- Tap plaster around the damaged area to 'see' (hear) if any part sounds hollow or loose.

'Hack off' existing
loose plaster

'Brush off' to remove
dust and loose particles

'Damp down'
with water

Mix plaster
in a bucket

Scoop up plaster from
hawk and apply to wall
in an upward sweep

Reinforce large
areas with repair
mesh or scrim

Comb or scratch area
to provide a 'key'

Brush off and apply
finishing plaster

'Rule off' using a sideways
sawing action,
working upwards

Trowel up to a
smooth finish

Repeat trowelling up whilst
splashing with water

Figure 6.31 *Patching plasterwork*

- Use a club hammer and bolster to hack off all existing loose plaster until the surface is sound.
- Brush down the surface to remove all loose particles and dust, using a stiff bristle or wire brush.
- Damp down the wall surface by brushing or spraying with water. This prevents the wall suction from drying out the plaster too quickly, which could result in cracking on drying. Some surfaces such as concrete, shiny or glazed bricks and impervious engineering bricks do not help the plaster to stick. In these cases brush on a PVC bonding agent before plastering to ensure good adhesion.
- Add a small amount of backing plaster into clean cold water in a bucket. Stir with a timber stick until a thick creamy consistency is achieved.
- Transfer some of the plaster to your hawk. With the hawk tilted away from the wall scoop up a small amount of plaster on the edge of the steel trowel and press the plaster against the wall using an upward sweep of the trowel. The trowel should be used at an angle to the wall, with the angle reduced as you sweep it up the wall. Take care not to allow the trowel to lay flat against the wall, as the suction will pull the fresh plaster off the wall.
- Continue adding plaster to the wall until the whole area to be repaired is covered, to within 2 to 3 mm below the surrounding wall finish. Larger areas may be reinforced by pushing into the backing coat a repair mesh or scrim.
- Before the backing plaster is completely set, scratch the surface with a comb. This provides a 'key' to help with the adhesion of the finishing coat.

219

- After about 3 to 4 hours the backing coat surface will be hard, but not dry. It is then ready for finishing. If allowed to dry further, it will require damping down again with water before finishing.
- Brush down the surface to remove any loose particles. Mix up a small batch of finishing plaster, by adding to a little water as before, except this time it should be a runnier consistency. Trowel on the plaster, aiming to leave it slightly proud of the surrounding area.
- Rule flat the surface, using a timber or metal straight edge. Start at the bottom of the patch, move it up the wall with a side-to-side 'sawing' action keeping it tight against the existing sound plaster as a guide. Trowel on more plaster to fill any hollows before ruling off again.
- The plaster will start to set within 30 to 45 minutes. At this stage smooth the surface with a plastering trowel. Again using upward sweeps with the trowel held at an angle. After 15 or so minutes lightly splash the surface with clean cold water, whilst trowelling up and over the surface, to provide a smooth hard finish. Ensure the trowel is kept clean and damp during this process, to prevent damaging the newly plastered surface. Regular brushing off in a bucket of cold water is ideal. **Note:** Small patches in rendering can be repaired in one or two coats, using the above procedure, except that a sand and cement mix is used in place of plaster.

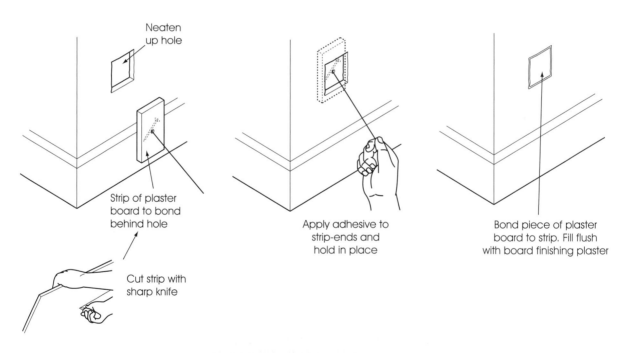

Figure 6.32 *Patching small holes in plasterboard*

Patching damage to plasterboard or lath and plaster surfaces – to repair small holes caused for example by striking the surface with the corner of a piece of furniture when moving it. The procedure to follow is illustrated in Figure 6.32.

- Neaten up the jagged edges using a sharp knife for plasterboard or a pad saw for lath and plaster.
- Cut a strip of plasterboard about 1½ times the length of the neatened hole and just narrower than it in width. Make a hole in its

centre, pass through a piece of string and knot it behind on a nail. **Note:** Plasterboard is simply cut by scoring on the face with a sharp knife, break along the line by applying pressure along from the scored side. Run the knife along the paper on the other side to separate.

- Mix up some plasterboard adhesive and apply to both ends of the strip. Feed the strip into the hole, using the string to pull it tight against the inner face of the board or laths. Tie off the string to a scrap of timber positioned over the face of the hole.
- When the adhesive has set, cut off the string. Cut another piece of plasterboard. This time to fit the hole and again bond in place using plasterboard adhesive. Press in until it is just below the surrounding wall surface, leave to set.
- Fill the patched hole using board finishing plaster and trowel up as before.

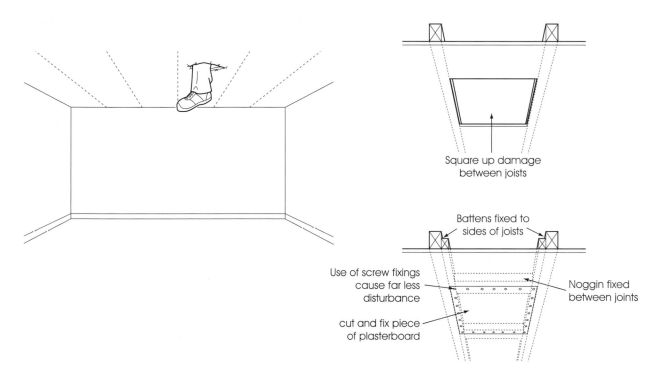

Figure 6.33 *Repairing large holes in plasterboard*

To repair large holes for example caused by a foot slipping through the ceiling when working in a loft, the procedure to follow is illustrated in Figure 6.33.

- Mark on the ceiling two lines at right angles to the joist direction and enclosing the damaged area.
- Use a pad saw to cut along these lines until the adjacent joists are reached after first checking for the presence of cables and plumbing.
- Again using the pad saw cut along the joist edges. Remove the damaged area, leaving a neat rectangular hole.
- Cut battens; fix to the sides of the joists.
- Cut and fix noggins between the battens at either end of the hole, ensuring the noggins centre lines straddle the cut line, to provide a bearing for both the existing sound ceiling and new plasterboard.

- Cut a piece of plasterboard 2 to 3 mm smaller than the hole in both directions. Fix in place using plasterboard nails or plasterboard screws into the noggins and battens.
- Use a sharp knife to cut away the finishing plaster about 25 mm all round the hole. Bed lengths of plasterer's scrim over the joints between the patch and existing sound ceiling, using a thin (runny) mix of board finishing plaster as an adhesive. This is to reinforce the joint and reduce the risk of later cracking.
- Fill the patched area using board finishing plaster and trowel up as before.

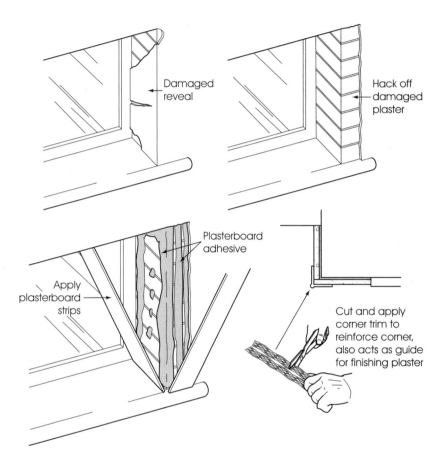

Figure 6.34 *Making good plasterwork to damaged reveals*

To make good the plaster work around the reveals of a replaced door or window: in most circumstances these can be patched using the two coat backing and finishing plaster method as before. Where there is extensive damage, or the plaster is loose, the entire reveal should be hacked off and replaced. Figure 6.34 illustrates the procedure to follow using plasterboard and board finishing plaster:

- Hack off plaster reveal back to the brick or blockwork surface and extending around the corner by about 75 to 100 mm.
- Cut two strips of plasterboard, one for the reveal and the other for the return.
- Brush down the wall surfaces. Mix up some plasterboard adhesive. Using a trowel or special caulker, apply dabs of adhesive up the centre of the reveal and continuously around the perimeter.

- Press plasterboard strips in place and check for plumb with a spirit level. The return strip should finish 2 to 3 mm below the adjacent plaster, to allow for a coat of board finish.
- Reinforce the corner with a length of metal plasterboard bead, (this also acts as a guide for the later board finishing plaster coat). Apply a bed of plasterboard adhesive or board finish to the corner. Press the bead in place, check with spirit level for plumb. Also ensure it is in line with existing wall surface. Remove excess adhesive and allow too dry for 2 to 3 hours.
- Reinforce the joint between return plasterboard strip and existing wall plaster, using a length of scrim as before.
- Complete repair by applying a coat of board finishing plaster and trowel up in the normal way.

Ceramic wall and floor tiles

You may be required to replace damaged tiles individually or lay a much larger area such as a whole wall or floor.

Rake out grout joint

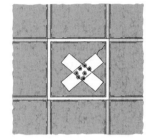

Drill holes around centre

Break out from centre

Scrape off old adhesive

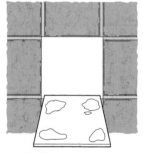

Press new tile in place

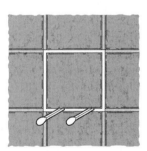

Insert spacers

Apply grout, then point

Polish to remove haze

Figure 6.35 *Replacing a damaged tile*

Replacing damaged tiles – Probably the hardest task is to find a good match for replacement. The building owner may have spares left over from the original work. Alternatively take a damaged piece to a tile supplier for them to find a match. Figure 6.35 illustrates the procedure to follow.

- Prepare the surrounding area and yourself. Cover the floor and surrounding units or bath and sanitary ware with dustsheets to protect from dust and possible scratching by the small sharp particles of broken tiles. Protect yourself by wearing eye protection goggles, gloves and a dust mask.

- Rake out grout joint around damaged tile, to relieve the perimeter stresses.
- Drill a series of holes around the centre of the tile and break out using an old chisel, working progressively towards the edges. Do not try to break out the tile by trying to prise it off from the edge joints, as almost inevitably you will damage the adjacent tiles. Masking tape can be applied when drilling out the centre, to prevent the masonry drill skidding across the ceramic surface.
- Scrape or chip off the old tile adhesive back to the surface, taking care not to damage the plaster base.
- Apply four dabs of tile adhesive to the back of the tile, or use a notched comb to provide a uniform ribbed layer.
- Press the tile in place, so that it lies flush with the surrounding ones. Insert tile spacers or matchsticks in the joints to position or support the tile. Adjust the tile as required to ensure a uniform gap all around.
- Allow the adhesive to set for about twenty-four hours and then remove the spacers.
- Fill the gap around the tile with grout, working in with a rubber squeegee. Point the joint with a finger tip or piece of wood dowel with a rounded end point.
- Finally when dry polish up the surface to remove the grout haze, using a clean dry cloth. **Note:** The long-term success of tiling

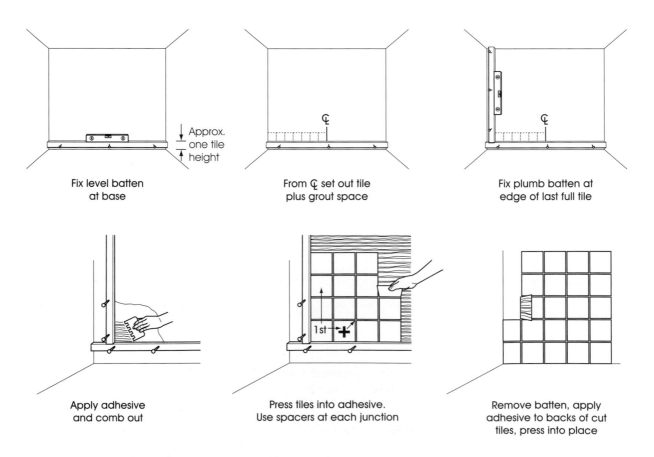

Figure 6.36 *Ceramic wall tiling*

depends on the adhesive and grout used. Most are available either in ready mixed or powder form for mixing with water to a creamy paste with water. A standard type mix is only suitable for dry areas. It may also tolerate a little condensation or occasional splashing with water. In areas subject to more prolonged condensation or extensive wetting such as a shower area, always use waterproof products.

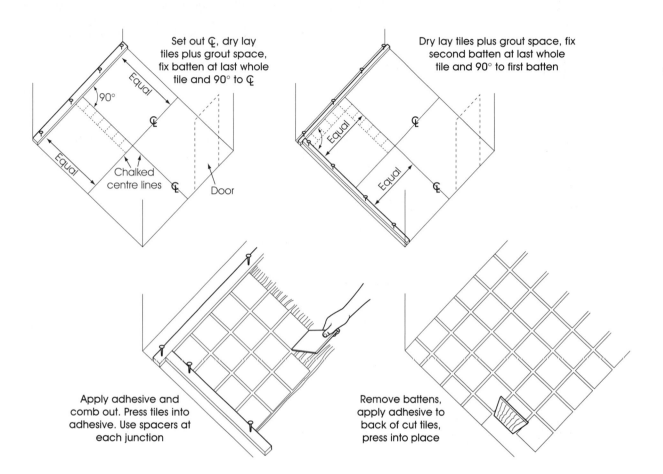

Set out ℄, dry lay tiles plus grout space, fix batten at last whole tile and 90° to ℄

90°

Equal

Equal

℄

℄

Chalked centre lines

Door

Dry lay tiles plus grout space, fix second batten at last whole tile and 90° to first batten

Equal

Equal

℄

℄

Apply adhesive and comb out. Press tiles into adhesive. Use spacers at each junction

Remove battens, apply adhesive to back of cut tiles, press into place

Figure 6.37 *Ceramic floor tiling*

Re-tiling a whole wall or floor – In circumstances where a match for a damaged tile is not possible, you may be required to replace the whole area. Figures 6.36 and 6.37 illustrate the procedures to follow.

Surface preparation – Protect yourself and the surrounding area as before.

● *Walls:* Remove all existing tiles and traces of the old adhesive back to a sound, level base. Walls not previously tiled should be thoroughly cleaned to remove all traces of dirt, grease and old wallpaper. Make good any holes or loose plaster
● *Floor:* Remove all existing tiles and traces of the old adhesive back to a sound, level base. Ensure the surface is clean and dry (there should be an effective damp proof membrane below the surface to prevent rising damp). Uneven or damaged surfaces can be repaired with a floor levelling compound to provide a level and smooth surface for tiling.

Setting out –

- *Walls:* Temporarily fix a straight timber batten to the wall surface, horizontally level with its top edge a little more than one tile height above the floor, skirting, worktop or bath. Check with a spirit level. This will ensure the tiling is straight and level even if the underlying surface runs out. **Note:** Where the underlying surface is way out of level, the batten should be positioned so that maximum distance is one tile in height. Cut tiles are then used to infill when the batten is removed. Measure the length of the wall to determine the centre point, mark along the batten from the centre a series of distances equal to a tiles width plus a 2-mm grouting space. Ensure you are not left with a narrow strip to tile as they will be difficult to cut. If this is the case re-mark, this time straddling the middle tile over the centre point. The aim is to end up with more or less a half tile at either end of the wall. Temporarily fix a straight batten to the wall surface, vertically plumb, with its edge next to the last full tile mark.

- *Floor:* Measure the length and width of the room to determine the centre lines. Mark in both directions using a chalk line. Dry layout tiles using 4 mm or 6 mm grout joint spacers from the centre point. Fix temporary batten at last whole tile position. This must be at 90º to one centreline and parallel with the other. Dry layout tiles plus grout space, from centre line along batten. Fix second temporary batten at last whole tile position. This must be at 90° to the first batten and again parallel to the centre line. This will determine the cut tile sizes around the perimeter. Again if either of these are narrow strips straddle the centre tiles over the centre lines.

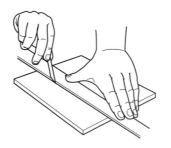

Score along line with
tile cutting point

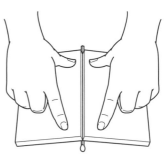

Place matchsticks under
score, press down to snap
tile in two

Figure 6.38 *Cutting ceramic tiles*

Laying tiles –

- *Walls:* Starting at the junction of the battens, apply adhesive to about 1 m^2 of wall and comb out. Press tiles into ribbed adhesive, with spacers set in between them. Continue working sideways and upwards about 1 m^2 at a time to lay all of the whole tiles. Allow to set for about 24 hours. Carefully remove battens. Cut tiles to fit around the perimeter and fix them in place, using adhesive dabbed or combed onto their backs. Use spacers or matchsticks to ensure even grout joints. Tiles are best cut using a proprietary tile cutter, or diamond tipped wet saw. However, small amounts can be cut by scoring the surface with a carbon tipped tile cutting point and snapping the tile along the scored line. Place two matchsticks under scored line. Press down firmly on either side to snap in two, see Figure 6.38. Corners and curves can be cut out of tiles to fit around projections using a tile saw blade in a coping saw frame. Alternatively the lines of the area to be removed may be scored and the waste nibbled away with a pair of pincers.

- *Floor:* Tiling starts at the junction of the two battens, working away from there in both directions. Trowel on the adhesive and comb out again working about 1 m² at a time. Press tiles into ribbed adhesive with spacers set in between them. Continue laying tiles, working out from the corner, aiming to lay the last whole tile next to the doorway (do not trap yourself into a corner as you will not be able to walk on the freshly laid area). Allow to set for about 24 hours. Cut tiles to fit around the perimeter and fix them in place with adhesive. **Note:** Floor tiles are often thicker than those for walls and may require the use of a heavy duty tile cutter or diamond tipped wet saw to cut them.

Grouting – When all cut tiling is complete allow to set for about 24 hours. The joints between them can then be grouted. Working grout with a rubber squeegee, point up with finger or a rounded end dowel. Allow to dry and polish off the haze with a dry clean cloth as before.

Finishing off – The joint between tiles and horizontal surfaces such as kitchen worktops, baths and sanitary ware will require sealing with a silicone sealant to prevent moisture penetration. Figure 6.39 illustrates the procedure to follow, which ensures a neat bead of sealant to these locations.

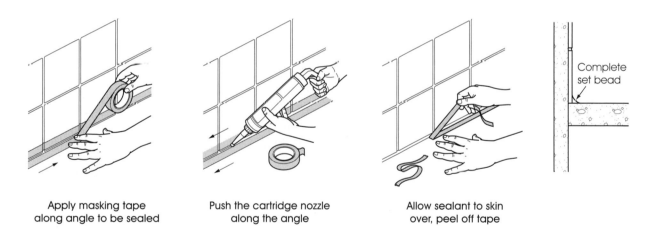

Apply masking tape
along angle to be sealed

Push the cartridge nozzle
along the angle

Allow sealant to skin
over, peel off tape

Complete
set bead

Figure 6.39 *Sealing tiles to a worktop*

Apply masking tape to both the vertical and horizontal surfaces, 2 to 3 mm away from the internal angle. Trim the cartridge nozzle off at an angle of 45° to give a bead just wide enough to fill the gap between the two taped edges. Gently squeeze the cartridge gun trigger until the sealant is just seen at the tip. Place the nozzle at one end of the angle to be filled, with the gun held at 45° to the wall. Apply steady, even pressure to the trigger whilst pushing the gun along the angle. The nozzle will form the sealant into a neat concave curve. To stop the flow at the corners and on completion, release the metal tag adjacent to the trigger. Any unevenness in the bead can be smoothed using a small paintbrush dipped in water. Leave sealant for a short while to skin over, then peel off the tape to leave a well-formed neat bead.

Glazing and painting

READ THIS PAGE

Maintenance of glazing work involving sealed double-glazing units and large window panes is best undertaken by specialist glaziers, who will be kitted up to undertake the work efficiently and safely.

Re-glazing

Re-glazing of small single-glazed panes can be undertaken by the carpenter and joiner. Wherever possible glass should be pre-cut to size by the glass supplier. Measure the timber rebate sizes and order glass 3 mm undersize in both directions. For example, a piece of glass for a rebate opening size of 150×250 mm should be ordered as a cut size of 147×247 mm. If necessary pieces of glass can be cut to size by scoring along the required line using a glass-cutting wheel. Lay the glass on a flat surface with matchsticks placed under the scored line at either end. Apply pressure on both sides to snap in two along the line. Never attempt to cut narrow strips and always wear eye protection and gauntlets.

The first stage is to remove the broken pane. Where practical, sash or casements should be removed from their frame so that broken glass can be removed and replaced with a new piece with relative safety, at ground level.

When replacing broken glass at high level ensure that the area below is cordoned off so that no one can enter the area below. Before starting to hack out the broken pane and hardened putty, ensure you are wearing eye protection goggles and gauntlets to protect hands, wrists and lower arms. These should be worn during the whole process as inevitably shards of glass and fine splinters will be created as the pane is removed and the rebates cleaned up.

Start at the top of the pane removing the old putty or glazing beads with a wood chisel or hacking knife. Remove glazing sprigs (flat or square nails) with pliers and then lever out remaining glass from behind again using a wood chisel. Finally continue hacking out remaining back putty to rebates.

The procedure for re-glazing is illustrated in Figure 6.40.

- Check glass is correct size.
- Ensure rebates are primed with paint.
- Work a bead of putty around the back of the rebate.
- Position plastic seating blocks in the bottom of the rebate to support the glass.
- Position the bottom edge of the glass on seating blocks. Gently push the glass into the rebate, applying pressure evenly around the edge until a back bed putty thickness of 1 to 2 mm is achieved.
- Use glazing sprigs to secure the glass in place. These may be driven in using a pin hammer or the edge of a firmer chisel. (Panel pins should not be used to secure the glass in place, as their round point of contact results in pressure points, which can lead to the formation of cracks.)
- Work a bead of putty all around the rebate in front of the glass. Only a small bead is required when using glazing beads to secure the glass.

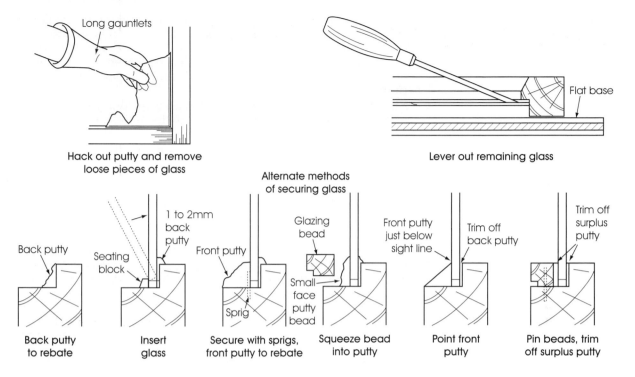

Figure 6.40 *Re-glazing procedure*

- Replace glazing beads squeezing putty into glass, or point up the front putty bead using a putty knife or chisel to form a bevelled fillet. Its upper edge in contact with the glass should be just below the rebate sight line. Slight imperfections in the putty fillet can be improved by running over with a wetted paint brush.
- Trim off the surplus putty to beads and then trim off the back bedding putty on the inside of the glass.
- Clean the glass to remove oil and putty marks before it dries.

Painting woodwork

Woodwork is painted to provide a decorative finish. However, more importantly it serves also to protect it from the elements. As a carpenter and joiner carrying out maintenance work you may be required to paint new replaced items as well as repaint existing items that have been eased or repaired. The paint system for wood normally consists of a primer to seal the surface and provide a bond for later coats, an undercoat which provides a smooth opaque covering coat and finally a decorative gloss or satin top coat.

Preparation – The key to a successful paint system is careful preparation. Paint will not last long on a defective surface.

Bare wood – should only need an initial rub down with glass paper to remove any roughness and sharp arrises. Knots in bare soft wood can be full of resin and may later 'bleed' through to the finished paint surface if not sealed. Firstly wipe over the surface with a cloth soaked in white spirit to remove any stickiness and excess resin. Then coat all knots with a knotting solution. On resinous hardwoods that are to be painted, wipe off excess resin using white spirit and seal the entire surface with an aluminium wood primer.

- Apply wood primer to all surfaces and edges taking particular care to achieve full penetration of any end grain. This is best undertaken prior to fixing in order to ensure full protection. For example, the backs of skirtings, architraves, door frames and linings etc. are inaccessible when fixed. This is particularly important for external timber.
- Fill any defects and open end grain with a wood filler. Always select a waterproof type for external use. Rub down flush with the surface using glass paper
- As priming tends to raise the grain of woodwork resulting in a felt-like hairy surface, the whole job will require rubbing down (de-nibbing) prior to over painting.
- Wipe off surface with a 'low tack' cloth to remove any surface dust; apply undercoat.
- When undercoat is dry, apply the topcoat. Refer to paint manufacturer's information with regard to minimum and maximum over-coating times. If the top coat is applied too soon, the undercoat will tend to bleed into the top coat causing defects; too long and it may not bond successfully to the undercoat, resulting in early breakdown and peeling off.

Previously painted wood – If in good condition, lightly rub down with glass paper or clean off using a sugar soap solution. This cleans the surface dirt or grease deposits and removes some of the gloss. New coats of paint will not key well on a gloss surface and will easily chip and peel, if not rubbed down or cut back.

- Knot and prime any eased edges or repairs. When dry, rub down to blend in primer to existing paint surface.
- Fill and rub down any minor defects and imperfections.
- Remove surface dust, apply undercoat followed by the top coat within recommended over-coating time.

When the old system has broken down, it is best to completely strip off the old paint, make good and start again from scratch using the same procedure as for bare wood.

Small areas showing signs of deterioration, may be repaired without fully stripping the area.

- Treat any minor areas of soft timber caused by wet rot with a wood hardener.
- Rub down the surface to remove all loose defective paint. **Note:** Always wear a dust mask when rubbing down paintwork. Surfaces painted before the 1960's may contain harmful lead within the paint. It is best in these circumstances to rub down using a wet process (wet and dry paper) to minimise the potential risk.
- Apply the paint system as before.

Painting procedure

Internal painting – Protect carpets and furniture with dustsheets. Doors to other rooms can be sealed with masking tape prior to any rubbing down. Open the window to ensure adequate ventilation. This is both for you and to help the paint dry. Always wear a dust mask when rubbing down and eye protection goggles when scraping off.

- Primers and undercoats are applied by brushing out along the grain.
- Top coats are initially applied along the grain, brushed out across the grain and finally 'laid off' finished with gentle brush strokes along the grain. The aim is to produce a thin, even paint film, which does not 'sag' on vertical surfaces or 'pond' on horizontal ones.

External painting – In general the same procedure for internal painting can be adopted, except for adverse weather conditions and taking extra care to ensure full paint coverage to avoid the possibility of moisture penetration.

● Do not work in strong sunlight, as this prevents paints drying properly and likely to cause it to 'blister'. Wait until the area is in shade before painting.
● Do not paint if rain is expected.
● Do not paint first thing in the morning or last thing in the evening, when there might be a 'dew'. The resulting moisture will spoil the paint finish.
● Do not paint when there is a risk of frost.
● Do not use paint intended for interior use only.

In these circumstances it is best to aim to paint from mid morning to just after lunch. This will allow the air to dry before starting and the paint film to dry before the early evening dampness starts to form.

Sequence of operations – A logical approach is required when painting framed joinery. The aim is to keep a 'wet edge' blending in adjacent areas of paint, so that joints are not seen when the paint dries.

Figure 6.41 illustrates typical numbered sequences for a range of joinery.

Doors: remove handles, paint in sequence shown. Leading edge should be painted to match the woodwork of the room it opens into

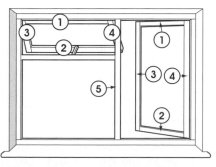

Casement window: paint opening parts before frame and interior sill

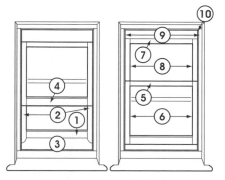

Sash window: from inside open sashes as far as they will go, paint all accessible surfaces, reverse sashes and complete painting

Figure 6.41 *Sequence for painting doors and windows*

231

Painting plasterwork

Walls and ceilings are normally painted using emulsion paint. Newly plastered and repaired surfaces should be left for seven to ten days to dry and then treated with a coat of plaster sealer before decoration. This prevents the new plaster showing through the paint finish as a kind of 'patchiness'. Alternatively, a thinned emulsion can be applied as a primer, before at least two full strength coats are put on. The priming coat should be about one part water to about three parts emulsion paint.

Before starting work, arrange for any furniture in the room to be removed. Protect carpets and fixtures with dustsheets. Wear a dust mask and eye protection goggles when rubbing down and scraping off.

The procedure to follow is illustrated in Figure 6.42

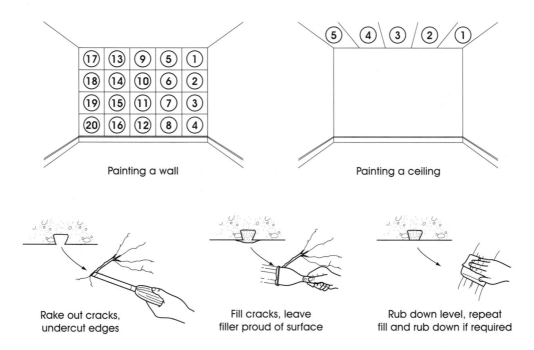

Figure 6.42 *Painting plasterwork*

- Remove all loose material such as dirt, dust and flaking paint.
- Rake out any minor cracks in the plaster surface, using the end of an old slot blade screwdriver. The raking out is to make the crack a little deeper and wider with undercut edges.
- Fill cracks with a plaster filler. Ensure filler is pressed well into the cracks in order for it to key on the undercut edges.
- Leave filler slightly proud of surrounding surfaces. Rub down level when dry. Fill the area again and rub down if required.
- Rub down the entire wall or ceiling surface.
- Wash down the surface and allow it to dry.
- Ceilings should be painted before walls. A small brush is used to cut into the corners and up to the frames and skirtings etc.
- Use a roller or large brush to cover an area of about 1 m² at a time. Apply paint in one direction, spread it out by brushing or rollering diagonally. Finally finishing off using light pressure only, in the same direction as you started.

- Using the numbered sequence continue painting the subsequent squares or strips, blending in the paint application of one with another whilst the paint is still wet. Otherwise pronounced lines will be apparent in the finished work, if wet paint is applied over a drying one.
- Clean all brushes/rollers and equipment in water on completion.

Paint coverage

This depends upon the absorbency of the surface to be painted and the quality of the paint. Typically:

- Primers and undercoats cover 12–14 m^2 per litre per coat;
- Gloss or satin top coats cover 14–16 m^2 per litre per coat.
- Emulsions cover 10–12 m^2 per litre per coat.

── Learning task ──

(Reference to *A Building Craft Foundation* may be required to complete this task.)

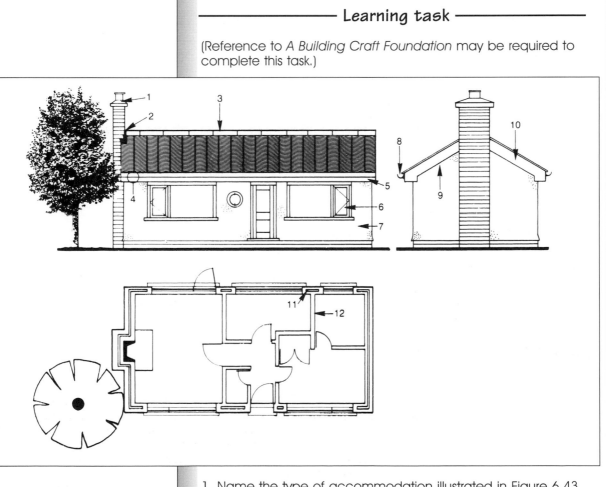

Figure 6.43 *Plan and elevation*

1. Name the type of accommodation illustrated in Figure 6.43

---

2. Using the following items, identify the numbered features shown in Figure 6.43; not all of the items are applicable: gable, ridge, sash, hip, verge, eaves, parapet, cavity, partition wall, cladding, lintel, flashing, casement, barge board, fascia board, gutter, rendering, casement, flaunching.

READ THE INSTRUCTIONS
AND COMPLETE
THE TASK

_____

_____

_____

_____

_____

_____

_____

_____

_____

_____

3. Define the following terms and indicate an example of each of them on the section shown in Figure 6.44:

(a) substructure

_____

(b) superstructure

_____

(c) primary element

_____

(d) secondary element

_____

(e) finishing element

_____

(f) component

_____

4. Name the type of foundations illustrated in Figure 6.44

_____

5. Sketch an alternative type of ground-floor construction

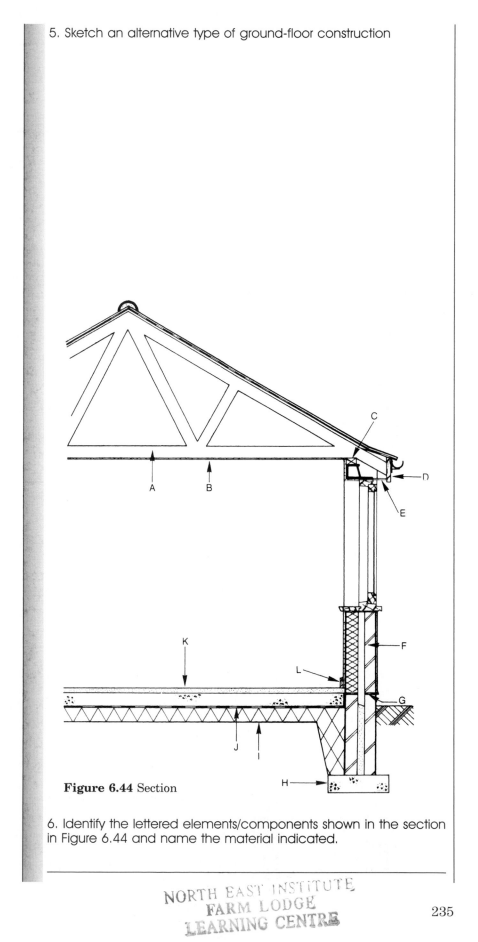

Figure 6.44 Section

6. Identify the lettered elements/components shown in the section in Figure 6.44 and name the material indicated.

_____

_____

_____

_____

_____

_____

_____

_____

_____

_____

_____

_____

7. During a close inspection of the building in Figure 6.43 you notice the following defects. State for each a possible cause and remedy:

(a) Small damp patch in the centre of the lounge floor.

_____

_____

(b) Rafters next to chimney stack are wet and show signs of fungal attack.

_____

_____

(c) Vertical cracks both internally and externally in walls down the side of the chimney and under the lounge window.

_____

_____

(d) Soft woodwork to external kitchen window sill.

_____

_____

(e) Front door has dropped at head, sticks on the threshold and shows signs of open/loose joints.

_____

_____

REFER BACK TO THE INDICATED SOURCES IF YOU HAVE ANY PROBLEMS

8. Write a letter to the building owner, informing them of the defects you identified during your survey visit and suggest appropriate remedial action.

_____

_____

_____

_____

_____

_____

_____

_____

_____

_____

_____

_____

_____

_____

_____

_____

_____

_____

_____

_____

_____

_____

_____

_____

_____

_____

_____

_____

TRY TO
ANSWER THESE

—————— Questions for you ——————

1. Name the work activities associated with the following operations:

Pointing

_____

_____

Splicing

_____

_____

Grouting

_____

_____

Ruling off

_____

_____

Cutting in

_____

_____

Laying off

_____

_____

Trowelling up

_____

_____

2. Describe two methods of cutting a ceramic tile.

_____

_____

_____

_____

3. State why screwing of plasterboard when repairing a ceiling is preferable to nailing.

_____

_____

4. A high level sash window requires re-glazing. Describe a safe method of work.

_____

_____

_____

5. You are asked to replace a badly decayed window frame with a new one. However, on examination there is no lintel or other means of support evident above the opening. Outline the procedure to follow.

_____

_____

_____

_____

_____

6. On lifting a floorboard, the underside is found to be soft, powdery and full of small holes. The most likely cause is:
(a) Wet rot attack
(b) Dry rot attack
(c) Wood boring insects
(d) Excessive floor load

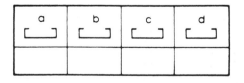

7. A maintenance carpenter has a 'mouse' in their tool bag. State what it would be used for.

_____

_____

_____

8. State or sketch the sequence of operations required to keep a 'wet edge' when applying the finishing coat of paint to a six panel door.

9. State the precautions to be taken before removing unsound plasterwork in a carpeted room.

_____

_____

_____

_____

10. Describe the procedure for disposing of old timber, shavings and swept up dust during the eradication of a dry rot attack.

_____

_____

_____

_____

WELL, HOW DID YOU DO?

WORK THROUGH THE SECTION AGAIN IF YOU HAD ANY PROBLEMS

COMPLETE THE WORD SQUARE

WORD-SQUARE SEARCH

Hidden in the word square are the following 20 words associated with '*maintenance*'. You may find the words written forwards, backwards, up, down or diagonally.

BRICK	PLASTER
PAINT	SPLICING
BACK PUTTY	SCRIM
PIPE	FUNGI
BATTEN	CERAMIC
POINTING	PLUMB
BONDING	LEVEL
GLAZING	SASHCORD
TROWEL	MORTAR
MIXING	GROUTING

Draw a ring around the words, or line in using a highlight pen thus:

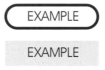

(EXAMPLE)

EXAMPLE

A	C	O	U	N	N	T	P	F	B	S	B	P	I	P	I	P	S
B	R	O	M	R	G	R	O	U	T	I	U	G	L	L	L	C	A
O	A	T	B	G	R	O	U	T	I	N	G	U	A	A	R	A	S
N	E	A	B	L	E	W	E	A	L	G	B	N	S	I	A	F	S
S	C	R	M	O	T	W	M	E	T	E	R	S	U	M	M	I	G
A	M	I	R	C	S	E	V	D	B	Q	I	O	W	F	O	R	N
S	O	C	O	K	A	E	U	R	R	U	C	G	U	U	R	F	I
C	R	R	B	N	L	L	B	O	T	A	K	N	A	T	T	U	Z
O	T	O	O	S	P	L	I	C	I	N	G	L	A	S	T	N	A
R	A	R	T	I	N	G	L	H	P	E	N	N	P	P	A	N	L
D	R	A	O	T	W	L	L	S	A	T	I	U	O	L	R	N	G
S	T	R	O	W	E	L	H	A	N	T	O	I	I	O	U	N	P
A	D	H	E	S	E	Y	O	S	Z	A	D	U	N	U	I	M	J
S	R	Y	T	T	U	P	K	C	A	B	N	F	T	X	I	R	B
H	E	A	D	I	N	I	G	P	R	A	B	N	I	P	A	N	T
C	E	R	A	M	I	P	A	I	N	T	G	M	N	O	I	N	T
O	C	I	M	A	R	E	C	P	N	N	R	O	G	R	I	P	P
R	D	D	P	O	E	K	E	I	I	G	O	T	E	A	S	L	A

WELL, HOW MANY DID YOU GET?

Index